MEDIA ACCLAIM

FOR THE

ENCYCLOPEDIA OF SANTA FE AND NORTHERN NEW MEXICO

Anyone who has lived in Northern New Mexico a day or a year has to own a copy of the *Encyclopedia of Santa Fe and Northern New Mexico*.

—— *Rio Grande Sun*

... an honest, tantalizing and truly informative history of the City Different.

—— *Santa Fe Reporter*

Cross's breezy style makes it easy to read. An entertaining and useful addition to any library...

—— *The Santa Fe New Mexican*

... a wonderful resource for Northern New Mexico history, geography, art, food, people and culture.

—— *Taos News*

Anything you want or need to know about Northern New Mexico is now at your fingertips.

—— *Las Vegas Optic*

From *Aamodt* to *Zuni*, this entertaining and informative book covers the region's history, literature, politics, geology, local lore, food, customs, gossip and much more.

—— *Green Fire Times*

When I first moved here, there were so many things that people referred to and assumed that I knew, and it would have been great to have a reference book like this.

—— Mary-Charlotte Domandi, *Radio Cafe*

... filled with fascinating information... an A-to-Z encyclopedia of all things Santa Fe.

—— Christopher Johnson, *Collected Words*

When your [home] buyers are new to New Mexico, give them a copy of Mark's book, the *Encyclopedia of Santa Fe and Northern New Mexico*. It's a handy guide to help them pronounce words like "Cerrillos," to know the meaning of words like "latilla," and to know what the word "Christmas" refers to when ordering dinner at Maria's.

—— *Santa Fe Real Estate Guide*

The encyclopedia goes well beyond [a] gringo's guide to include a more elaborate and subtle appreciation for the complexities and complications of Northern New Mexico's struggle for identity.

—— *Pasatiempo*

ENCYCLOPEDIA OF SANTA FE
AND NORTHERN NEW MEXICO

ENCYCLOPEDIA *of*
SANTA FE

and Northern
New Mexico

To Morgan, Jin + Wyatt —
Welcome to Santa Fe!

MARK H. CROSS

Caminito Publishing LLC
Santa Fe, NM

Listen to audio pronunciations of
New Mexico place names at

encyclopediaofsantafe.com

Encyclopedia of Santa Fe and Northern New Mexico
ISBN: 978-0-9834194-2-6
E-book ISBN: 978-0-9834194-3-3
Library of Congress Control Number: 2011919395

Book design by Kathleen Dexter
Cover art by Pamela Jensen
Cover photo of the Rio Chama by Laird Graeser

Caminito Publishing LLC
P.O. Box 31385
Santa Fe, New Mexico 87594

~ TABLE OF CONTENTS ~

MAPS

CHARTS AND GRAPHS

~ ACKNOWLEDGEMENTS ~

A project this ambitious will incur many debts. I am beholden to the friends, coworkers, and helpful strangers who assisted in the creation of this book.

The late Ellie Becker endorsed the idea of a regional reference book early on, and her advice determined the project's general direction. Donna Cross read a draft, and Bruce Cross helped with research. Ruth Kirkpatrick fact-checked the first few hundred entries.

Thanks to Dr. Donald Shina, Carl Flock, and Jan Meyers at the St. Vincent Hospital Cancer Center for their care in 2005. The book would not have been completed without their intervention.

As the project progressed, it was helped along by many knowledgeable friends. They all answered questions about the meaning of this or the pronunciation of that, but Annie Rodriguez deserves special thanks. Her cheerfulness and consistent willingness to help are much appreciated.

Others read a late draft and made invaluable suggestions. Raúl Burciaga, Steven Davis, Jeret Fleetwood, Renée Gregorio, Jonelle Maison, and Jim Meyer read most of the book, and Pam Ray and Jim Terr read selected parts. Their comments and error catches were critical. It must be noted, however, that their suggestions were not always accepted and that errors belong solely to the author.

Many people in Santa Fe and elsewhere provided help in other ways. There is not enough space to name them all individually, but I am grateful for their courtesy and competence in response to requests for images and information. Particular thanks are due John Pen La Farge for the use of his family's photographs and for sharing his thoughts on Santa Fe's evolution over the last 30 years.

Laird Graeser, economist, trailmaster, and photographer, took most of the pictures. It would be a poorer book without his contribution.

Thanks also to Steven Davis, Marinha Santos, and Jim Meyer for their photos and drawings, and to Carrie McGovern for proofreading the manuscript. Pamela Jensen created the cover art and the book's web site, and Jon Boller contributed the audio for the site's pronunciation guide.

Kathleen Dexter created the maps and designed the book. Her skill, patience, and awesome stamina are much appreciated.

Finally, the encyclopedia would not have been completed without the help of Beth Nommensen. She tolerated the obsession, copyedited the manuscript, and most importantly, declared the book finished.

Regional encyclopedias are usually compiled by teams of academicians and librarians. They assign topics to local writers, and the encyclopedia is published in two or three years. This book has a different history.

When I moved to New Mexico in 1996, I was, like most newcomers, confused by the odd place names and unfamiliar colloquialisms, and I looked for a book to explain them. Santa Fe is a world-class tourist destination, so there were plenty of guides to its restaurants and hotels. And it is home to more writers per capita than any other city in the country, so there were dozens of books on topics of regional interest. I could not, however, find the kind of reference book I was looking for. The *Encyclopedia of Santa Fe and Northern New Mexico* was born of that frustration.

It started as a hobby, as an informal glossary with entries for architectural features such as *viga* and *latilla*, local foods like *posole* and *sopaipilla*, and physical features like *arroyo* and *bosque*. As I read New Mexico history, I added biographical sketches of Po'pay, who led the 1680 Pueblo Revolt; Doña Tules, who ran a house of ill repute in the 1840s; and Thomas B. Catron, suspected leader of Territorial New Mexico's shadowy Santa Fe Ring.

Reading *The New Mexican* every day, I soon realized that contemporary Santa Feans were every bit as colorful as the historic figures. The glossary was expanded to include people like Santa Fe mayor Debbie Jaramillo, who personifies Hispanic resistance to the city's gentrification; actor Val Kilmer, who complained to *Rolling Stone* magazine that "eighty percent of the people in my county are drunk"; and financier Eddie Gilbert, who made and lost two fortunes and served time in federal prison before moving to Santa Fe to make his third fortune.

My education in regional colloquialisms began when I got a job at the New Mexico Legislature. Some of my coworkers were native Santa Feans, some came here as hippies in the 1960s, some grew up speaking Spanish, and some spoke Tewa or Keres. They introduced me to terms like *lambe*, "flatterer"; *movida*, "a secret move"; and *borracho*, "drunkard." And I learned that New Mexicans have their own versions of English phrases: they say "baby-cry" rather than "crybaby," and "box of Pandoras" rather than "Pandora's box."

After listening to the way my friends pronounced place names, I created phonetic pronunciation guides. And I started referring to the project as the "Santa Fe Dictionary."

The years went by, and I learned more about the towns and villages to the north. I discovered that Taos honors Padre Antonio José Martinez, the rebellious priest who defied Archbishop Jean Baptiste Lamy, as much as Santa Fe honors Lamy himself. And that Los Alamos was not always a nuclear laboratory; before the Manhattan Project, it was the site of Los Alamos Ranch School, a rustic prep school for troubled rich boys like Gore Vidal and William S. Burroughs. These stories were added to the dictionary.

I finally decided to publish the book but was undecided about what to call it. A friend said he thought that it had evolved into an encyclopedia. That term seemed slightly presumptuous at first, but the book had grown to more than 1,000 entries.

The project then became more of a collaborative effort. Friends read each entry and pointed out inconsistencies. Others contributed photographs and drawings. Charts and graphs of things like temperature, population, and voting histories were added to the text.

Now, many years after the first entry in the "glossary," the *Encyclopedia of Santa Fe and Northern New Mexico* is finally in print.

This book is not so complicated as to require an owner's manual, but there are a few issues that merit a short explanation.

The encyclopedia is intended to be simple and intuitive, so entries are listed the way that one would hear them in ordinary conversation. The Cathedral Basilica of St. Francis of Assisi, for instance, is listed as St. Francis Cathedral. People's names are also simplified. United States Senator Thomas Stewart Udall is universally known as Tom Udall, and that is how he is listed. Some people, like author N. Scott Momaday and architect John Gaw Meem, are known by an initial and two names or by all three names. In their cases, the listing includes the initial and two names or the three names.

Some place names have been capitalized and some have not. Northern New Mexico is capitalized because it is a distinct region, like Southern California. And although most Spanish towns in New Mexico have a "plaza," when capitalized, that word refers specifically to the Santa Fe Plaza. Santa Fe's Eastside, Westside, and Southside have been capitalized and rendered one word because, though they may not have definite boundaries, they are spoken of and thought of as having definite characteristics. The north side, on the other hand, is relatively undefined, and so remains two words in lower case.

Reference books have different ways of coping with cross references. Some insert *see entry* after the word and some format the word in small capitals so that readers will know that it appears as an entry elsewhere in the book. Both methods were attempted, but neither solution was satisfactory as they both cluttered the text. I decided not to make any attempt to identify cross references on the assumption that readers who encounter an unfamiliar word will look for it under its own entry.

Pronunciation is confusing in New Mexico. The regional lexicon includes English corruptions of Spanish corruptions of Indian words, so, depending which New Mexican one asks, the same word may be pronounced in different ways. *Tesuque*, for example, is the name of a pueblo and a village, both just north of Santa Fe. Pueblo people pronounce the name tuh-SUE-*key*, as do most of the Anglos who live near the village. But because *que* is pronounced kay in Spanish, most Spanish speakers say tuh-SUE-*kay*. The encyclopedia does not pretend to settle the debate about the right way to pronounce Tesuque, or any other word. When a word is pronounced in more than one way, both pronunciations are included.

The phonetic pronunciation guides are intended to help English speakers avoid glaring errors, but they do not necessarily reflect the way a Spanish speaker would pronounce a word. In *Rio Grande*, for example, it is perfectly acceptable to say GRAND, rather than the Spanish GRAHN-day. And, while (almost) all New Mexicans pronounce *coyote* in three syllables, English speakers say kye-YO-tee, not ko-YO-tay, which is how the word is pronounced in Spanish. In cases where both English and Spanish pronunciations are included, the English versions are listed first. Umlauts, tildes, and stress marks have been omitted in favor of sound-alike syllables. Those who would like to hear how a word sounds should visit the encyclopedia's web site, encyclopediaofsantafe.com, which includes audio pronunciations for most of the place names.

The encyclopedia was compiled entirely from secondary sources: books, newspapers, magazines, and, in some cases, blogs and online journals. There is no suggested reading list because most sources are listed as entries in the text.

Various businesses, including restaurants, hotels, and stores, are referenced in the book, but a mere listing should not be considered an endorsement. Some business entries are included simply because they have been around for so long that most Santa Feans know them. Some are landmarks that locals use when giving directions, and others are included because they are associated with an historical event. It must be noted, however, that these business entries are not inclusive. Many old Santa Fe establishments meet one of the foregoing criteria but have not been included simply because they did not occur to me until after the final copy was set. Such omissions will be corrected in the next edition.

Even with multiple fact-checks and numerous pre-publication readings, it is inevitable that the encyclopedia will contain errors. I would appreciate it if readers would email me at mark@encylopedia-ofsantafe.com to point out mistakes. The encyclopedia will be reissued in two or three years, and it would be good to eliminate existing errors before creating new ones.

"Every calculation based on experience elsewhere fails in New Mexico."

- Governor Lew Wallace

- A -

Aamodt case (*A-mutt)

Lengthy court case that illustrates the dizzying complexity of New Mexico water law. Filed in 1966, *State Engineer vs. R. Lee Aamodt et al.* is the oldest case on the federal docket. The lawsuit is an attempt by the state to preemptively resolve the potential conflict between the senior water rights of Indians and the junior water rights of non-Indians in the Pojoaque Valley. There are more than 2,800 claimants (Aamodt is first alphabetically), including dozens of acequia associations and the Nambé, Pojoaque, Tesuque, and San Ildefonso pueblos.

A 2006 settlement agreement is contingent on combined county, state, and federal expenditures of almost $300 million, most of which will be used to build a regional water system. The federal portion was approved in 2010, so a final settlement is in sight.

*First-year law students at the University of New Mexico often mispronounce the name. A learning tool was created when a frustrated professor exclaimed, "It's Aamodt, dammit!".

Abiquiu (A-bih-cue)

New Mexico village best known as the longtime home of reclusive artist Georgia O'Keeffe. From 1949 to 1984, O'Keeffe lived in her Abiquiu house in the winter and her Ghost Ranch house in the summer. The name is a Tewa word of unknown origin. (It is sometimes written "Abiquiú," with an accent over the final *u*.)

The village is 48 miles northwest of Santa Fe via US 84. Abiquiu Lake, a reservoir on the Rio Chama, is created by a dam seven miles northwest of the village.

Abruzzo family (ah-BROO-zo)

Owners of Ski Santa Fe, the Sandia Peak Ski Area, and the Sandia Peak Tramway. Ben Abruzzo, the Albuquerque family's patriarch, was a real estate developer and adventurer who set several ballooning records, including the first trans-Atlantic and trans-Pacific balloon crossings. He and his wife died in a private plane crash in 1985. The Anderson-Abruzzo Albuquerque International Balloon Museum is co-named for him.

Ben's three sons took over the family businesses after his death. Richard, the youngest, was killed in 2010 when his balloon plummeted into the Adriatic Sea.

abuelo/a (ah-BWAY-lo/la)

"Grandfather" and "grandmother." *Abuelito* and *abuelita* are affectionate diminutives. In some contexts, a grandfather can be a bogeyman. In the Matachines dance, the abuelo character maintains order – and provides comic relief – by bullying the spectators.

acequia (ah-SAY-key-uh)

Acequia headgate

An irrigation ditch, an essential element of Northern New Mexico agriculture. The parciantes, those who draw water from the ditch, are organized into an acequia association headed by a mayordomo, or ditch boss. The annual cleaning of the acequia is a centuries-old rite of spring in Northern New Mexico's farming communities.

Acequias are man-made ditches. They should not be confused with arroyos, which are natural streambeds.

acequia madre (ah-SAY-key-uh MAH-dray)

The "mother ditch" or main trunk of a local acequia system. Santa Fe's Acequia Madre dates from the early 17th century and is mentioned on the National Register of Historic Places. It runs from the foothills east of Santa Fe to the village of Agua Fria on the city's Westside. The Railyard features an *Acequia Niña*, "Daughter Ditch," that has been diverted from the Acequia Madre.

Acequia Madre is also the name of a street that parallels a length of the ditch. The street runs from Canyon Road to Paseo de Peralta, through some of Eastside Santa Fe's priciest real estate.

Acoma Pueblo (ACK-uh-muh)

The oldest continuously occupied community in the United States. Acoma is known as Sky City because the original pueblo sits atop a 350-foot-high mesa. A few Acomas stay on the mesa, but most live in nearby villages.

In 1599, the Keresan-speaking pueblo was the site of a fierce battle between the Acomas and Spanish soldiers under Don Juan de Oñate. When the pueblo surrendered, Oñate ordered its population enslaved and the amputation of one foot from each captured warrior. In 1998, protestors calling themselves the "Friends of Acoma" retaliated by cutting the right foot off of the equestrian statue of the conquistador at the Oñate Monument and Visitors Center in Alcalde.

Acoma Pueblo is 120 miles southwest of Santa Fe, 13 miles south of I-40.

Adams, Ansel

(1902-1984) World-famous photographer who made multiple visits to New Mexico, often as a guest of Mabel Dodge Luhan. Adams collaborated with writer Mary Austin in a 1930 book titled *Taos Pueblo*. His most famous photograph, *Moonrise, Hernandez, New Mexico*, was taken in 1941. *Moonrise* has been described as the best known and most sought after fine art photograph.

adobe (uh-DOE-be)

A sun-dried brick made of clay, sand, and straw. Unlike kiln-dried bricks, adobes "melt" after prolonged exposure to the elements, so they must be covered with a protective coat of mud or stucco.

Santa Fe-style architecture is sometimes called "adobe architecture" because the adobe brick was the basic building block for the original style.

In modern Santa Fe, however, most buildings are faux adobe, built with other materials but made to look as though they are constructed of adobe bricks. *Adobe* also means "earth-colored."

adobe camouflage

Author Chris Wilson's term for disguising a non-adobe building to make it conform to Santa Fe style. In *The Myth of Santa Fe*, he cites the Catron Block building on the northeast corner of the Plaza as the best example of adobe camouflage. Constructed in 1891 with an Italianate façade, the building was later disguised with adobe-brown paint and a Territorial-style portal.

adobe Disneyland

Dismissive term for Santa Fe. Most Santa Feans think that the comparison to Disneyland is silly. While the city's architecture is carefully controlled and tourism is an important industry, Santa Fe's cultural foundations are real. Anyone who has attended a pueblo feast day or the processioning of La Conquistadora knows that these are authentic religious and cultural events, not shows staged for tourists.

African Americans

The most underrepresented ethnicity in Northern New Mexico.

Blacks have a long history in the region (see ESTEVAN THE MOOR), but they are underrepresented in New Mexico today, just as they are in the country of Mexico. This is because the black servants and slaves who accompanied the Spanish to the New World intermarried with both the Indians and the Spanish, and their descendants were absorbed into the larger culture.

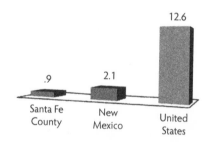

African-American Percentage of Population

Santa Fe County .9
New Mexico 2.1
United States 12.6

Blacks are even less numerous in Northern New Mexico than they are in the state at large. The few black immigrants who came to New Mexico in the 19th and 20th centuries – the Blackdom settlers, Buffalo Soldiers who stayed after their enlistments were up, and African Americans who worked on the Santa Fe Railway – tended to settle around Las Cruces or Albuquerque rather than Santa Fe.

Santa Fe's most memorable African American was Donald Grady, who served as police chief from 1994 to 1996. Originally from Wisconsin, Grady was hired by Mayor Debbie Jaramillo to reform the police department, but his policies were unpopular with the rank and file. He prohibited policemen from accepting free coffee and banned the wearing of bolo ties by plainclothes officers, a policy that was seen as culturally insensitive by Santa Fe's largely Hispanic police force. Grady resigned and left the state after his officers gave him a 103-5 vote of no confidence. He later earned a doctorate at the University of Minnesota and worked in peacekeeping efforts in Bosnia, Kosovo, Israel, and Palestine.

Agua Fria (AH-gwah FREE-uh)

A village and a street. The village of Agua Fria, whose name means "cold water," occupies about two square miles on Santa Fe's western boundary, some six miles southwest of the Plaza. Agua Fria, population 2,800, has been designated a Traditional Historic Community, so it cannot be easily annexed, although it is in danger of being completely surrounded by the city.

Agua Fria Street begins downtown at Guadalupe Street and runs southwest for seven-plus miles before terminating at Airport Road.

Akal Security (ah-CALL)

The most visible of the Sikhs' many businesses. Founded in 1980, Akal is one of the largest security companies in the United States. It holds contracts to guard courthouses, military bases, and other federal facilities around the country.

alacena (ah-la-SEH-nuh)

A recessed cupboard built into an interior adobe wall. Alacenas often feature decorative wooden doors.

Alameda Street (*al-uh-MEE-duh, ah-la-MEH-duh)

Santa Fe's riverside drive. Alameda Street parallels the Santa Fe River, beginning at Camino Cabra on the city's Eastside and running west for six and a half miles. It is divided into East and West Alameda, with Don Gaspar Avenue as the dividing line.

Santa Fe author John Pen LaFarge suggests in *Turn Left at the Sleeping Dog* that the word *street* is redundant since *alameda* means "tree-lined boulevard." Some Santa Feans do refer to the street as "the Alameda."

*Many Anglos pronounce the word al-uh-MEE-duh; others say something closer to the Spanish ah-la-MEH-duh.

alamo (AL-uh-mo)

"Poplar" or "cotton-wood." People and trees both need water, so they tend to congregate in the same places. Variations of *alamo* – Los Alamos, Alamogordo, and Alameda Street, for example – are common in New Mexico place names.

Alamo (cottonwood)

Alamogordo (al-uh-muh-GORE-doe)

New Mexico's ninth most populous city. Alamogordo, population 30,403, is associated with nearby Holloman Air Force Base and White Sands National Monument. The city's name means "fat cottonwood."

Alamogordo is 221 miles south of Santa Fe on US 54/70.

Albuquerque (AL-buh-kirk-ee)

New Mexico's largest city, by far. Albuquerque's population is 545,852, compared to Las Cruces at 97,618, Rio Rancho at 87,521, and Santa Fe at 67,947.

Most Santa Feans have clear feelings about their larger neighbor: they like having an airport, university, zoo, and big-city shopping an hour

Albuquerque in 1880, just before the boom

away – but they would not want to live there. Traffic is one reason, but heat is a bigger factor. In the summer, Albuquerque is seven or eight degrees hotter than Santa Fe.

The Duke City, which is named for the Spanish Duke of Alburquerque (the first *r* was later dropped), grew exponentially after the Santa Fe Railway arrived in 1880. Albuquerque is 59 miles south of Santa Fe via I-25.

Albuquerque Journal

Albuquerque's morning newspaper, the most-read paper in New Mexico. A modified version of the paper called the *Journal Santa Fe* is sold in the City Different as an alternative to *The New Mexican*. Publisher Tom Lang has run the family-owned *Journal* since 1971. The Republican-leaning paper endorsed George W. Bush for president in 2000 and 2004 and John McCain in 2008.

alcalde (all-CALL-day)

"Mayor" or "official." Alcalde is the name of a community 32 miles north of Santa Fe on NM 68. The Oñate Monument and Visitors Center is in Alcalde.

The Railyard's Alcaldesa Street (*alcaldesa* means "lady mayor") is named for former Santa Fe Mayor Debbie Jaramillo, who presided over the city's acquisition of the Railyard property in 1995.

Algodones (al-go-DOAN-es)

Small community named for *algodón*, "cotton." The name derives from the fluff produced by the village's many cottonwood trees.

Algodones is off I-25, 40 miles south of Santa Fe.

Alianza (ah-lee-AHN-zuh)

The *Alianza Federal de Mercedes*, "Federal Alliance of Land Grants," a 1960s protest organization led by fiery Mexican-American preacher Reies Lopez Tijerina. The Alianza argued, sometimes violently, that Northern New Mexico Hispanics had been cheated out of their land in violation of the Treaty of Guadalupe Hidalgo.

In June 1967, two people were wounded and two others held hostage when the group staged a raid on the Rio Arriba County Courthouse in Tierra Amarilla. Reies Tijerina successfully defended himself when tried for his part in the courthouse raid but was later jailed for other offenses related to the movement. The Alianza eventually faded away, though a billboard that reads *Tierra o Muerte*, "Land or Death!", still stands on US 84 near the turnoff for Tierra Amarilla.

American Indian

One of the names for the original inhabitants of the Americas. (See INDIAN.)

American Spirit cigarettes

Principal product of Santa Fe Natural Tobacco Company. The additive-free cigarettes come in packages bearing the image of a pipe-smoking Indian chief.

Anasazi (ah-nuh-SAH-zee)

Ancient ancestors of most of today's Pueblo Indians. (New Mexico's Zuni tribe and Arizona's Hopi tribe are thought to be descended from the

Mogollon rather than the Anasazi.) The Anasazi once inhabited pueblo towns at New Mexico's Bandelier and Chaco Canyon sites, in Arizona's Canyon de Chelly, and around Colorado's Mesa Verde. These and other settlements were abandoned in the 1300s when their inhabitants migrated to lands closer to the Rio Grande. Drought is the usual explanation for the moves, though there is speculation that they were accelerated by Navajo and Apache raids.

The Navajo, who are not Pueblo people, came up with the name *Anasazi* when they found the abandoned pueblos. Some Pueblo Indians dislike the term, which they say means "alien ancestor" or "ancestor of my enemy." The National Park Service recognizes their objection and uses "Ancestral Puebloan" instead. But the Navajo say that *Anasazi* means nothing more than "ancient ones," and the term is still widely used.

Anaya (ah-NIGH-ya)

Prominent New Mexico surname. Toney Anaya served as New Mexico's governor from 1983 to 1987. Rudolfo Anaya is the author of the coming-of-age novel *Bless Me, Ultima.*

Rudolfo Anaya

Angel Fire

Northern New Mexico village and ski resort. Angel Fire, population 1,216, is known for the nearby Vietnam Veterans Memorial State Park, where Victor Westphall erected a monument in memory of his son, Marine First Lieutenant David Westphall. The Westphall memorial was the first monument in the country to honor Vietnam veterans. It was designated a state park in 2005.

The ski area sponsors an annual shovel race, where competitors sitting on grain shovels race down the slopes at speeds of up to 70 miles per hour.

Like Red River and Eagle Nest, Angel Fire is what is sometimes called an "Anglo village," one established in the 19th or 20th century, as opposed to a much older, historically Hispanic village like Chimayó or Truchas.

Angel Fire is just south of the Enchanted Circle, 95 miles northeast of Santa Fe and 25 miles east of Taos.

Anglo

Inclusive ethnic and cultural term. Derived from *Anglo-Saxon*, the word usually means a non-Spanish-speaking white person of European descent. In New Mexico's tricultural society, however, all people who are neither Hispanic nor Indian – including African Americans, Asians, and East Indians – are categorized as Anglos.

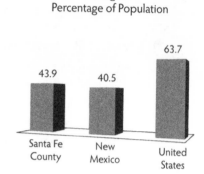

Anglo
Percentage of Population

Unlike *gringo*, a term that carries a newcomer connotation, *Anglo* is never construed as even mildly pejorative.

Annual Manual

The *Santa Fe Reporter*'s "Locals' Guide to Living in Santa Fe." The *Annual Manual* lists the addresses, phone numbers, and web sites of government offices, animal shelters, restaurants, medical clinics, and schools, and other information useful to residents and visitors.

Apache

One of New Mexico's three major Indian groups, along with the Pueblo and the Navajo. The name is a variation of the Zuni word *apachu*, "enemy."

Like the Navajo, the Apache are Athabascans who migrated to the Southwest from the Pacific Northwest between 1300 A.D. and 1500 A.D. The most warlike of the regional tribes, Apaches raided the indigenous Pueblo Indians, the Spanish, and the Americans until Geronimo's capture in 1886.

The Mescalero Apache reservation is in the southern part of New Mexico, northeast of Alamogordo. The Jicarilla Apache reservation is in the northern part of the state, on the Colorado border.

Apache Canyon

Narrow defile 15 miles southeast of Santa Fe. Traffic between Santa Fe and the plains to the east has always passed through Apache Canyon: the Santa Fe Trail ran through it in the 1820s; General Stephen Watts Kearny marched his troops through it in 1846; Confederate invaders were stopped in it in 1862; and I-25 runs through it today.

The canyon's name stems from the frequent Indian raids on people traveling through it, though some historians think the raiders were more often Comanches than Apaches.

Apodaca (ah-po-DAH-cuh)

Prominent New Mexico surname. Democrat Jerry Apodaca was New Mexico's governor from 1975 to 1979. Apodaca Hill is an old address on Santa Fe's Eastside.

Aragon, Manny (*AIR-uh-gone, ah-rah-GOAN)

(1947-) Disgraced state politician.

Former Senate President Pro Tempore Manny M. Aragon was for many years the most powerful man in the New Mexico Legislature. After representing Albuquerque's South Valley for 29 years, the Democratic leader resigned from the Senate in 2004 to become president of Highlands University. Four years later, he was charged with illegally profiting from a courthouse construction project undertaken during his tenure in the legislature. Aragon ultimately pled guilty to the charge and was sentenced to five and a half years in federal prison. His friends, including a former chief justice of the New Mexico Supreme Court, held a party for him before he reported to prison in 2009.

*The Anglo pronunciation of the name (AIR-uh-gone) is how gringos hear it in world history class in the lesson on Catherine of Aragon. The Spanish pronunciation (ah-rah-GOAN) requires a slight roll on the r.

araña (ah-RAHN-yuh)

"Spider" or "chandelier."

Archuleta (ar-choo-LEH-tuh)

Prominent surname in Northern New Mexico and southern Colorado. Felipe Archuleta was a santero from the village of Tesuque. Archuleta County, Colorado, which includes the town of Pagosa Springs, is just north of the New Mexico state line.

Arkin, Alan

Alan Arkin

(1934-)   Oscar-winning actor (*Little Miss Sunshine*) and Santa Fe resident. The multi-talented Arkin co-wrote *The Banana Boat Song* made famous by Harry Belafonte, was a founding member of the Second City comedy troupe, and directed *The Sunshine Boys* on Broadway. He has appeared in scores of movies and was nominated for a Best Actor Academy Award for his first screen role in *The Russians Are Coming, the Russians Are Coming*. He has authored ten books, including his 2011 memoir, *An Improvised Life*.

Arkin moved to Santa Fe in 2004. Asked why he chooses to live in Northern New Mexico, he explained that, "It's the only place in the world where you can wear a cowboy hat and Birkenstocks and not look out of place. I have both."

Armijo, Manuel (ar-MEE-ho)

(1793-1854) New Mexico's colorful governor for much of the Mexican Period. The portly and elaborately uniformed Armijo was instrumental in putting down the Chimayó Rebellion of 1837 and in apprehending members of the Texas-Santa Fe Expedition of 1841. But he is suspected of collaborating with the Americans in the 1846 Mexican-American War. Historians speculate that money changed hands when Armijo met with an American trader just before the arrival of the invading army. Whether he accepted a bribe or not, Armijo did abandon his soldiers in Apache Canyon, and the Americans occupied Santa Fe without resistance.

Locally sold T-shirts credit Armijo with the phrase, "Poor New Mexico, so far from God, so close to Texas."

Manuel Armijo

arroyo (uh-ROY-o)

A streambed. Arroyos are harmless rivers of sand when they are dry, which is most of the time, but they can be dangerous in flash floods. Also, because ne'er-do-wells often loiter in arroyos, Santa Feans usually avoid them at night. Parents used to keep their children out of arroyos by scaring them with the story of La Llorona.

Arroyos are natural streambeds. They should not be confused with acequias, which are man-made ditches.

Ashley Pond Park

Park in downtown Los Alamos centered around Ashley Pond. The pond was just a low spot where water stood after a rain until the boys of the Los Alamos Ranch School dug it out and made it a permanent water feature. Whimsy compelled the boys to name it Ashley Pond after Ashley Pond, Jr., founder of the Ranch School.

Aspenization

The process of becoming like Aspen, Colorado, where wealthy newcomers have raised property values so high that middle-income people can no longer afford to live there. Many Santa Feans, particularly Hispanics whose families have lived in the city for centuries, fear that their hometown is becoming like Aspen.

Because Santa Fe is the state capital, there will always be middle-class government jobs available to locals, something that is missing in Aspen, but Santa Fe still has what is called an "hourglass" economy, with many people in the upper- and lower-income brackets and relatively few in the middle. And, with property values rising much faster than wages, it has become increasingly difficult for middle-class workers to buy homes in the city. Some people commute to work from Rio Rancho or Albuquerque; others live within the city limits, but mostly on the Southside. The old residential areas on Santa Fe's Eastside have become prohibitively expensive, and the downtown area that was once a shopping center for locals is now devoted to art galleries and other tourist-oriented businesses.

Atalaya Mountain (at-uh-LIE-uh)

"Watchtower" mountain, Santa Fe's premier in-town hiking locale. The three-and-a-half-mile Atalaya Trail begins at the parking lot of St. John's College and climbs 1,781 feet to the top of the mountain. The trail is popular with hikers, runners, and sightseers.

Atalaya Mountain was rescued from development in the early 1990s when local conservationists protested Shirley MacLaine's plan to build a home near its summit. Opposition from Dale Ball, Stewart Udall, and the Trust for Public Land ultimately quashed the project.

Atchison, Topeka and Santa Fe Railway

See SANTA FE RAILWAY.

Athabascan (ath-uh-BASK-un)

Indian language group, and the people who speak it. The Apache and the Navajo are Athabascans who migrated from the Pacific Northwest to present-day New Mexico, Arizona, and southern Colorado between 1300 A.D. and 1500 A.D.

Austin, Mary

(1868-1934) Author, social activist, and co-founder of the Spanish Colonial Arts Society. A prolific writer, Austin is best known for *The Land of Little Rain* (1903), a collection of short stories and essays dealing with the Southwest.

Austin was already famous when she visited Northern New Mexico in 1918 at the invitation of Mabel Dodge Luhan. She moved to Santa Fe in 1924, and she and artist Frank Applegate formed the Spanish Colonial Arts Society in 1925. The society sponsored the first Spanish Market a year later.

Mary Austin

Austin was a serious person, and she was committed to protecting Indian and Spanish culture. An acquaintance said of her: "Crowned in queenly braids, wrapped in a Spanish shawl ... she pushed for action. Her followers laughed at her, but they loved her ...."

avenida (ah-veh-NEE-duh)

"Avenue." Avenida Vista Grande is the main entrance to the Eldorado subdivision south of Santa Fe.

Aztlán (*AHZ-lahn, ahz-LAHN)

"Land of the Aztecs," the mythical homeland of the ancient Aztecs and, by extension, modern Indo-Hispanics. Chicano activists have argued that Aztlán was in the Four Corners region and that, because of this prehistoric connection, Mexicans and Mexican-Americans have more right to the American Southwest than the Anglos who came later. Some, including former UNM professor Charles Truxillo, have even advocated the establishment of a separate country in the part of the United States that was taken in the Mexican-American War. For most Chicanos, however, the Aztlán concept has always been more of a talking point than a real goal.

*Anglos tend to emphasize the first syllable, as in AHZ-lahn. Spanish speakers obey the accent mark and stress the second syllable, saying ahz-LAHN.

- B -

baby-cry

Local reversal of "crybaby." Baby-cry is heard in schoolyards throughout Northern New Mexico.

Baca (BAH-cuh)

Prominent New Mexico surname. (See C De Baca.)

bagolito (bag-o-LEE-toe)

Cynic's name for an electrified farolito. The Christmas lantern is traditionally fashioned from a brown-paper bag, sand, and a candle, but some businesses use a manufactured version made from a plastic bag and an electric bulb.

baile (BY-lay)

"Ball" or "dance." In the 19th century, a Santa Fe baile could be a refined affair or a wild bacchanal attended by rowdies and ladies of the evening. In March 1869, *The New Mexican* quoted a young man who said that he attended a baile and saw 16 fights before he was himself knocked out.

The *Gran Baile*, "Grand Ball," is held each year during Fiesta.

Ball, Dale

(1923-) Retired banker and conservationist. As director of the Santa Fe Conservation Trust, Ball worked with Stewart Udall and others to stop residential development on Atalaya Mountain. He is best known as the driving force behind the Dale Ball Trails.

Albuquerque International Balloon Fiesta

Balloon Fiesta, Albuquerque International

The largest gathering of hot air balloons and, purportedly, the most-photographed annual event in the world. The nine-day festival takes place in Albuquerque in early October.

banco (BAHN-co)

A bench built into an adobe wall, usually an interior wall.

Bandelier, Adolph (ban-duh-LEER)

(1840-1914) Swiss-born ethnographer, archaeologist, and novelist. In 1890, Bandelier published *The Delight Makers*, a fictionalized account of prehistoric life in Frijoles Canyon. Bandelier National Monument was named for him when it was created in 1916.

The Bandelier Garden at El Zaguán is also named for Adolph. He and his wife lived in the Canyon Road hacienda in 1891 and 1892, but there is no evidence that they designed or planted the garden.

Bandelier National Monument

One of the most popular places for Santa Feans to take visitors. The 32,000-acre monument includes over 70 miles of hiking trails, but its main attractions are the Anasazi ruins and cave dwellings. An easy trail meanders up Frijoles Canyon past the ruins, and a steep ladder ascends to the cave dwellings, which include Alcove House (once known as Ceremonial Cave) and a reconstructed kiva.

The monument closed briefly after the Las Conchas fire of 2011 because of the danger of flash floods through Frijoles Canyon.

Bandelier National Monument is on the Jemez Mountains' Pajarito Plateau. The entrance is 40 miles from Santa Fe on NM 4.

Kiva at Bandelier National Monument

bark beetle

Parasitic killer of piñon trees. The *ips confusus*, a beetle about the size of a grain of rice, burrows through the bark of drought-weakened trees, carrying with it a blue fungus that shuts off the flow of moisture in the trees' trunks. There is no treatment for an infected tree. The drought of the early 2000s led to a bark beetle infestation that destroyed thousands of piñons.

barranca (bah-RAHN-cuh)

"Ravine" or "gorge," though in New Mexico the more common meaning is "hill." The hilly area just west of US 84/285 between Pojoaque and Española is known as Las Barrancas.

barrio (BAH-ree-o)

"Neighborhood" or "district." In Santa Fe, the word does not imply an urban ghetto, or even an area with a majority of Hispanic residents, as it does in Los Angeles and elsewhere. Barrio de la Cañada is an older, middle-class subdivision on Santa Fe's Westside.

Barrio de Analco (ah-NAHL-co)

Historic district along East DeVargas Street, just south of the Santa Fe River. The area was originally settled by Mexican Indians who accompanied the Spanish to New Mexico. It was called *analco*, "other side of the water," because the Santa Fe River separates it from the Plaza and the Palace of the Governors. San Miguel Mission and what is reputed to be the Oldest House in America are in Barrio de Analco.

Bataan Memorial Military Museum (buh-TAN)

Museum honoring New Mexico veterans, particularly those who served in the Pacific Theater in World War II. In January 1941, the New Mexico National Guard was called up and sent to the Philippines. When the islands fell to the Japanese in April 1942, over 1,400 of the unit's men were captured, and New Mexico instantly became the state with the most soldiers held prisoner by the Japanese. Nearly half of the New Mexican POWs died in captivity – on the infamous Bataan Death March, on transport ships, or in prisoner of war camps.

Feelings about the Japanese run deep among New Mexico veterans. In October 1999, a Santa Fe City Council meeting became heated over a proposal to erect a memorial to Japanese civilians interned in Santa Fe during World War II. (See JAPANESE INTERNMENT CAMP.) When council members approved the memorial, a protester accused them of "kick[ing] the Bataan veterans in their teeth in the twilight of their years."

The Bataan Memorial Military Museum and Library is on Old Pecos Trail in what was once the National Guard armory. The Bataan Memorial Building is a state-government office building on Don Gaspar Avenue, near the Roundhouse. An eternal flame honoring the Bataan veterans burns outside the building.

Battle of Glorieta Pass

See GLORIETA PASS, BATTLE OF.

Baumann, Gustave

(BOW-mun, rhymes with COW-mun)

(1881-1971) One of Santa Fe's best-known artists. Baumann was already a recognized printmaker when he visited the Taos art colony in 1918. Finding Taos too crowded, he settled in Santa Fe instead, and he lived and worked in the City Different until his death in 1971. The German-born artist is known for his color woodcut prints, but he also painted in oils and made fanciful marionettes that he used in puppet shows

Gustave Baumann, John Gaw Meem, and Ernest Blumenschein in 1957

for Santa Fe children. His puppet work included construction of the head of the first Zozobra and the reconstruction of La Conquistadora.

Cards, calendars, and posters of Baumann's work outsell those of any other artist at the New Mexico Museum of Art gift shop.

Baumann's ashes are buried beneath an aspen tree off Hyde Park Road.

Begay (bih-GAY)

One of the most common Navajo names, *Begay* is derived from *bii ye*, which means "son of" in Navajo. When Navajo parents delivered their children to boarding schools in the late 19th century, confused Anglo registrars often noted Begay as the child's last name.

Professional golfer and Albuquerque native Notah Begay III was Tiger Woods's roommate at Stanford and the best man at his wedding.

Belen (beh-LIN)

City named for Bethlehem. Belen, current population 7,269, originated as a paraje, or rest stop, on the Camino Real. Apache raiders made life precarious for people who settled between Belen and El Paso del Norte, so for most of the Spanish Colonial Period, Belen marked the southern extension of Spanish New Mexico.

Today, Belen is the southern terminus of the Rail Runner Express. The city is 93 miles south of Santa Fe via I-25.

Benitez, Maria (beh-NEE-tez)

(Ms. Benitez does not disclose her age.) Noted flamenco dancer and choreographer. Born Maria Diaz in Taos, Benitez began performing in Santa Fe in the 1960s. The Lodge at Santa Fe presents flamenco performances in the Maria Benitez Cabaret.

Bent, Charles

(1799-1847) The first governor of the New Mexico Territory. Bent was a graduate of West Point, a trader on the Santa Fe Trail, and a partner in Bent's Fort. He was also Kit Carson's friend and brother-in-law. (Bent was married to Maria Ignacia Jaramillo, sister of Carson's wife, Josefa Jaramillo.) Both men maintained houses in Taos.

Bent was appointed New Mexico's first American governor by General Stephen Watts Kearny in 1846, but he was murdered in the Taos Revolt after only four months in office. Bent Street, just off the plaza in Taos, is named for Charles Bent. He is buried in Santa Fe National Cemetery.

Bent's Fort

Adobe fort in southeast Colorado established by Charles Bent and his brother William. From 1833 to 1849, the fort served as a trading post for Indians and fur trappers and as a way station for travelers on the Mountain Branch of the Santa Fe Trail.

Bent's Fort has been reconstructed and is now a National Historic Site. It is eight miles east of La Junta, Colorado.

Bernalillo (burn-uh-LEE-o)

Town named for the Bernal family. Bernalillo, population 8,320, originated as a paraje, or rest stop, on the Camino Real, became a farming town, and is now a bedroom community for Albuquerque and Santa Fe.

Bernalillo is not in Bernalillo County but is, rather, the county seat of Sandoval County. The town is 47 miles southwest of Santa Fe, at the US 550 exit off I-25.

Bernalillo County

The most populous of New Mexico's 33 counties. Bernalillo County's population of 662,564 in the 2010 census dwarfs that of runner-up Doña Ana County, at 209,233, and third-place Santa Fe County, at 144,170. Bernalillo County encompasses most of the Albuquerque metro area. Like the town of Bernalillo, it is named for the Bernal family.

Best of Santa Fe

The *Santa Fe Reporter*'s annual popularity contest for restaurants, politicians, opticians, auto repair shops, and other entities. The paper lists the top vote-getters in reader polls in late summer, and winners' names appear on the *Reporter*'s web site through the following year.

bienvenido (be-en-vuh-NEE-doe)

"Welcome." *Bienvenidos* is *The New Mexican*'s annual summer guide to Santa Fe. It is also the name of the Santa Fe Chamber of Commerce's volunteer division. In the summer, Bienvenidos volunteers staff a tourist information booth on the west side of the Plaza.

Big I

Albuquerque's "Big Interchange" of I-25 and I-40. In most large cities, interstate traffic is routed around the downtown area via a beltway. In Albuquerque, the interstate highways meet in the middle of the city.

bigote (bih-GO-tay)

"Mustache." An old dicho goes: *Un beso sin bigote es como un huevo sin sal*, "A kiss without a mustache is like an egg without salt."

Billy the Kid

(1859-1881) New Mexico's most notorious outlaw. William McCarty, a.k.a. Henry Antrim, a.k.a. William Bonney, a.k.a. Billy the Kid, was born in an Irish slum in New York and came to New Mexico with his tubercular mother in the early 1870s. While still in his teens, he earned notoriety as a cattle rustler and as an enthusiastic participant in the Lincoln County War.

The Kid was no ordinary gunslinger. He spoke fluent Spanish to his girlfriends and carried on a lengthy correspondence with Territorial Governor Lew Wallace. Wallace had promised Billy a pardon for crimes committed during the Lincoln County War if he would testify to other crimes he had witnessed. Billy did testify, but, for reasons that are not clear, the governor did not issue the pardon. The Kid vowed "... to ride into the

Billy the Kid, circa 1879

plaza at Santa Fe, hitch my horse in front of the palace, and put a bullet through Lew Wallace," but he died at age 21 in a shootout with Sheriff Pat Garrett before he could carry out the threat. He is buried near Fort Sumner.

Talk of granting Billy the Kid a posthumous pardon comes up every few years, mostly because it guarantees national publicity. Governor Bill Richardson raised the subject in the waning days of his administration, but the idea was not well received. Descendants of Governor Lew Wallace and Sheriff Pat Garrett opposed a pardon, as did Santa Fe author Hampton Sides. Sides wrote a letter to the editor of *The New York Times* in which he wondered what would be gained by dredging up stories about a "trigger-happy sociopath who's been moldering in his grave for almost 130 years." On his last day in office, Richardson announced that he would not pardon the Kid.

Bingaman, Jeff (BING-uh-mun)

(1943-) New Mexico's long-serving United States senator. Bingaman, who grew up in Silver City, was the state's attorney general before being elected to the Senate in 1982. Bingaman announced in early 2011 that he would not seek reelection in 2012. As of this writing, the frontrunners for his seat are Democrat Martin Heinrich and Republican Heather Wilson.

Jeff Bingaman

Bishop's Lodge

Exclusive resort on the site of what was once the private retreat of Archbishop Jean Baptiste Lamy. The secluded, 450-acre property includes 111 rooms in 15 lodges, riding stables, tennis courts, a skeet range, a trout pond, and hiking trails. Lamy's well-preserved private chapel and gardens are open to the public. The facility is on Bishop's Lodge Road, just under four miles from the Plaza.

bizcochito (biss-co-CHEE-toe)

New Mexico's anise-flavored official state cookie. The word is sometimes spelled "biscochito."

black bear

New Mexico's official state animal. The Department of Game and Fish estimates that there are 6,000 black bears in the state. (Grizzlies, also called brown bears, are no longer found in New Mexico.) Black bears can live in close proximity to humans, though encounters are rare. Sightings are more common in years in which the bears' natural forage is reduced because of a late freeze or a particularly dry winter. In those years, hungry bears have been seen throughout the state, including in the city of Santa Fe.

Smokey Bear is New Mexico's most famous black bear.

Black Hole

Scientific equipment surplus store and nuclear-age museum. The store

The Black Hole

was founded by the late Ed Grothus, a former Los Alamos National Laboratory employee who became an antinuclear activist. Grothus collected recycled hardware from LANL, both for display and for resale to artists and amateur scientists.

The Black Hole is on Arkansas Avenue in Los Alamos.

Black Legend

Widespread belief that the colonial Spanish were unusually cruel, particularly to Indians. The Black Legend served as anti-Catholic and anti-Spanish propaganda in an era when Spain was often in conflict with England and other Protestant countries. While the conquistadors were brutal, it is difficult to argue that indigenous people suffered more under the Spanish than the English.

Black Mesa (MAY-suh)

Rock formation that served as a refuge for the San Ildefonso Indians when they were attacked by Don Diego de Vargas in the 1693 reconquista.

Black Mesa is 24 miles north of Santa Fe, just east of NM 30 and the Rio Grande.

Black Mesa

black widow

Poisonous black spider with red hourglass markings. The spiders are found throughout New Mexico, and Albuquerque is said to have more black widows than people. (The much-feared brown recluse spider is not indigenous to Northern New Mexico.)

Blackdom

Community founded around 1900 by Francis Marian Boyer, an African American who walked all the way from Georgia to establish a "black kingdom" free from the racism of the post-Civil War South. The experiment was a social success, but lack of water for irrigation was a serious problem, and the community lasted only about 20 years.

Blackdom was in Chaves County, 16 miles south of Roswell. Some residents, including Boyer and his family, moved to Vado, south of Las Cruces, where their descendants can be found today.

black-on-black pottery

Pueblo pottery in two shades of black, one matte and the other highly polished. The ancient style was revived in the 1920s by Maria Martinez of San Ildefonso Pueblo.

Bless Me, Ultima (ULL-tih-muh)

Prize-winning 1972 novel by Rudolfo Anaya. The story revolves around six-year-old Tony Marez's attempt to reconcile the multiple traditions of his rural New Mexico village. Ultima is the name of the curandera, or folk healer, who comes to live with Tony's family.

Blood and Thunder: An Epic of the American West

Santa Fe author Hampton Sides's nonfiction bestseller about Kit Carson and his times. The book was published in 2006.

blue corn

An ingredient in many New Mexico dishes. Blue corn meal is coarser and has a nuttier taste than other types of corn meal. Blue corn tortillas are a regional favorite.

Blue Hole

Naturally flowing artesian well used by scuba divers. The Blue Hole is 60 feet in diameter and 81 feet deep, with an outflow of 3,000 gallons per minute. Its water stays at a constant temperature of 63 degrees. The Santa Rosa spring is open to scuba divers as well as those who just want to take a dip.

The town of Santa Rosa, which bills itself as the "Scuba Capital of the Southwest," is off I-40, 121 miles southeast of Santa Fe.

Blue Lake

Sacred site that was confiscated from Taos Pueblo by the federal government and returned 64 years later. In 1906, President Theodore Roosevelt authorized the creation of the Taos National Forest (later incorporated into the Carson National Forest), which included Blue Lake and surrounding lands claimed by Taos Pueblo. The pueblo was particularly disturbed by the loss of the lake because it was a sacred site to which pueblo members made a yearly pilgrimage.

For decades, the pueblo and sympathetic Anglos like Oliver La Farge lobbied for the return of the lake and the land. Finally, in 1970, President Richard Nixon signed the bill that restored Blue Lake to Taos Pueblo. It was a rare example of the United States government returning confiscated land to an Indian tribe.

Bobcat Bite

Diner known for its green chile cheeseburgers. The cozy, 26-seat restaurant, which dates from 1953, acquired its name from the bobcats that used to come down from the hills to be fed treats at the back door. It is currently owned by John and Bonnie Eckre. Bobcat Bite is on Old Las Vegas Highway, about eight miles south of the Santa Fe Plaza.

Bode's store (BO-dee's)

General store on US 84 across from the village of Abiquiu. The store, which sells gas, groceries, deli food, hardware, horseshoes, and camping and fishing equipment, was frequented by Georgia O'Keeffe when she lived in Abiquiu.

Bode's is 48 miles northwest of Santa Fe.

bolo tie

Western neckwear, a braided-leather string tie held together with a sliding clasp of bone, silver, or turquoise.

There was once an intense debate about whether Santa Fe's plainclothes police officers should be allowed to wear bolo ties. The rank and file liked them, but Chief Donald Grady, who was originally from Wisconsin, thought they were unprofessional. The New Mexico Legislature has since named the bolo the official tie of New Mexico.

Bonanza Creek Movie Ranch

Western-town movie set, also a working cattle ranch. Bonanza Creek Ranch has been the setting for numerous movies, television shows, and commercials.

The ranch is 17 miles south of the Santa Fe Plaza via the La Cienega exit off I-25.

Bonney, William

See BILLY THE KID.

borracho/a (bore-AH-cho/cha)

"Drunkard." Borrachos are frequently haunted by La Llorona, the ghostly "weeping woman" who wanders through acequias and arroyos at night.

borrego (buh-RAY-go)

"Sheep." In *Commerce of the Prairies*, published in 1844, Josiah Gregg writes that sheep were the principal product of New Mexico but that their numbers were reduced by the "lords of the soil" (Indians), who frequently raided the herds, murdering the shepherds, and driving off thousands of sheep. In fact, Gregg notes, Indians had been heard to say that they could have captured every sheep in New Mexico but preferred to leave a few as breeding stock so that the New Mexicans could produce more animals for future raids.

The Borrego Trail off Hyde Park Road is popular with hikers.

bosque (BAH-skay, BO-skay)

Wooded area around a body of water.

Bosque del Apache

National Wildlife Refuge on the banks of the Rio Grande near San Antonio. Established in 1939 as a cold-weather habitat for sandhill cranes, the bosque's marshlands now host migratory geese, ducks, eagles, kestrels, and great blue herons, numbering in the tens of thousands.

Bosque del Apache

The 57,000-acre Bosque del Apache is 153 miles south of Santa Fe via I-25.

Bosque Redondo (reh-DON-doe)

Site on the Pecos River in eastern New Mexico where some 8,500 Navajos and 450 Mescalero Apaches were interned between 1863 and 1868.

The reservation experiment was a disaster, and thousands of internees died from malnutrition and other causes before the Mescaleros escaped the reservation in 1865 and the Navajos were allowed to leave in 1868. The Navajo refer to the sad trek from their homelands to Bosque Redondo as The Long Walk.

The Bosque Redondo Memorial is near Fort Sumner, 160 miles southeast of Santa Fe.

box of Pandoras

The inadvertent reversal of the expression "Pandora's Box" by the late Bruce King, three-time governor of New Mexico and master of the malapropism. In New Mexico, one hears King's version almost as often as the original.

Bradbury Science Museum

The Los Alamos National Laboratory's museum. Founded in 1963, the museum's purpose is to interpret LANL's history and current research. It is named for Norris E. Bradbury, who succeeded J. Robert Oppenheimer as director of the Lab. The Bradbury Science Museum is at 15th and Central in downtown Los Alamos.

Bradbury Science Museum

Bradford, Richard

(1932-2002) Author of Red Sky at Morning and So Far from Heaven, novels set in New Mexico. For many years, Bradford wrote a column for El Palacio, the Museum of New Mexico's quarterly publication. After his death, the magazine ran a tribute to him entitled "The Man Who Loved New Mexico."

Turn Left at the Sleeping Dog, a history of Santa Fe by John Pen La Farge, is named for directions that Bradford once gave a visiting motorist.

Breaking Bad

Emmy-winning TV show filmed and set in Albuquerque. The show, which premiered in 2008, revolves around a high school chemistry teacher with terminal lung cancer who teams up with a former student to manufacture methamphetamine. *Breaking Bad* has won multiple Emmys, including awards for Best Actor for Bryan Cranston, who plays teacher Walter White, and Best Supporting Actor for Aaron Paul, who plays accomplice Jesse Pinkman.

Breaking Bad realistically portrays Albuquerque's seamy underside. In 2001, Mayor Marty Chavez asked the TV show *Cops* to stop filming in Albuquerque because it was making the city look bad. No other city has ever made such a request.

broomstick skirt

Long, pleated Santa Fe-style skirt. The name comes from the old Navajo practice of tying a wet, bunched-up skirt to a broomstick so that creases are set as the garment dries.

brujo/a (BROO-ho/ha)

"Sorcerer" or "witch." Ghost Ranch, now a Presbyterian conference center, was originally named *Rancho de los Brujos*, "Ranch of the Witches," because it was thought to be haunted by evil spirits.

Buckaroo Ball

Santa Fe fundraiser. The first Buckaroo Ball was held in 1994. The upscale party, loosely based on the Dallas Cattle Baron's Ball, was held at Eaves Movie Ranch and featured singer Willie Nelson. For the next 14 years, affluent buckaroos (the word derives from *vaquero*, Spanish for "cowboy") paid up to $700 per person for the three-day event, which culminated in a fancy Western-dress party.

The last full-scale Buckaroo Ball was held in 2008. The sluggish economy was blamed for the event's cancellation in 2009 and 2010, but a scaled-down version called "A Little Bit of Buckaroo Ball" was held at the Railyard in 2011. As in previous years, proceeds from the event were donated to Santa Fe-area charities.

Buckman Water Treatment Plant

The source of much of Santa Fe's drinking water. The treatment plant, which went online in early 2011, draws water directly from the Rio Grande, supplementing the existing wells that pump water from the aquifer rather than from the river itself. The $216 million construction project was a partnership between the city of Santa Fe and Santa Fe County. The Rio Grande wells and the Buckman plant together supply about 60 percent of the city's water, with the balance coming from the Santa Fe Municipal Watershed.

The Buckman Water Treatment Plant is downriver from Los Alamos National Laboratory, and some people are concerned that the river water could contain traces of plutonium and uranium. The facility's engineers say that the state-of-the-art treatment plant is designed specifically to monitor and remove such contaminants.

The Buckman plant is on the east bank of the Rio Grande, three and a half miles downstream from the Otowi Bridge.

Budaghers (BUD-uh-gurs)

Exit off I-25 halfway between Santa Fe and Albuquerque. Joseph M. Budagher came to New Mexico from Lebanon in the early 1900s. The exit named for him leads to a curiously situated shopping center that has seen more wind than commercial success. Most recently called iTraditions!, the mall is currently unoccupied.

An obelisk honoring the Mexican-American War's Mormon Battalion stands just south of the shopping center.

bueno (BWAY-no)

All-purpose acknowledgment. *Bueno* is literally translated "good," but when used to close a conversation, it means something like "OK, see you later." *Bueno bye* is a Spanglish variation.

Buffalo Soldier

An African-American soldier in one of the segregated United States Army units of the late 19th century. The men were called "buffalo soldiers" by the Plains Indians because of their wooly hair and their ferocity

9th Cavalry Band on the Santa Fe Plaza in 1880

in battle. The best-known Buffalo Soldier units were the 9th and 10th Cavalry Regiments, which fought the Apaches, attempted to quell the Lincoln County War, and manned forts throughout New Mexico in the 1870s and 1880s. Three Buffalo Soldiers are buried in Santa Fe National Cemetery.

The Buffalo Soldiers Society of New Mexico is an Albuquerque-based group of reenactors and educators who visit area schools in period uniforms.

Buffalo Thunder Resort

Luxury hotel, casino, and golf resort owned by Pojoaque Pueblo and operated by Hilton Hotels. The 395-room hotel boasts a significant collection of Native American art.

Buffalo Thunder has struggled financially since its opening in 2008. The recession limited the convention business that the hotel had hoped to attract, and the casino has not thrived as expected. Some say that the casino's problem is its location halfway between Santa Fe and Española –

gamblers have to drive past Camel Rock Casino, which is closer to Santa Fe, or Cities of Gold Casino, which is closer to Española, to gamble in the new casino.

Buffalo Thunder is on US 84/285, 12 and one-half miles north of the Santa Fe Plaza.

bulto (BULL-toe)

Carved, three-dimensional santo, or depiction of a saint. Bultos should not be confused with retablos, which are two-dimensional paintings.

burrito (buh-REE-toe)

Warm tortilla wrapped around meat and beans, usually accompanied by chile, cheese, and other ingredients. Breakfast burritos normally include eggs and potatoes.

Burrito means "small burro." The name may derive from the wrapped tortilla's resemblance to a burro's ear.

burro

"Donkey." Burros were introduced into what is now the United States by the Spanish in 1598. In 1884, a visitor noted that Santa Fe had more burros than any other town in the country, and the animals could still be seen on the Plaza as late as the 1940s.

Burro Alley statue

Burro Alley is a pedestrian-only walkway between Palace Avenue and San Francisco Street in downtown Santa Fe. For 300 years, burros were tethered in the alley while their owners peddled firewood hauled down from the Sangre de Cristo Mountains. The patient beast is commemorated in a statue at the San Francisco Street entrance to Burro Alley.

butte (BEAUT)

Steep, flat-topped hill rising abruptly from the surrounding landscape. Lone Butte, some 17 miles south of the Santa Fe Plaza off NM 14, is the best-known local example.

The difference between a butte and a mesa is a topic of much discussion. One explanation is that buttes are taller than they are wide, while mesas are wider than they are tall.

Bynner, Witter

(1881-1968)   Poet Harold Witter Bynner, called Hal by his many friends. Bynner arrived in Santa Fe in 1922 and quickly positioned himself at the center of the city's social scene, where he remained for almost five decades.

A poet, former instructor at Berkeley, and translator of Chinese texts, Bynner lived openly as a homosexual, which was a rare thing in his time. Boozy "teas" in his Eastside home were attended by friends as diverse as physicist J. Robert Oppenheimer and writer Hart Crane, who quipped, "It's going to be a bitter winter, Mr. Witter Bynner."

Bynner could be touchy. He and poet Robert Frost had been classmates at Harvard, but Frost was much more famous, and Bynner was jealous. He hosted a luncheon when Frost came to Santa Fe in 1935 but lost his temper during a poetry discussion and poured a beer on Frost's head. Relations between Bynner and Taos social diva Mabel Dodge Luhan were also strained. Resentful of his friendship with D.H. and Frieda Lawrence, Luhan complained that Bynner "single-handedly brought homosexuality to New Mexico."

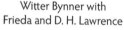
Witter Bynner with Frieda and D. H. Lawrence

- C -

CCA

The Center for Contemporary Arts, a nonprofit arts center and theater founded in 1979. CCA is behind the Santa Fe Children's Museum on Old Pecos Trail, between Paseo de Peralta and Cordova Road.

C de Baca (SEE deh BAH-cuh)

One of New Mexico's oldest and most intriguing surnames. Short for Cabeza de Baca, a variant of *cabeza de vaca*, "head of a cow," the name was awarded to a scout who marked a river crossing with a cow's skull during Spain's Moorish wars.

Alvar Nuñez Cabeza de Vaca made the name famous in the New World. In 1528, he and three companions, including Estevan the Moor, were shipwrecked near present-day Galveston, Texas, and spent the next eight years on an epic overland trek to Mexico City. Cabeza de Vaca and his companions passed on to the Spanish viceroy stories they had heard of Indian cities teeming with precious stones and minerals. Their report was the beginning of the legend of the Seven Cities of Cibola and the impetus for Coronado's 1540 exploration of the Southwest.

Ezequiel C de Baca was New Mexico's second governor after statehood.

caballero (cah-bah-YEAH-ro)

"Horseman" or "gentleman." Caballeros de Vargas is a service organization made up of men who have played Don Diego de Vargas or one of his attendants in the Santa Fe Fiesta. The group escorts La Conquistadora on her annual procession to Rosario Chapel.

cabra (CAH-bruh)

"Goat," specifically a she-goat. Camino Cabra is a street on Santa Fe's Eastside.

cabrón (cah-BROAN)

All-purpose epithet. Depending on the context, *cabrón*, which is literally translated "billy goat," can be either a playful greeting to a friend or a serious insult. Inserting the adjective *pinche* before *cabrón* creates an insult as offensive as anything in the English language.

A cabrón is a male goat, so the word is ordinarily applied to a man. One Santa Fean recalls, however, that when she was a little girl and her mother was really mad, she would refer to her daughters as *cabróncitas*, which means something like "little female billy goats."

Café Pasqual's

See PASQUAL'S.

calabacitas (cal-uh-bah-SEE-tas)

A traditional New Mexico side dish of late-summer vegetables like summer squash (*calabacita* means "little squash"), zucchini, green chile, and, often, corn.

caldera (call-DAIR-uh)

A collapsed volcano, from the Spanish for "cauldron." The Valles Caldera National Preserve in the Jemez Mountains surrounds an ancient caldera.

caliche (cuh-LEE-chay)

Crust of calcium carbonate on or just beneath the surface of the soil. Caliche clay is extremely slippery when wet, and an otherwise serviceable caliche road may become nearly impassable after a rain.

caliente (cah-lee-EN-tay)

"Hot," as in temperature. *Caliente* should not be confused with *picante*, which means "spicy."

Californication

A pejorative combination of *California* and *fornicate*. The word was coined in the 1960s (long before the Red Hot Chile Peppers song or the David Duchovny TV show) to describe the ill effects of California's uncontrolled urban sprawl. *Time Magazine* used the term in a 1972 story describing grassroots resistance to over-development in New Mexico and other Western states.

Today, in New Mexico, the perceived problem with Californians is not their number, but their self-absorption. In the introduction to *Turn Left at the Sleeping Dog*, John Pen La Farge writes: "In the 80's, Santa Fe's immigrants became more determinedly wealthy, more West Coast... more the sort who has little interest in the two old cultures and so thinks of them as a mere background to their lives." People from Texas and Oklahoma were once characterized as having more money than manners. Californians are accused of having more money than curiosity.

calle (CAH-yay)
"Street." Santa Fe's *Calle Estado*, "State Street," is a continuation of Mansion Drive, where the Governor's Mansion is located.

Camel Rock
Land form that looks remarkably like its namesake. The sizable rock formation is on the west side of US 84/285, 11 miles north of the Santa Fe Plaza. Tesuque Pueblo's Camel Rock Casino is across the highway from Camel Rock.

Camel Rock

camino (cah-MEE-no)
"Road" or "way."

Camino del Monte Sol (MON-tay SOLE)
"Sun Mountain Road," one of Eastside Santa Fe's premier addresses. When Los Cinco Pintores, "The Five Painters," lived on Camino del Monte Sol, it was referred to as simply "The Camino."

Camino Real (ray-ALL)

"Royal Road," the 1,500-mile trail from Mexico City to Santa Fe. Officially known as *El Camino Real de Tierra Adentro*, "The Royal Road to the Interior," the route served as New Mexico's primary connection to the outside world during the Spanish Colonial Period. The arduous trip from Mexico City could take up to six months, making Santa Fe one of the most isolated European outposts in the New World.

El Camino Real's importance waned after 1821, when Americans began bringing in trade goods via the Santa Fe Trail.

Campbell, Nancy

(1907-1981) Respected physician and perpetrator of one of Santa Fe's strangest crimes.

In November 1950, developer Allen Stamm's nine-year-old daughter, Linda, was walking home from school when she was kidnapped at gunpoint by a person described by a witness as an "oddly dressed man." The family notified the police, who staked out the drop-off location for the $20,000 ransom. Police officers were shocked when the money was picked up by Dr. Nancy Campbell, a 43-year-old Yale graduate and local obstetrician.

Campbell confessed to being the "oddly dressed man" and told authorities where to find the girl. Santa Feans expressed different views of Campbell's motive for the crime. Local artist Jerry West suggested that Dr. Campbell had suffered a psychological breakdown because Santa Fe's male doctors refused to share her workload. Calla Hay, a reporter for *The New Mexican*, said that Campbell was part of a "lesbian ring" and needed money for a girlfriend.

Campbell returned to Santa Fe after serving seven years in prison. She never regained her medical license and died in her home in 1981. Linda Stamm, now known as Linda Lee Strong, is an accomplished sculptor who lives south of Santa Fe.

campo santo (CAHM-po SAHN-toe)

"Holy ground," a cemetery. The colorful cemeteries in the villages of Northern New Mexico are a favorite subject of photographers.

Campo santo

cañada (cahn-YA-dah)

"Canyon." Barrio de la Cañada and Cañada de los Alamos are Santa Fe-area place names.

canales (*cuh-NAHL-ees)

Rain spouts that extend through the parapets of Santa Fe-style buildings to channel rainwater off the roof and away from the wall. Newcomers like the romantic effect of long icicles hanging from canales in winter, but the ice blocks the drains, and the water that backs up behind the canales causes leaks in flat roofs.

Canales is the plural of the singular *canal* (cuh-NAHL). But most Anglos say *canale* (cuh-NAHL-ee), just as they say *tamale* when the proper singular of that word is *tamal*.

Canales and exposed vigas

Canjilon (cahn-he-LOAN)

Northern New Mexico village whose name means "deer antler" in Northern New Mexico Spanish. The village was probably named for nearby Canjilon Mountain. It is in Rio Arriba County, 78 miles north of Santa Fe, 16 miles south of Tierra Amarilla, and three miles east of US 84.

cañon (can-YOAN)

Like *cañada*, a word for "canyon."

Cañoncito (can-yon-SEE-toe)

Settlement 15 miles southeast of Santa Fe. Cañoncito was the last stop on the Santa Fe Trail before Santa Fe itself.

Because of its location – where the Santa Fe Trail enters narrow Apache Canyon – Cañoncito was the site of two significant military events. In 1846, in the Mexican-American War, Governor Manuel Armijo ordered works placed there in a planned defense against invading American troops, though he abandoned the effort before the Americans arrived. In 1862, Confederate supplies and mules stored at Cañoncito were destroyed by Union troops in the Battle of Glorieta Pass.

Canyon de Chelly (CAN-yon deh SHAY)

Complex of wide chasms in northeast Arizona. Once home to the Anasazi, the abandoned canyons were later occupied by the Navajo.

In 1863, the Navajo made their last stand at Canyon de Chelly before surrendering to Colonel Kit Carson. They were subsequently interned at the Bosque Redondo reservation. Released in 1868, many Navajos returned to the canyons, where their descendants live today. The 83,000-acre national monument is a destination for those interested in Anasazi and Navajo culture.

Canyon Road

Santa Fe's most popular tourist stroll. Eighty-odd art galleries and scores of other shops and restaurants line Canyon Road between Paseo de Peralta and Palace Avenue. Walking this three-quarter-mile section of the narrow street is a must for most visitors.

Canyon Road is one of the oldest roads in the country. Even before the Spanish conquest, an Indian trail followed the Santa Fe River up into the Sangre de Cristo Mountains and then down to now-abandoned Pecos Pueblo. The early Spanish called it *El Camino del Cañon*, "The Road of the Canyon," and used it to haul wood from the mountains. Centuries later, Anglo artists moved into the lower Canyon Road area because it offered cheap housing. Galleries and shops followed, and the street now commands some of Santa Fe's highest rents.

Upper Canyon Road, which starts opposite Cristo Rey Church, runs uphill for a little over three and a half miles, ending at the Randall Davey Audubon Center.

capilla (cah-PEE-yuh)

"Chapel." Families in Northern New Mexico sometimes build private chapels on their property. The stone capilla pictured was constructed by the late Luis Atencio, founder of Española's El Paragua Restaurant. It is just off US 84/285, near the highway's intersection with County Road 88.

Capilla

Capital High School

One of Santa Fe's two public high schools. By most measures, Capital, which opened in 1988, compares poorly with the older Santa Fe High. Capital's attendance rate and test scores are lower and its dropout rate is higher. The reason for the disparity is clear: the school is on the less affluent southwest side of town, and many of its approximately 1,200 students are considered financially disadvantaged. Also, since most of the city's recent Latino immigrants live in that area, many of the children assigned to Capital are not native English-speakers.

Capital's sports teams are called the Jaguars. The school is off Airport Road, on Paseo del Sol.

Capitol Art Collection

The New Mexico state capitol's collection of almost 600 works by Anglo, Hispanic, and Indian artists from around the state. The collection was established in 1992 in conjunction with a major renovation of the Roundhouse, as the capitol building is known. It has been said that the Roundhouse is the best place in Santa Fe to see the variety of art produced in the state.

Capitol, State

See Roundhouse.

Carlsbad

Southeast New Mexico city associated with Carlsbad Caverns. The city, population 26,138, is New Mexico's tenth most populous.

A visitor to the state capitol posing by "Buffalo," a mixed-media piece by artist Holly Hughes

The people of Eddy, New Mexico, voted to change its name to Carlsbad in 1899. A spring near Eddy was said to have the same mineral content as the springs in the famous spa town of Karlsbad, Germany (now in the Czech Republic). The townspeople hoped that the association with Karlsbad would attract health seekers.

Carlsbad is 270 miles from Santa Fe via US 285 south. The famous caves are 25 miles south of the city.

carne (CAR-nay)

"Meat." Carne adovada (ah-doe-VAH-duh) refers to cubes of pork marinated in red chile sauce. Carne asada (ah-SAH-duh) is roasted meat, and carne seca (SEH-cuh) is dried meat.

carnitas (car-NEE-tuhs)

"Little meats," small cubes or strips of beef or pork. In the summer, Santa Fe street vendors peddle carnitas from carts set up around the Plaza.

carpe mañana (CAR-pay mahn-YA-nuh)

T-shirt witticism. *Carpe mañana*, "seize tomorrow," is the laid-back local version of the more ambitious *carpe diem*, "seize the day."

carreta (car-EH-tuh)

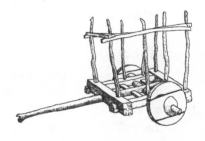

Carreta

Two-wheeled ox cart used by Hispanic New Mexicans in the Spanish Colonial and Mexican periods. Carretas were usually constructed of cottonwood, with each wheel made of two or three solid pieces of wood. The axles were not lubricated, making the carts so noisy that some Anglos called them "screaming woodpiles."

La Carreta de la Muerte, "The Death Cart," is a familiar image in New Mexican folk art.

Carrizozo (care-ih-ZO-zo)

Small town in south-central New Mexico. Carrizozo, population 996, is in Lincoln County at the intersection of US 54 and US 380. The name is derived from *carrizo*, which means "reed grass." According to *The Place Names of New Mexico*, the second *zo* was added by a ranch foreman in 1907 to indicate abundance. Carrizozo is 162 miles south of Santa Fe via US 285 south and US 54 west.

Carson, Kit

(1809-1868) Famous mountain man and army officer. Though he was himself illiterate, Christopher "Kit" Carson's exploits throughout the West made him the subject of heroic tales in the penny press of his day.

Carson left Missouri as a teenager in 1826 and headed west on the Santa Fe Trail. In the 1830s, he roamed the Rockies as an itinerant fur trapper. In the 1840s, he served as a hunter and guide with John C. Fremont's expe-

Kit Carson

ditions across the West. Fremont's widely read reports made the frontiersman a popular hero to the American public.

In 1861, Carson accepted an appointment as a lieutenant colonel in the New Mexico militia. He fought the invading Confederates at the Civil War Battle of Valverde and reluctantly conducted a campaign against the Navajo that resulted in their confinement at Bosque Redondo. He retired from the army as a brigadier general in 1867.

Carson's domestic life was equally eventful. His first two marriages were to Indian women. He and his first wife, an Arapaho, had two children. Their son was killed in an accident, and when his wife died of fever soon after, Carson enrolled his motherless daughter in a St. Louis boarding school. His brief second marriage, to a Cheyenne, ended when she left him. In 1843, Carson courted and wed a 14-year-old Taos girl named Josefa Jaramillo. The couple raised seven children. Kit and Josefa died within months of each other in 1868 and are buried in Taos's Kit Carson Park.

An obelisk honoring Kit Carson stands in front of the Federal Courthouse in Santa Fe. Santa Fe author Hampton Sides's 2006 book, *Blood and Thunder: An Epic of the American West,* illuminates Carson and his times.

Carson National Forest

One of two national forests in Northern New Mexico, the Santa Fe National Forest being the other. Named for Kit Carson, the Carson National Forest encompasses 1.5 million acres, mostly in Rio Arriba, Taos, and Colfax counties. It includes parts of the Tusas and Sangre de Cristo mountain ranges and the northern portion of the Pecos Wilderness. Wheeler Peak, New Mexico's highest mountain, is in the Carson National Forest.

casa (CAH-suh)

"House" or "home." Santa Fe developer Allen Stamm's projects include neighborhoods named *Casa Linda*, "Pretty Home," *Casa Alegre*, "Happy Home," and *Casa Solana*, "Sunny Home."

casino

See INDIAN CASINOS.

casita (cah-SEE-tuh)

"Little house," usually a guest house on a larger property. Some casitas are rented out year-round, some are occupied by caretakers, and some are reserved for guests.

Cathedral Basilica of St. Francis of Assisi

See ST. FRANCIS CATHEDRAL.

Cather, Willa

(1873-1947) Author of *Death Comes for the Archbishop*, a fictionalized biography of Archbishop Jean Baptiste Lamy published in 1927. Like D.H. Lawrence, Ansel Adams, and many other writers and artists, Cather visited New Mexico as a guest of Mabel Dodge Luhan.

Catron Block building (CAT-trun)

Santa Fe's best example of adobe camouflage. Named for political boss Thomas B. Catron, the Catron Block (the name is engraved at the top of the building) was erected on the northeast corner of the Plaza in 1891. Its

Italianate facade was later disguised with adobe-brown paint and a Territorial-style portal.

Catron, Thomas B. (CAT-trun)

(1840-1921) Territorial-era businessman and political boss. Catron graduated from law school in his home state of Missouri before serving in the Confederate Army during the Civil War. He left Missouri after the war because he believed that lingering animosity against former Rebels would limit his career in that state. Like many Anglos before and after him, he came to New Mexico to make a new start.

Thomas B. Catron

Catron became rich and powerful in New Mexico. He was a lawyer, a politician, and, reputedly, the leader of the shadowy Santa Fe Ring. For decades, he bought up land grants and eventually became one of the largest landowners in the United States. He served as mayor of Santa Fe and became one of New Mexico's first United States senators in 1912. Catron County, the Catron Block building, and Catron Street are all named for him. He is buried in Fairview Cemetery.

Thomas Benton Catron and his Era, published in 1973, was written by historian Victor Westphall. (Westphall is also known as the founder of the Angel Fire monument to Vietnam veterans.)

Catron's descendants still practice law in Santa Fe. His grandson, Thomas B. Catron III, was designated a Santa Fe Living Treasure in 2007. He was a founding member of the Santa Fe Opera Board and has held leadership positions with the Boy Scouts, The United Way, and other civic and charitable organizations.

Cebolla (seh-BOY-uh)

Northern New Mexico village whose name means "onion." The name comes from the wild onions that grow in the valley in which the village is located. Cebolla is in Rio Arriba County, on US 84, 78 miles north of Santa Fe and 13 miles south of Tierra Amarilla.

cedro (SEH-dro)

"Cedar pole." Cedros are used as latillas in Santa Fe-style ceiling construction and as poles in coyote fences.

centipede

Nocturnal arthropod that preys on insects and the morbid fear of humans. Because they crave dampness, centipedes live under rocks or in mulch, often in planted areas around a house. Indoors, they are often found in a sink or bathtub after crawling up a drain in the middle of the night. They can also use electrical wiring as a means of entry, creeping through the walls of a house and dropping into a room from an overhead light fixture.

Centipedes are found throughout the United States, but encounters with them are especially upsetting to people in the Southwest. Desert centipedes can get much bigger than the eastern variety and, because of the arid climate, they are more likely to enter a house in search of moisture. For all of their quick-slithering creepiness, centipedes are only mildly venomous and pose no threat to humans.

Cerrillos (suh-REE-yos)

Old mining town 20 miles south of Santa Fe off NM 14 (the Turquoise Trail). Named for the hills three miles to its northwest, Cerrillos came to life in 1879 in a short-lived gold and silver rush. It later supplied coal to the Santa Fe Railway.

Like Madrid four miles to the south, Cerrillos lost most of its population when the mining petered out. Today, it is an occasional stop for

Cerrillos in 1884

tourists and day-trippers driving NM 14 south from Santa Fe. The Turquoise Mining Museum and the Casa Grande Trading Post and Petting Zoo are the town's main attractions.

Cerrillos Hills

The "small hills" 17 miles southwest of Santa Fe. The hills were a source of turquoise for Anasazi traders and the focus of a brief gold and silver rush in 1879. The town of Cerrillos and Santa Fe's Cerrillos Road are named for them. Cerrillos Hills is, of course, a redundancy as *cerrillos* means "small hills."

Cerrillos Road

Santa Fe's longest, busiest, and most commercial street. From downtown, Cerrillos Road's four to six lanes run southwest for about eight miles to I-25. The road then becomes NM 14 (the Turquoise Trail) and continues south through the towns of Cerrillos, Madrid, and Golden.

cerro (SAIR-o)

"Hill" or "mountain."

Cerro Grande fire (SAIR-o GRAHN-day)

Forest fire that swept through Los Alamos in May 2000, the most destructive fire in New Mexico history. The fire began as a controlled burn on *Cerro Grande*, "Big Mountain," a 10,000-foot peak west of Los Alamos in Bandelier National Monument. It rapidly blazed out of control and ultimately consumed 280 homes and more than 47,000 acres, including 7,500 acres of Los Alamos National Laboratory property.

Cerro Pedernal (SAIR-o peh-der-NALL)

"Flint Hill." See PEDERNAL.

Chaco Canyon (CHA-co)

Expansive Anasazi site. Chaco Canyon was the thriving center of an extensive pre-Columbian trade network before it was abandoned in the 1300s. The Chaco Culture National Historical Park encompasses 18 major ruins, including Pueblo Bonito, an 800-room building that once housed as many as 1,500 people.

Chaco Canyon is 181 miles northwest of Santa Fe via I-25 south, US 550 north, and a 21-mile, mostly unpaved access road.

Chama (CHA-muh)

Northern New Mexico village. Originally called Chama Crossing, the settlement languished until the Chili Line transformed it into a small boomtown in the 1880s. Today, the Chama area is popular with outdoorsmen, particularly out-of-state hunters and fishermen. Chama (probably from the Tewa *tzama*, or "red," for the color of the Rio Chama) is the southern terminus of the Cumbres & Toltec Scenic Railroad.

The village, population 1,022, is eight miles south of the Colorado border. It is 106 miles north of Santa Fe via US 84.

Chama River

One of Northern New Mexico's principal rivers, a tributary of the Rio Grande. In New Mexico, a waterway is usually called either a rio or a

Chama River

river, but the Chama is referred to as the Rio Chama in some places and the Chama River in others. (See also RIO CHAMA.)

chamisa (cha-MEE-suh)

Greenish-gray shrub ubiquitous throughout Northern New Mexico. The plant, known as rabbitbrush in English, grows from three to five feet in height and width and produces bright yellow flowers. Its pollen is a notorious fall allergen. The word is sometimes spelled "chamiso."

Chávez (*CHA-vez)

One of New Mexico's prominent Hispanic surnames. *The Place Names of New Mexico* counts 69 places that are named either Cháves or Chávez. (Chaves County is spelled in the older style, but the *z* spelling is much more common today. The inclusion of the accent varies.)

*In New Mexico, the name is usually pronounced CHA-vez, not SHA-vez or sha-VEZ.

Chavez, Dennis

(1888-1962) The first person born in New Mexico to serve in the United States Senate. Democrat Dionisio "Dennis" Chavez was first appointed, then elected, to serve out the unexpired term of Republican progressive Bronson Cutting, who was killed in a 1935 plane crash. He was reelected in subsequent elections and served until his death in 1962.

Chavez was a tireless advocate for civil rights. Protesting the treatment of Hispanic veterans after World War II, he said, "We are 'Americans' when we go to war, and when we return, we are 'Mexicans'." He was also one of the first legislators to denounce the practices of Senator Joseph McCarthy.

Dennis Chavez

Dennis Chavez is one of two New Mexicans to be honored with a statue in the National Statuary Hall of the United States Congress. (The other is Po'pay, leader of the 1680 Pueblo Revolt.)

Chávez, Fray Angélico (fry ahn-HELL-ee-co)

(1910-1996)   Franciscan priest, artist, and Northern New Mexico historian. *Fray*, "Friar," Angélico Chávez was born in Wagon Mound in 1910 and ordained a priest in 1937. His books include *Origins of New Mexico Families*, a genealogical study of the region's first Hispanic families, and *My Penitente Land*, an essay on traditional life in Northern New Mexico.

A statue of the padre stands in front of the Fray Angélico Chávez History Library, a repository for historic books and manuscripts in downtown Santa Fe. Fray Angélico is buried in Rosario Cemetery.

chica (CHEE-cah)

"Girl," or "young woman," the equivalent of the English word *chick*. Regional poets Joan Logghe, Miriam Sagan, and Renée Gregorio operate a collaborative press called Tres Chicas Books.

chicano/a (chee-CAH-no/nah)

Term derived from "Mexicano" for a politically aware Mexican-American. *Chicano* conveys a greater ethnic and political consciousness than either *Latino* or *Hispanic*.

chicharron (chee-cha-ROAN)

Fried pork skin. Like posole and sopaipillas, chicharrones are a particularly New Mexican food. A candidate for statewide office believed that a photograph of himself stirring a pot of chicharrones would help his campaign, but his plan backfired when aficionados called him a gringo for using a metal ladle instead of the more traditional wooden ladle.

chicos (CHEE-cos)

Dried corn kernels.

child of the earth

Creepy, flesh-colored insect also known as the Jerusalem cricket and the potato bug. Children of the earth are subterranean creatures that eat roots. They are not pests and are not harmful to humans. The Navajo call the big-headed bug *Woh-seh-tsinni*, "Old Man Bald Head."

Children's Museum, Santa Fe

Nonprofit, interactive children's museum next to CCA on Old Pecos Trail. Established in 1989, the museum is housed in what was originally the garage for the New Mexico National Guard.

chile (CHILL-ee)

Any of the many varieties of the fiery pepper essential to New Mexico's cuisine, economy, and culture, or a sauce made from the pepper. (New Mexico *chile* should never be confused with Tex-Mex *chili*, a dish of kidney beans, tomatoes, ground beef, and red chile seasoning.)

Chiles intended for culinary purposes are harvested when they are green or after they have ripened and turned red. Each color has its own flavor, and each can be more or less hot. Aficionados have strong opinions as to which chile to eat with what dish, so waiters always ask for a preference. The New Mexico Legislature has gone so far as to adopt "Red or green?" as the official state question and "Christmas," which indicates a desire for both, as the official state answer.

Chile is big business. New Mexico is the country's largest producer of the pepper, and it is consistently one of the state's most profitable crops. The town of Hatch, in southern New Mexico's Mesilla Valley, is the world capital of chile production.

Although its growing season is shorter, Northern New Mexico also produces chile. The village of Chimayó is known for the red variety, which is used for both culinary and decorative purposes. Most of the ristras seen around Santa Fe are made from Chimayó red chile.

chile con queso (con KAY-so)

"Chile with cheese," chile and melted cheese mixed together in a dip.

chile relleno (reh-YEH-no)

Stuffed green chile pepper. The pepper is peeled and stuffed with cheese, then dipped in batter and fried.

Chili Line (CHILL-ee)

Narrow-gauge railroad that ran between Santa Fe and Antonito, Colorado, from 1887 to 1941. Officially known as the Denver and Rio Grande Railroad, it may have been called the Chili Line because of the ristras hanging from the adobe homes along its route. ("Chile" is the more common spelling in New Mexico. The origin of the railroad's aberrant Texas-style spelling is unknown.)

The Chili Line's old depot in the Santa Fe Railyard is now occupied by Tomasita's restaurant. Embudo Station, which has also been converted into a restaurant, is another vestige of the old railroad.

Chimayó (chee-my-O)

Quintessential Northern New Mexico village. Chimayó's main attraction is the Santuario de Chimayó, whose holy dirt is reputed to have curative powers. The village is also known for weaving, red chile, lowriders, and the Rancho de Chimayó restaurant. Unfortunately, like much of Rio Arriba County, Chimayó is also known for drug abuse. (See CHIVA.)

The village, population 3,177, is 30 miles north of Santa Fe on NM 76, the High Road to Taos.

Chimayó Rebellion

Uprising by Northern New Mexicans against the Mexican governor, also known as the Revolt of 1837. New Mexico's Mexican Period (1821-1846) was characterized by Norteño dissatisfaction with increased taxes, decreased services, and government corruption. Simmering resentment exploded in August 1837 when rebels based around Chimayó staged an armed insurrection. Governor Albino Pérez was decapitated, and the jubilant rebels played kickball with his severed head. The rebellion was ultimately put down by loyalist troops under the command of former governor Manuel Armijo, who resumed office after the capture and execution of the insurrection's leaders.

chipotle (chee-POAT-lay)

Smoke-dried jalapeño chile pepper.

chiva (CHEE-vuh)

Slang for heroin. *Chiva: A Village Takes on the Global Heroin Trade* (2005), by Chellis Glendinning, describes the village of Chimayó's struggle with drugs.

cholla (CHOY-uh)

A cactus shrub found throughout the Southwest. Cholla spines are unique in that they are encased in papery sheaths. Most chollas display colorful flowers in spring and early summer.

cholo/a (CHO-lo/la)

Hispanic hoodlum. The classic image of a Los Angeles cholo is that of a young man sporting tattoos, baggy pants, and a bandana pulled low over his forehead. In Santa Fe, the look often includes a wife-beater T-shirt and a shaved head. Gringos should use the term advisedly.

chorizo (cho-REE-so)

Spicy sausage made with pork and red chiles.

Christ in the Desert Monastery

Isolated Benedictine monastery. Founded in 1964, the monastery is home to 25 to 30 monks, with half a dozen nuns living in the adjacent

Our Lady of the Desert community. Guests are accepted for retreats. The monastery brews Monk's Ale and operates a gift shop called The Monk's Corner in downtown Santa Fe.

Christ in the Desert is 75 miles northwest of Santa Fe, on the banks of the Rio Chama. The drive includes 13 miles of scenic-but-unpaved road off US 84.

Christmas

The official state answer to New Mexico's official state question. Diners are routinely asked whether they want red or green chile with their meal. Those who want both answer "Christmas."

Christus St. Vincent Regional Medical Center

Northern New Mexico's principal hospital. Licensed for 268 beds, St. Vincent is the largest medical facility between Albuquerque and Pueblo, Colorado.

The first hospital in the New Mexico Territory, St. Vincent was established in downtown Santa Fe in 1865 by the Sisters of Charity. In 1977, it was moved to its present location at the intersection of St. Michael's Drive and Hospital Drive.

"St. Victim's" was not highly regarded in the late 1990s, but it has a much better reputation today. In 2008, the hospital joined Christus Health, a Catholic group based in Texas that operates over 40 hospitals. Its name was then changed to Christus St. Vincent Regional Medical Center, though most people call it "Christus St. Vincent" or just "St. Vincent." (See also OLD ST. VINCENT HOSPITAL.)

chupacabra (choo-puh-CAH-bruh)

"Goatsucker," a mythical creature said to suck the blood from domestic animals. The name is a combination of the Spanish words *chupar*, "to suck," and *cabra*, "goat."

Chupacabra

Biologists consider the chupacabra a contemporary legend. The supposed chupacabra carcasses that have been studied have proved to be coyotes with extreme cases of mange. Tales of the creature are not as prevalent in New Mexico as they are in Texas, Louisiana, and parts of Latin America.

Chupadero (choo-puh-DAIR-o)

Northern New Mexico community three miles northeast of Tesuque. *Chupadero* means "sinkhole."

cibola (SEE-bo-la)

Indian word for buffalo, which for unknown reasons the early Spanish applied to Zuni Pueblo and the surrounding lands. Coronado's 1540 expedition was a search for the mythical Seven Cities of Cibola, which he believed contained vast riches. Cibola County and the Cibola National Forest perpetuate the name.

cibolero (see-bo-LAIR-o)

"Buffalo hunter," a Nuevomexicano who rode out onto the *Llano Estacado*, "Staked Plains," of eastern New Mexico and west Texas to hunt buffalo in the 18th and 19th centuries. Ciboleros were colorful and brave. Dressed in buffalo skins, they rode among the 1,800-pound animals armed only with bows and arrows and lances, which they used to great effect.

Josiah Gregg extols the skill of the cibolero in *Commerce of the Prairies*. He wrote, "I once went on a hunting expedition with a Cibolero, who carried no arms except his bow and arrows and a butcher's knife. Espying a herd of buffalo, he put spurs to his horse, and, though I followed as fast as a mule I rode could trudge, when I came up with him, after a chase of two or three miles, he had the buffalo partly skinned!"

The ciboleros were greeted as heroes when they returned to their Northern New Mexico villages with their carretas, or carts, loaded with meat and hides.

Cieneguilla (see-en-ah-GHEE-uh)

Small community nine miles southwest of Santa Fe. The name is a diminutive of *cienega*, "marsh."

Cimarron (SIM-uh-ron)

Northern New Mexico town. *Cimarron*, which means "wild," is an apt name for a town that epitomized the Wild West. In Cimarron's heyday, when it flourished as a stop on the Santa Fe Trail, the St. James Hotel hosted Buffalo Bill Cody, Jesse James, and Wyatt Earp, among other renowned cowboys, outlaws, and lawmen. Shootouts were common, and the dining room of the restored hotel still has over 20 bullet holes in its ceiling.

Cimarron withered when the Santa Fe Trail was made obsolete by the Santa Fe Railway. Today, the town, population 1,021, is associated with nearby Philmont Scout Ranch.

Cimarron is 156 miles northeast of Santa Fe via I-25 north and NM 58 west.

Cimarron Cutoff

See SANTA FE TRAIL.

Cinco de Mayo (SINK-o deh MY-o)

The "Fifth of May," a holiday commemorating Mexico's victory over the French in the 1862 Battle of Puebla.

For Santa Feans, Cinco de Mayo is an excuse to drink tequila, even though the Battle of Puebla had no particular significance for New Mexico. By 1862, the Territory had been part of the United States for 16 years, and New Mexicans were too preoccupied with the American Civil War to be much concerned about events south of the border.

Cinco Pintores (pin-TOR-ehs)

See LOS CINCO PINTORES.

City Council, Santa Fe

Santa Fe is governed by an eight-member city council, with two councilors representing each of four districts. Councilors are elected for staggered, four-year terms, so one councilor from each district is elected every two years. The mayor votes only in the event of a tie.

Santa Fe in 1890, before it became the City Different

City Different

Santa Fe's nickname for itself. In the early 1900s, when cities across the country were reinventing themselves as part of the "City Beautiful" movement, Santa Fe took a different approach. City leaders incorporated Spanish Pueblo-style architecture into the city's 1912 urban plan, and the local Chamber of Commerce began marketing Santa Fe as the "City Different."

climate

Santa Fe's climate is determined by its relatively low latitude and high altitude. The city's 7,000-foot elevation ensures moderate summers, and fall is mild and pleasant. Santa Fe is cold in winter, but because the humidity is low, the cold is not as bone-chilling as in other places. Spring winds are irritating, particularly for those who are bothered by allergies. Santa Fe's skies are usually clear, with sunshine over 300 days per year.

Clines Corners

Service station, restaurant, and the state's largest gift shop. The business grew from a Route 66 gas station established by Roy E. Cline in the mid-1930s. Clines Corners is 55 miles south of Santa Fe at the intersection of US 285 and I-40.

MONTH	AVG HIGH	AVG LOW	MEAN	RECORD HIGH	RECORD LOW
January	43	15	29	65 (1986)	-14 (1974)
February	49	21	35	73 (1986)	-10 (1975)
March	56	26	41	77 (2004)	-6 (2002)
April	64	32	48	84 (2000)	10 (1973)
May	73	40	57	96 (2000)	23 (1999)
June	83	49	66	99 (1998)	31 (2007)
July	86	54	70	99 (2003)	38 (1999)
August	83	53	68	96 (2007)	36 (1992)
September	77	46	62	94 (1984)	26 (2000)
October	66	35	51	87 (1980)	5 (1996)
November	52	24	38	75 (1980)	-12 (1976)
December	44	16	30	65 (1980)	-17 (1990)

SANTA FE TEMPERATURES (°F)

Clovis

Eastern New Mexico city best known as the home of Norman Petty Studios, where Texans like Buddy Holly, Roy Orbison, and Waylon Jennings recorded hit records. Cannon AFB, seven miles southwest of Clovis, is home to the 27th Special Operations Wing. The city's population of 37,775 makes it New Mexico's seventh most populous.

Clovis is eight miles west of the Texas border, 216 miles southeast of Santa Fe via US 285 south and US 60 east.

Cochiti Pueblo (CO-chih-tee)

Pueblo best known for its Rio Grande reservoir. The man-made lake, with 22 miles of shoreline, was created on pueblo land in 1975 by the Army Corps of Engineers for water storage and recreation. The town of Cochiti Lake was later developed as a retirement and vacation community on land leased from the pueblo.

Cochiti, whose name means "stone kiva," is the northernmost of the

Keresan-speaking pueblos. Helen Cordero, creator of the storyteller tableau, was from Cochiti.

The pueblo is 36 miles southwest of Santa Fe via I-25 south and NM 16 north.

Collected Works Bookstore & Coffeehouse

Independent bookstore in downtown Santa Fe. The store opened in 1978 and is owned by Dorothy Massey and her daughter Mary Wolf. It is on the corner of Water Street and Galisteo Street.

College of Santa Fe

See Santa Fe University of Art and Design.

Colter, Mary Jane

(1869-1958) Architect and designer employed by the Fred Harvey Company in the early 20th century to design and decorate buildings at stops along the Santa Fe Railway. Many of Colter's works are listed on the National Register of Historic Places. These include Santa Fe's La Fonda, on which she collaborated with John Gaw Meem, and La Posada, a hotel in Winslow, Arizona. (Santa Fe also has a hotel called La Posada.)

Female architects were rare in her day, but the chain-smoking, Stetson-wearing Colter easily held her own with bosses and construction workers. She died in Santa Fe in 1958.

comadre (co-MA-dray) and compadre (come-PA-dray)

"Co-mother" and "co-father," terms used by a child's godparents to refer to the child's biological parents and by the biological parents to refer to the godparents. Parents-in-law also use the terms to refer to each other. Unrelated people occasionally use *comadre* and *compadre* to mean "friend."

Commerce of the Prairies

Josiah Gregg's two-volume, 1844 book about trade along the Santa Fe Trail and life in Northern New Mexico. Gregg learned to speak Spanish during his years as a trader. His descriptions of the flora and fauna of the region, the habits of its inhabitants, and the personalities of Santa Fe's leading citizens were eagerly consumed by a curious American public.

Compound, The

Fine dining restaurant on Canyon Road. The Compound, which serves "contemporary American cuisine," opened in the 1960s. Current owner-chef Mark Kiffin, who worked with Mark Miller at the Coyote Café for eight years, bought and renovated the restaurant in 2000.

The Compound has always been more formal than other Santa Fe restaurants. As recently as the late 1990s, waiters wore white gloves, gentlemen were required to wear neckties, and children were banned. While those policies are no longer in effect, diners at The Compound still tend to be better dressed than those at other Santa Fe restaurants. The entrance to The Compound is on Canyon Road, across the street and a couple of hundred feet west of the Geronimo restaurant.

concha (CON-cha)

A silver disc used for decoration on belts and hatbands. *Conchas*, "shells," are a prominent feature in Santa Fe-style clothing.

Concha belt

Connie's

See KAUNE'S.

conquistador (con-KEY-stuh-dor)

"Conqueror." In the Americas, the term is used to describe the Spanish explorers who subjugated the indigenous Indians and claimed their land for Spain. Historian Marc Simmons's 1991 biography of Don Juan de Oñate is titled *The Last Conquistador*. (See also LA CONQUISTADORA.)

corbel (CORE-bull)

Wooden brace that extends from a wall to distribute the weight of a viga or carrying beam. (The two-sided brace that sits atop a post is properly called a zapata, though the distinction is not always observed.)

Cordova (CORE-duh-vuh)

Northern New Mexico village named for the Córdoba family. Cordova is in Rio Arriba County, 39 miles north of Santa Fe and one mile south of NM 76 (the High Road to Taos).

Corbels supporting vigas

Santa Fe's Cordova Road runs between Cerrillos Road and Old Pecos Trail.

Coronado, Francisco Vasquez de

(1510-1554) Leader of the first major Spanish exploration of the Southwest. In 1540, Coronado led an expedition into New Mexico in the hope of finding gold and silver in the fabled Seven Cities of Cibola. Misguided by an Indian from Pecos Pueblo, the Spanish marched as far as what is now Kansas before realizing that they were being led astray. Coronado had the guide strangled before leading his bedraggled men back to Mexico in 1542.

Coronado State Monument, near the town of Bernalillo, marks the ruins of a pueblo village once occupied by Coronado's expedition.

Corrales (co-RAL-es)

Town between Albuquerque and Rio Rancho. Corrales, whose name means "corrals," is a bedroom community for people who commute to work in Albuquerque or Santa Fe. The town, population 8,329, is in Sandoval County, 55 miles southwest of Santa Fe via I-25.

corrido (co-REE-doe)

"Ballad" or "folk song."

Coss, David

(1954-) Santa Fe's mayor. Coss was elected mayor in 2006. He is a former labor organizer, retired state employee, and former city manager. As a city councilor, he sponsored the city's Living Wage Ordinance.

David Coss

cottonwood

A type of poplar tree called *alamo* in Spanish. The cottonwood is the predominant deciduous tree in New Mexico bosques and other riparian areas. In the Spanish Colonial and Mexican periods, people found multiple uses for its wood, including for the construction of primitive carretas, or carts. The coarse wood is not highly valued today, though it is used for wood pallets and shipping crates.

The big trees along the downtown stretch of the Santa Fe River are cottonwoods. The chainsaw carvings along East Alameda Street are fashioned from the trunks of trees that died in the drought of the early 2000s.

Cowan, George

(1920-) Senior scientist at Los Alamos National Laboratory, founder of Los Alamos National Bank, and one of the founders of the Santa Fe Institute. Cowan participated in the Manhattan Project soon after graduating from college. After the war, he earned a Ph.D. and then returned to LANL, where he worked for 39 years.

In 1963, he founded Los Alamos National Bank as a place for Los Alamos families to get mortgages, and he served as the bank's chairman for 30 years. In 1984, Cowan, Murray Gell-Mann, and others founded the Santa Fe Institute. He is still active on the SFI board. Cowan was also an early board

George Cowan

member of the Santa Fe Opera. His memoir, *Manhattan Project to the Santa Fe Institute*, was published in 2010.

cowboy boot

New Mexico's dress shoe. Exuberant celebrants of Santa Fe style wear expensive boots, both new and vintage, that feature colorful patterns and elaborate stitching. The author of three books on the subject notes that, of all Westerners, Santa Feans wear the flashiest boots.

There are many boot outlets in Santa Fe. Enterprising thieves once burgled three stores and made off with over 100 pairs of custom cowboy boots. Valued at $500 to $2,500 per pair, the boots were being sold on eBay until a store owner recognized them as stolen merchandise.

Cowgirl BBQ

Western-themed bar and restaurant that originated in New York City. The original Cowgirl Hall of Fame opened in the West Village in 1988. Barry Secular, one of the partners in the New York operation, opened the Santa Fe restaurant on Guadalupe Street in 1993.

The Cowgirl specializes in barbeque and burgers, but it is also appreciated for its atmosphere and entertainment. The operation includes an outdoor patio, pool hall, and Kiddie Corral, and the bar offers live music or karaoke every day of the week. The Cowgirl is on Guadalupe Street, at its intersection with Aztec Street.

coyote (*kye-O-tee, ko-YO-tay)

Wild canine common in New Mexico and, increasingly, throughout the United States. Coyotes are more often heard than seen, and their nocturnal yipping holds an eerie fascination for humans and domestic dogs alike.

The howling coyote is a much overused art theme. By the early 1990s, representations of bandana-wearing coyotes had become so clichéd that Santa Feans displayed bumper stickers reading "Help Stamp Out Coyote Art." (Kokopelli has since replaced the coyote as the most overused image.)

*The Anglo pronunciation of this word is subject to regional variation. Most Westerners use the two-syllable version (KYE-oat). In Arizona and

New Mexico, however, where Spanish pronunciation patterns are more influential, the three-syllable variation (kye-O-tee) holds sway. And, of course, the three-syllable version comes naturally to gringos whose first exposure to the creature was the Wile E. Coyote cartoon character. The Anglo pronunciation is generally used in reference to the animal.

The Spanish pronunciation (ko-YO-tay) is appropriate when the word is used to mean a person of mixed Anglo and Hispanic heritage (though this meaning seems to be fading) or a smuggler of illegal immigrants. The two New Mexico villages that are named Coyote also use the Spanish pronunciation.

Coyote Café (kye-O-tee)

Santa Fe fine dining restaurant started by chef Mark Miller in 1987. The Water Street establishment features modern Southwest cuisine. Miller sold the restaurant in 2007 to a group that includes Geronimo chef Eric DiStefano.

coyote fence (kye-O-tee)

Rustic pole fence. The fence's vertical poles are typically saplings that are two to four inches in diameter, with the bark left on to retard rot. The poles are usually held together with baling wire. As the name implies, the fence was originally designed as a barrier to coyotes.

Coyote fence

Crawford, Stanley

(1937-) Novelist, essayist, and organic farmer. In 1970, Crawford was living off the proceeds of *Gascoyne*, his first novel, when he felt a call to a simpler life. He and his wife, Rose Mary, moved to Northern New Mexico, built an adobe home, and began farming near the community of Dixon. He has since written four more novels, as well as three books of essays describing life on El Bosque Farm: *Mayordomo* (1988), *A Garlic Testament* (1992), and *The River in Winter* (2003). Crawford sells his produce at the Santa Fe Farmers Market.

crime

Santa Fe and Northern New Mexico are not exempt from crime. As in most cities, the young and the poor are often both the perpetrators and the victims of violent crimes, which usually occur away from the downtown areas frequented by visitors. On the rare occasion when an armed robber or mugger targets a tourist, the crime becomes the immediate focus of law enforcement and the perpetrator is usually apprehended in short order.

Property crime, which is epidemic in Santa Fe, occurs citywide. The FBI reported that in 2009 the Santa Fe area had 2,083 burglaries per 100,000 residents. The agency cautions against using its statistics to compare metropolitan areas because not all cities define "burglary" the same way (e.g., some count auto break-ins and some do not). Still, comparisons are inevitable, and, using the FBI statistics, the Santa Fe area has the country's second worst per capita burglary rate. There are a number of reasons for this: Santa Fe's "hourglass" economy in which there are many rich people and many poor people, with few in the middle; the region's perpetual problem with drug addiction; the large number of second homes, which are often vacant and therefore tempting to burglars; and, in recent years, the entry of juvenile gangs like the West Side Locos into the organized burglary business.

Cristo Rey Church (CRISS-toe RAY)

"Christ the King" Church. Designed by John Gaw Meem, the Catholic church was built in 1940 using 180,000 adobe bricks made on-site from the soil on which the building stands. The church was designed to display the stone reredos (altar screens) that once graced *La Castrense*, a Spanish military chapel that was demolished in 1859.

Cristo Rey Church is at the intersection of Canyon Road and Camino Cabra.

Cristo Rey Church

Crosby, John

(1926-2002) Founder and, for 43 years, general director of the Santa Fe Opera. In 1957, after studying music at Yale and Columbia, Crosby borrowed money from his father, a prominent New York attorney, to start the SFO. Crosby served in the army in World War II and is buried in Santa Fe National Cemetery.

Cross of the Martyrs

Monument commemorating the 21 priests killed in the 1680 Pueblo Revolt. The white, 20-foot-high metal cross stands on a hill near the ruins of old Fort Marcy, off Paseo de Peralta between Marcy and Otero streets. Santa Fe's Fiesta concludes with a candlelight procession

Cross of the Martyrs

from St. Francis Cathedral to the Cross of the Martyrs.

There are in fact two Crosses of the Martyrs. The original, 25-foot-high concrete cross was erected in 1920 and still stands off Paseo de la Loma, just north of Old Taos Highway. The Fiesta Council constructed the newer cross in 1977 to shorten the candlelight procession.

cruising

Driving to nowhere, seeing and being seen. A lowrider is the vehicle of choice for cruising, but almost anything with chrome wheels will do. Santa Fe's Alameda Street, which was once the most popular venue for cruisers, became so jammed on Friday and Saturday nights that the police banned them from that street.

Cruising the Plaza is the subject of an ongoing debate. Downtown merchants argue that motorized traffic is unsafe for tourists. They advocate making the streets around the Plaza pedestrian-only. Many native Santa Feans, mostly Hispanics, counter that cruising the Plaza is a time-honored cultural tradition.

crypto Jews

Secret Jews who converted to Christianity in name only. Some historians believe that many of New Mexico's first families were crypto Jews trying to escape the Spanish Inquisition.

King Ferdinand and Queen Isabella expelled the last of the Moors from Spain in 1492. They then decreed that Spain would henceforth be an exclusively Catholic country, and the sizable Jewish population was required to leave or convert to Catholicism. Of the several hundred thousand *conversos* who chose to stay, many became Christians in name only and continued to pass on Jewish traditions within their families. This was a dangerous ruse in the days of the Spanish Inquisition.

Historian Stanley Hordes has concluded that many secret Jews migrated to Mexico, and eventually to New Mexico, to escape close scrutiny. Hordes's theory was bolstered when he was appointed New Mexico state historian in 1981 and Hispanic New Mexicans began approaching him with stories of how their abuelas, or grandmothers, lit candles on Friday night, refrained from eating pork, or observed other Jewish traditions.

The New Mexico crypto-Jew theory is not without critics. A December 2000 article in *The Atlantic Monthly* questions Hordes's research methods and accuses him of overstating his conclusions.

cuartocentenario (cwar-toe-sen-teh-NAH-ree-o)

Four-hundred-year anniversary. New Mexico celebrated its cuarto-centenario in 1998. Santa Fe's 400th birthday was celebrated in 2010. (Although there was a Spanish presence on the site before then, 1610 is generally accepted as the year of the city's founding by Don Pedro de Peralta.)

Cuba (*CUE-buh, COO-bah)

Small Northern New Mexico community on US 550. *The Place Names of New Mexico* discounts the idea that the village was named by Rough Riders returning from the country of Cuba and suggests instead that the name derives from the Spanish word for "sink" or "draw." Cuba is 110 miles from Santa Fe via I-25 south and US 550 north.

*Anglos usually say CUE-buh, as in the Caribbean island. Spanish-speakers say COO-bah.

cuento (KWEN-toe)

"Story" or "folktale."

Cumbres & Toltec Scenic Railroad (COOM-bress and TOLL-teck)

Narrow-gauge railroad that runs along a section of the old Chili Line. Tourists ride the train for 64 miles between Chama, New Mexico, and Antonito, Colorado. The Cumbres & Toltec is the country's highest and longest steam railroad. It is jointly owned by the states of New Mexico and Colorado.

Cundiyo (coon-DEE-yo)

Northern New Mexico village on NM 503, 22 miles north of Santa Fe. Cundiyo was once known as the "Village of Vigils" because everyone living there was named Vigil. *Cundiyo* is a Spanish corruption of a Tewa word that means "round hill of the little bells."

curandero/a (coo-ron-DEH-ro/ruh)

A folk healer, one who understands the medicinal uses of plants and the healing power of ritual.

Cutting, Bronson

(1888-1935) Newspaper publisher and politician who brought Hispanics into New Mexico's political process. Cutting was born into a wealthy New York family. He left Harvard in 1910 in his senior year and moved to New Mexico for "health reasons," which probably meant tuberculosis. By 1912, he had decided to stay and was well enough to buy *The New Mexican.*

Cutting gradually became interested in politics. He was a progressive with independent means, so he had neither the

Bronson Cutting

inclination nor the need to participate in New Mexico's corrupt politics-as-usual. He served as a military attaché in London during World War I, and when he returned to New Mexico, he used the American Legion as a springboard to political power. Cutting had to overcome many obstacles in his courtship of Hispanic voters – he was Anglo, Protestant, a newcomer, and gay (something he never openly acknowledged) – but he used his fortune wisely. He traveled the state visiting Hispanic veterans and making "loans" to needy families. It was said that if you went into any house in Northern New Mexico, you would see a picture of Jesus Christ on one wall and a picture of Bronson Cutting on the other.

Cutting was elected to the United States Senate in 1928 and was reelected in 1932. A nominal Republican, he was a strong supporter of FDR's New Deal and a vocal opponent of government censorship. He died in an airplane crash in 1935 and was succeeded as senator by Democrat Dennis Chavez.

Cuyamungue (coo-yuh-MOON-gay)

Northern New Mexico community 12 miles north of Santa Fe. The name became more familiar when the Cuyamungue exit was added to US 84/285 in the 2002-2004 reconstruction of that highway. *K'uuyemugeh*, which is how the word is spelled on an overpass, is a Tewa word that means "place of the sliding rock." Gabriel's New Mexican restaurant is off the Cuyamungue exit.

- D -

Dale Ball Trails

Hiking and biking trails that run through the Sangre de Cristo foothills. The 22-mile network was the brainchild of retired banker Dale Ball, who raised the money and spearheaded the trails' construction. The project was completed in 2005.

Davis, Andrew

(1963-) Owner of the largest house in Santa Fe. Davis is a third-generation money manager. His grandfather, Shelby Davis, built the family fortune in New York through investments in insurance companies. His father, also named Shelby, moved to Tucson, where he has been described as the "Warren Buffet of the Southwest." Andrew followed his brother, Chris, into the family business.

In 1993, Andrew moved to Santa Fe, where he and his wife, Sydney, are active in community affairs. He has served on the New Mexico State Investment Council and on the boards of Santa Fe Prep and the Georgia O'Keeffe Museum.

A hill above the Santa Fe Institute was flattened to accommodate the Davis's 23,000-square-foot house and 3,000-square-foot "casita." In 2005, Santa Fe Mayor David Coss, then a city councilor, told *The New Mexican,* "I think they've basically manipulated the [escarpment] ordinance to build a trophy home that the rest of us have to look at ...."

Day Hikes in the Santa Fe Area

The local Sierra Club book about ... day hikes in the Santa Fe area. The popular guide was first published in 1981 and is now in its sixth edition.

Day of the Dead

Mexican celebration and remembrance of dead friends and family held on All Saints Day and All Souls Day, November 1 and 2. Like Cinco de Mayo, the Day of the Dead (*El Dia de los Muertos* in Spanish) is primarily a Mexican, rather than New Mexican, tradition. Still, folk art images like La Catrina, an elegantly dressed skeleton lady, are becoming increasingly popular in New Mexico.

Deaf School

See SCHOOL FOR THE DEAF, NEW MEXICO.

Death Comes for the Archbishop

Willa Cather's 1927 fictionalized biography of Archbishop Jean Baptiste Lamy. Some New Mexico historians, including Fray Angélico Chávez, have taken issue with Cather's unflattering depiction of New Mexico's Hispanic priests, Padre Antonio José Martinez of Taos in particular.

DeBuys, William (duh-BWEEZ)

(1949-) Author and environmentalist. Born and raised in Baltimore, deBuys moved to the Northern New Mexico village of El Valle in 1972 after graduating from the University of North Carolina. He earned a Ph.D. in American Studies at the University of Texas in 1982. DeBuys's books about Northern New Mexico include *Enchantment and Exploitation* (1985); *River of Traps* (1990), which was a finalist for the Pulitzer Prize in nonfiction in 1991; and *The Walk* (2007). His latest book, *A Great Aridness: Climate Change and the Future of the American Southwest*, was published in 2011. DeBuys served as founding chairman of the Valles Caldera National Preserve from 2001 to 2004.

Delgado, Larry (del-GAH-doe)

(1936-) Santa Fe's mayor from 1998 to 2006. Delgado's conciliatory manner came as a relief after the often-confrontational tactics of his predecessor, Debbie Jaramillo. He was succeeded as mayor in 2006 by David Coss.

Larry Delgado

Denish, Diane (DEN-ish)

(1949-) New Mexico's first female lieutenant governor. The Hobbs native is the daughter of the late Jack Daniels, a businessman and state legislator who lost the 1972 race for the United States Senate to Pete Domenici. She served as chair of the state Democratic Party before being elected lieutenant governor in 2002.

Denish had planned to take over the governor's office in early 2009 when Bill Richardson was appointed Secretary of Commerce in the Obama administration, but that chance evaporated when Richardson's appointment was withdrawn because of an investigation into alleged corruption in his administration. Denish was defeated by Republican Susana Martinez in the 2010 gubernatorial race.

descanso (dess-CAHN-so)

"Resting place." The word originally referred to a place where pallbearers rested as they carried a coffin from church to graveyard. These days, it means a roadside memorial dedicated to a person who was killed near that spot, usually in a traffic accident. The original descansos were rock cairns topped with rustic wooden crosses. Modern versions still feature crosses but are often embellished with teddy bears, plastic flowers, and Mylar balloons.

Descanso

De Vargas, Don Diego (duh VAR-gus, don dee-AY-go)

(1643-1704) Spanish governor who led the 1692-1693 reconquista, or reconquest, of New Mexico after the 1680 Pueblo Revolt. De Vargas served two terms as governor of New Mexico. He died in 1704 of a fever that he contracted on an expedition against Apache raiders.

De Vargas's entrada, or procession, into Santa Fe in 1692 is celebrated in the city's annual Fiesta.

DeVargas Center

The older and smaller of Santa Fe's two enclosed shopping malls. (Santa Fe Place, on the Southside, is both bigger and newer.) The 248,000-square-foot DeVargas mall was built in 1973 and is, of course, named for Don Diego de Vargas.

The mall's location at the intersection of Guadalupe Street and Paseo de Peralta makes it the ideal staging area for Fiesta parades.

Dia de los Muertos (DEE-uh day los MWAIR-toes)

See DAY OF THE DEAD.

Don Diego de Vargas

Diablo Canyon (dee-AH-blow)

Narrow canyon 18 miles northwest of Santa Fe, near the Rio Grande. Diablo, "Devil," Canyon's 300-foot vertical cliffs are a favorite with Santa Fe-area hikers and rock climbers. Unfortunately, the area is also popular with beer drinkers, recreational shooters, and litterers.

Diablo Canyon is known as *Caja del Rio*, "Box of the River," Canyon on USGS maps.

dicho (DEE-cho)

"Proverb" or "saying." *Pa pendejo no se necesita mestro*, "To be a fool one needs no school" is an example of a Northern New Mexico dicho.

Dictionary of New Mexico and Southern Colorado Spanish, A

COLORADO

NEW MEXICO

Range of unique Spanish dialect

The late Professor Rubén Cobos's study of the Spanish language as spoken in Northern New Mexico and southern Colorado. Northern New Mexicans developed a unique dialect during their centuries of isolation from the rest of the Spanish-speaking world, and those who moved into southern Colorado in the 19th century introduced it to that region. Cobos's dictionary was first published in 1983, with a revised edition issued in 2003.

Diné (dee-NAY)

"The People," what the Navajo call themselves. Diné is the tribe's traditional name. *Navajo*, which means "place of large cultivated fields," is a Tewa word assigned to the tribe by the Pueblo Indians.

Dixon

Northern New Mexico village. The community was originally named Embudo but its name was changed to Dixon, in honor of a local schoolteacher, when the Chili Line railroad station a few miles west was also named Embudo.

The village is home to author Stanley Crawford and hosts the annual Dixon Studio Tour. (Dixon is *not* the home of Dixon's Apple Orchard, which is in a canyon six miles north of the village of Cochiti Lake.) Dixon is 45 miles north of Santa Fe on NM 75, two miles east of NM 68.

Domenici, Pete (duh-MEN-ih-chee)

(1932-) New Mexico's longtime Republican United States senator. The son of Italian immigrants, Domenici was first elected to the Senate in 1972. Poor health precluded his running for reelection in 2008, and his seat was claimed by Democrat Tom Udall.

Pete Domenici

Don/Doña (DON, DOAN-yuh)

Spanish title of respect for a socially elevated man or woman. The title is seldom heard today, although a recent New Mexico state official let it be known that he expected to be called "Don Francisco." His subordinates were compelled to comply, but his insistence on the title earned him as much ridicule as respect.

Don Gaspar Avenue (gas-PAR)

Santa Fe street named for Don Gaspar Ortiz y Alarid, a merchant who became wealthy trading between the Indians, Mexicans, and Americans in the Mexican and Territorial periods. He died in Santa Fe in 1882.

Don Gaspar Avenue is a one-way street that runs south from downtown to just below San Mateo Road. It is the dividing point between East and West Alameda, East and West De Vargas, East and West San Francisco, and East and West Water streets.

Doña Ana County (DOAN-yuh AN-uh)

The second most populous, after Bernalillo County, of New Mexico's 33 counties. Doña Ana County, population 209,233, is in the southern part of the state and it borders both Texas and Mexico. It is known for the agricultural bounty of the Mesilla Valley and for New Mexico State University, which is located in the county seat of Las Cruces.

The county's name may have originated with Doña Ana Maria de Córdoba, a 17th-century lady who owned a ranch in the area.

Doña Sebastiana (DOAN-yuh seh-bahs-tee-AH-nah)

Skeletal figure representing Death in New Mexican folk art. Doña Sebastiana is most often seen in *La Carreta de la Muerte*, "The Death Cart," wearing a hooded black robe and holding a drawn bow and arrow. Like the Grim Reaper, Doña Sebastiana is sometimes the object of fun. New Mexican cuentos, or folk tales, tell of Norteños negotiating with her and occasionally outwitting her.

Doña Tules (DOAN-yuh TOO-less)

(circa 1800-1852) Maria Gertrudis Barcelo, colorful operator of a famous gambling room, saloon, and brothel in Santa Fe's Mexican Period.

Nicknamed La Tules because of her thin frame (*tules* means "reeds"), she is often mentioned in the accounts of American visitors. In 1846, Susan Magoffin described her as "a stately dame of a certain age, the possessor of a ... shrewd sense and fascinating manner necessary to lure the wayward, inexperienced youth to the hall of final ruin."

Doña Tules

Doña Tules was close to Mexican Governor Manuel Armijo and is said to have helped smooth Santa Fe's transition to American rule in the Mexican-American War. She paid newly arrived Bishop Jean Baptiste Lamy $2,000, a vast sum in those days, to be buried in the parroquia, or parish church, that stood on the current site of St. Francis Cathedral. Bishop Lamy himself conducted the funeral service in 1852.

Doodlet's

The source for whimsical knickknacks, toys, and books. Doodlet's store has a genuine Santa Fe pedigree. It was established in 1952 by Theo Raven, a native of Santa Fe whose mother, Helene Ruthling, came to New Mexico to work as a governess for Mabel Dodge Luhan. Artist Will Shuster, who was a family friend, called Helene "Doodles" and daughter Theo "Doodlet." His nickname for Theo became the store's name.

Theo Raven retired and sold the business to Lisa Young in 2010. Doodlet's is on the corner of Don Gaspar Avenue and Water Street, across Don Gaspar from Pasqual's restaurant.

Downs at Santa Fe, The

Horse racetrack in La Cienega, 10 miles southwest of Santa Fe. Since its opening in June 1971, the racetrack's numerous owners have at various times announced plans for luxury hotels, golf courses, and other improvements, but the facility has never been profitable enough to allow for expansion.

Pojoaque Pueblo bought The Downs in 1996 but stopped the horse racing there in 1997. The pueblo had hoped to reopen the track as a racino but was unable to obtain a license, and Santa Fe County refused to approve any other improvements until the pueblo removed the massive pile of horse manure that had accumulated over more than 20 years.

A seasonal flea market called The Flea at the Downs opened at the racetrack in 2010.

downtown

Loosely, the part of Santa Fe within the "D" defined by Guadalupe Street on the west and the loop of Paseo de Peralta on the south, east, and north. The Plaza is at the center of downtown. Old-time Santa Feans complain that the downtown area no longer holds any attraction for them because the drugstores and grocery stores that they used to frequent have been replaced by expensive art galleries. (See the following page for a map of downtown Santa Fe.)

Dragon Room

The Pink Adobe's world-famous watering hole. Founder Rosalea Murphy opened the bar in 1978, and in 1986, *Newsweek* magazine cited it as one of the two best bars in the United States. The Dragon Room is on Old Santa Trail, one block north of the Roundhouse.

drought

Insufficient precipitation and its effect on the environment. Santa Fe averages about 14 inches of precipitation per year, but there have been periods of serious drought.

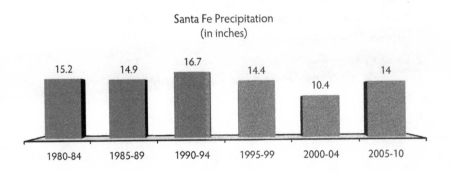

Santa Fe Precipitation
(in inches)

1980-84	1985-89	1990-94	1995-99	2000-04	2005-10
15.2	14.9	16.7	14.4	10.4	14

Downtown Santa Fe

1	Bataan Memorial Building	11	Museum of Art, New Mexico
2	Catron Block	12	Old Fort Marcy Park
3	City Hall	13	Palace of the Governors
4	Cross of the Martyrs	14	Plaza
5	Federal Courthouse (Santiago E. Campos United States Courthouse)	15	Post Office (Joseph M. Montoya Federal Building)
6	Georgia O'Keeffe Museum	16	Roundhouse
7	Institute of American Indian Arts	17	San Miguel Mission
8	La Fonda	18	Santuario de Guadalupe
9	Lensic Performing Arts Center	19	Sena Plaza
10	Loretto Chapel	20	St. Francis Cathedral

The most recent drought occurred in the early 2000s, when average annual precipitation between 2000 and 2004 dropped to just 10.4 inches, with a low of 7.2 inches in 2003. The dry spell was particularly painful because the 1980s and 1990s had been unusually wet, averaging over 15 inches of precipitation per year.

Santa Fe still shows the effects of the drought. Rosario Cemetery, and many homeowners, replaced dying grass with rocks. And millions of weakened trees were killed by bark beetles and other parasites – the chain-saw carvings on East Alameda Street are all that remain of the tall cottonwoods that died as a result of the drought.

Duke City

Albuquerque's nickname. The city is named for the Spanish Duke of Alburquerque. (The extra *r* in the city's name was later dropped.)

Dulce (DULL-say)

Principal city on the Jicarilla Apache Reservation. Dulce, whose name means "sweet," was established in 1883 when the reservation's headquarters were moved from nearby Amargo, whose name means "bitter." The city's population is 2,743.

Dulce is 131 miles northwest of Santa Fe via US 84 west and US 64 west.

Durham, Linda

(1942-) New York City Playboy bunny turned Cerrillos hippie turned Santa Fe art dealer. Originally from New Jersey, Linda Graves was working at the Manhattan Playboy Club in 1966 when she chucked it all to pursue an alternative lifestyle with her new husband in an off-the-grid house near the town of Cerrillos. She eventually migrated to Santa Fe, where she worked as a researcher for gallery owner Forrest Fenn. By the mid-1970s, she was on her own and dealing in artwork by New Mexico artists.

Durham was a pioneer in bringing contemporary art to Santa Fe. She admitted in a 1997 *Newsweek* article that it had been hard to overcome the preconception that the Santa Fe art scene was all regional kitsch. She recalled an East Coast art critic asking her, "So what do you specialize in, little Indian angels floating up to heaven?" Durham closed her gallery in 2011 after 33 years in business.

- E -

Eagle Nest

Northern New Mexico village on the Enchanted Circle, 30-odd miles northeast of Taos. Eagle Nest Lake was created and stocked with trout in 1919, and the village developed soon after. The community exists mostly to serve visiting anglers.

Like Angel Fire and Red River, Eagle Nest is what is sometimes called an "Anglo village," one established by Anglos in the 19th or 20th century, as opposed to a much older, historically Hispanic village like Chimayó or Truchas.

earthship

Eco-friendly house designed or built by Taos architect Michael Reynolds. Reynolds incorporated bottles, discarded tires, and solar energy features into the earthships that he constructed in the 1970s, 1980s, and 1990s. While his ideas were good, their execution was not, and his ar-

Earthship

chitect's and contractor's licenses were revoked in 2000 after repeated complaints from clients. Reynolds's travails are recounted in a 2008 documentary film titled *Garbage Warrior*.

The Greater World Earthship Community and the Earthship Visitor Center are on US 64, a mile and a half west of the Rio Grande Gorge Bridge.

Easter pilgrimage

Hike to the Santuario de Chimayó. Each year during the Holy Week preceding Easter, thousands of peregrinos, or pilgrims, walk from the city of Albuquerque and from towns and villages all over Northern New Mexico to the old church in the village of Chimayó. They make the pilgrimage in remembrance of a departed loved one, to atone for their sins, or to collect some of the Santuario's holy dirt.

Eastside

Santa Fe's oldest and, in the eyes of many, most desirable residential area. The Eastside is characterized by narrow streets, authentic adobe homes, and old-growth trees.

Most of what is considered the Eastside is within the area bounded by Cerro Gordo Road on the north, the Sangre de Cristo foothills on the east, Camino de Cruz Blanca on the south, and Old Santa Fe Trail and Paseo de Peralta on the west. Canyon Road, Acequia Madre Street, Garcia Street, East Palace Avenue, East Alameda Street, and Camino del Monte Sol are signature Eastside addresses. Boundaries are inexact, and homebuyers should exercise caution: because of the cachet attached to "Eastside," real estate agents often stretch its boundaries to include newer housing developments that clearly lack the essential age or ambiance.

Eastsiders are sometimes stereotyped as rich Anglo snobs, a perception once reinforced by the *Santa Fe Reporter*. The *Reporter*'s endorsement of the Hispanic candidate in a Santa Fe mayoral race generated lots of phone calls to the paper, and the editors later wrote that it was possible to predict a caller's opinion by inflection alone. They noted that the candidate's supporters spoke with "melodic Spanish accents," while her opponents evinced that "irritating Eastside whine." In fact, many old

Hispanic families still live on the Eastside, though it is becoming increasingly difficult for them to resist the astronomically high offers for their property.

Eaves Movie Ranch

Western-town movie set named for its owner, rancher and raconteur J. W. Eaves. The facility, which opened in the early 1960s, has been the setting for over 250 television and film productions. Eaves Movie Ranch is 18 miles south of Santa Fe, off Bonanza Creek Road.

Eaves Movie Ranch
and
Lone Butte

Echo Amphitheater

Natural echo chamber created by a concavity in sandstone cliffs. The amphitheater is on US 84, 65 miles northwest of Santa Fe, four miles north of Ghost Ranch.

eee!

Exclamation associated with Norteños, a shortened version of *hijole*. A popular joke goes, "How do people in Española communicate? By eee!-mail."

Eight Northern Indian Pueblos

Consortium of the eight pueblos north of Santa Fe: Nambé, Ohkay Owingeh, Picuris, Pojoaque, San Ildefonso, Santa Clara, Taos, and Tesuque.

The group is governed by the Eight Northern Indian Pueblos Council, which maintains its offices at Ohkay Owingeh. The council sponsors a collaborative arts and crafts show, which is held at Ohkay Owingeh the third week of July.

El Farol (fuh-ROLL)

"The Lantern," Santa Fe's oldest bar and restaurant. There has been a commercial enterprise of some sort in the Canyon Road building since 1835. The property was owned by the Vigil, Serna, and Tapia families until 1968, when it was purchased by Bob Young, who named it El Farol. Current owner David Salazar bought it in 1985.

The restaurant and nightclub was embroiled in controversy in 1998 when some of its Eastside neighbors complained about the noise, noting that the bar's presence was a violation of the area's residential arts and crafts zoning. Salazar responded that the bar predated both the neighbors and the zoning. Then things got ugly. The spokesman for the neighbors received a death threat, and, soon after, the bar was extensively damaged by a fire that investigators concluded was arson. To the relief of all, the city negotiated a compromise and the bar reopened after repairs.

El Farol is one of Santa Fe's most popular restaurants. It is known for its tapas and as one of the city's best venues for listening and dancing to live music. It is on Canyon Road, just east of Camino del Monte Sol.

El Guique (WEE-kay)

Northern New Mexico community on the west side of the Rio Grande, opposite Alcalde. The name is of unknown origin, though it was probably a Tewa word. El Guique is two miles north of Ohkay Owingeh, 31 miles north of Santa Fe.

El Malpais National Monument (mal-pie-EESE)

"The Badlands" National Monument, 115,000 acres of uninhabitable land covered by dark lava flows from ancient volcanoes. The monument's information center is near Grants, 160 miles from Santa Fe via I-25 south, I-40 west, and NM 117 west.

El Morro (MORE-o)

Sandstone butte that has served as a message board since pre-Columbian times. In Spanish, *El Morro* means "The Bluff." In English, the butte has long been known as Inscription Rock. The 200-foot-high prominence rises above a fresh-water pool that has for centuries been a stopping place for travelers between Zuni Pueblo and Acoma Pueblo.

Pre-Columbian Indians carved petroglyphs into the stone, and Spanish explorers later contributed their inscriptions. The first of hundreds of Spanish and English messages reads: "There passed by here the Governor Don Juan de Oñate from the discovery of the sea of the south [the Gulf of California] on the 16th of April, 1605."

El Morro National Monument is 180 miles southwest of Santa Fe via I-25 south, I-40 west, and NM 53 west.

El Museo Cultural de Santa Fe (moo-SAY-o cool-too-RALL deh SAHN-tah FAY)

"The Cultural Museum of Santa Fe," a nonprofit organization dedicated to the preservation and showcasing of the art and culture of Hispanic New Mexico. El Museo was organized in 1995 and has occupied a former warehouse in what is now the Railyard since 1998. It is on Paseo de Peralta, across from SITE Santa Fe.

El Niño (NEEN-yo)

"The Little Boy," a periodic weather pattern caused by the warming of eastern Pacific waters. In the United States, the effect of El Niño is that the Pacific jet stream blows cooler, wetter weather across the southern half of the country, including New Mexico.

El Niño is so named because Peruvian fishermen first noticed it in the month of December and named it after the Christ child. *La Niña*, "The Little Girl," is caused by cooler-than-usual Pacific waters, and it usually produces warmer, drier weather.

El Norte (NOR-tay)

"The North," or Northern New Mexico. The local news section of *The New Mexican* is called *Santa Fe & El Norte*. Natives of Northern New Mexico are called Norteños, or Northerners.

El Palacio (puh-LAH-see-o)

The Museum of New Mexico's quarterly publication. *El Palacio*, "The Palace," is named for the Palace of the Governors. Established in 1913, it is the oldest museum publication in the United States.

El Paso

Texas city on the north bank of the Rio Grande. In the Spanish Colonial Period, a settlement on the south bank of the river was known as *El Paso del Norte*, "The Northern Pass." During the 1680 Pueblo Revolt, Spanish colonists fleeing south down the Camino Real did not feel safe until they had crossed the Rio Grande and entered El Paso del Norte.

Over time, a settlement developed on the north side of the river as well. This city, which was incorporated into Texas, later became known as El Paso. The old Mexican city of El Paso del Norte is now known as *Ciudad Juárez*, "The City of Juárez."

El Paso, Texas, is 328 miles south of Santa Fe via I-25.

El Rancho de Las Golondrinas (go-lahn-DREE-ness)

See Las Golondrinas.

El Rito (REE-toe)

Northern New Mexico village known for its artists and writers. El Rito, whose name means "The Creek," is 57 miles northwest of Santa Fe via US 84.

Public art in El Rito

El Vado Lake (VAH-doe)

One of three reservoirs, along with Heron Lake and Abiquiu Lake, on the Rio Chama. There was once a shallow ford across the Chama, and a community named *El Vado*, "The Crossing," grew up next to it. The town, which was at one time the largest in Rio Arriba County, was drowned when the river was dammed to create the lake in 1935.

~ 95

El Vado Lake is 109 miles from Santa Fe, 14 miles southwest of Tierra Amarilla.

El Valle (VIE-yay)

Northern New Mexico community whose name means "The Valley." The Taos County village is home to author William de Buys. El Valle is three miles southeast of Las Trampas, 49 miles from Santa Fe via US 84/285 and NM 76.

El Zaguán (zah-GWAN)

Historic building on Canyon Road named for its zaguán, or long breezeway. The building is owned by the Historic Santa Fe Foundation, which uses part of it as its headquarters. Other spaces within the building are rented out as artists' residences.

The Bandelier Garden at El Zaguán is named for anthropologist and author Adolph Bandelier. Bandelier and his wife lived in the house in 1891 and 1892, though there is no evidence that they designed or planted the garden.

Eldorado

Housing development south of Santa Fe. Eldorado is Santa Fe County's largest housing development and is one of the largest unincorporated communities in New Mexico. Established in 1972, the development currently has about 2,700 homes, with a population of 6,130. At one time, it boasted the highest percentage of solar-powered homes of any place in the United States. Eldorado can be very windy: a new resident who wrote a memoir of her first year there titled it *Blown Away*.

Eldorado is an affluent, predominantly Anglo community. A Hispanic candidate for state office once referred to its residents as "bigoted Anglos" who would not vote for a Hispanic. Political blogger Heath Haussamen, who grew up in Eldorado, pointed out that in the 2008 congressional race Ben Ray Luján received 60 percent of the Eldorado vote, while his Anglo opponents split the other 40 percent.

Eldorado's main entrance is 12 miles south of Santa Fe, off US 285.

Eldorado Hotel

Santa Fe's largest hotel. The 219-room, upscale Eldorado is downtown on the corner of San Francisco and Sandoval streets.

In 1983, the former site of Big Jo Lumber Company was purchased by developers Bill and Nancy Zeckendorf. The hotel they opened two years later was immediately criticized for being too big for its Spanish Pueblo-style architecture.

electrosensitivity

Real or imagined sensitivity to electromagnetic transmissions. Activist Arthur Firstenberg and LANL physicist Bill Bruno, both claiming to suffer from electrosensitivity, led the opposition to expanding Wi-Fi access in Santa Fe. Firstenberg sued his neighbor because he believed her computer and cell phone exacerbated his existing illness. Bruno appeared at public meetings wearing a chain-mail-like headdress that he thinks protects him from damaging waves.

Some Santa Feans characterize their claims as pseudoscience. When the city appointed Firstenberg to a technology advisory committee, science writer George Johnson likened it to "a planetarium hiring a court astrologer." In April 2010, Johnson outlined the controversy in an article for *Slate* magazine titled "On Top of Microwave Mountain."

Because it is in many ways a refuge from mainstream America, Santa Fe attracts people who are distrustful of mainstream technology. If letters to *The New Mexican*'s editorial page are any indication, more than a few Santa Feans believe that vapor trails from overhead jets are "chemtrails" that make people sick.

Elephant Butte Lake

The state's largest lake and most popular fishing and boating destination. The Rio Grande reservoir is named for a nearby rock formation that resembles an elephant. Elephant Butte Lake is 208 miles south of Santa Fe, off I-25 just north of Truth or Consequences.

Embudo Station (em-BOO-doe)

Railway station turned restaurant and microbrewery. The seasonal restaurant is on the banks of the Rio Grande, on what was once the site of a depot for the Chili Line.

Embudo Station is on NM 68 (the low road to Taos), 41 miles north of Santa Fe.

Encantado (en-cahn-TAH-doe)

High-end Tesuque resort. The 57-acre facility includes a restaurant, a spa, an art gallery, and 65 guest casitas. Encantado, whose name means "Enchanted," is the only hotel in New Mexico to hold the AAA five-star rating. The resort is in Tesuque on NM 592, eight miles north of the Santa Fe Plaza.

Enchanted Circle

Scenic drive. The 84-mile circle passes through or near the Northern New Mexico communities of Taos, Arroyo Hondo, Questa, Red River, Eagle Nest, and Angel Fire.

enchilada (en-chih-LAH-duh)

A tortilla served with beans, cheese, and, sometimes, meat, smothered in chile. In Mexico, the tortilla is rolled; in New Mexico, it is usually served flat and is often made with blue corn. The name derives from *enchilar*, "to season with chile."

entrada (en-TRAH-duh)

"Entrance" or "procession." In New Mexico, the term most often refers to Don Diego de Vargas's march into Santa Fe 12 years after the 1680 Pueblo Revolt. Local Hispanics playing De Vargas and his entourage solemnly reenact the Entrada in the Santa Fe Fiesta's opening parade.

escarpment ordinance

Santa Fe ordinance that prohibits building on certain ridge tops. Some Santa Feans were upset when designer Tom Ford was granted a waiver for his 16,000-square-foot home on the grounds that his lot offered no suitable building site other than the top of the ridge. The loophole was later closed with an amendment to the original ordinance.

Española (ess-pan-YO-luh)

Largely Hispanic city that bills itself as the "Lowrider Capital of the World." Española, population 10,244, is Northern New Mexico's fourth most populous city, after Santa Fe, Las Vegas, and Los Alamos. Blue-collar Española stands in stark contrast to upscale Santa Fe.

Though it is literally translated "Spanish lady," Española's name probably derives from *San Gabriel de los Españoles*, "Saint Gabriel of the Spanish," the first Spanish settlement in New Mexico. Don Juan de Oñate founded the settlement near present-day Española in 1598. It served as the Spanish capital until 1610, when Santa Fe was established as the new capital.

Española sprawls across the Rio Grande Valley, just south of the Rio Grande's confluence with the Rio Chama. The city is 25 miles north of Santa Fe via US 84/285.

Española joke

Jest at the expense of hard-luck Española. Examples include "Who discovered Española? Marco Cholo," and "What do you call a man wearing a suit in Española? The defendant."

In *Dancing to Pay the Light Bill*, Jim Sagel writes, tongue in cheek, that the people of Española created the jokes to keep out snobs from Santa Fe. University of New Mexico professor Michael Trujillo suggests in *Land of Disenchantment* that while they may not have authored the jokes, the people of Española do appreciate them because they represent the real, unvarnished Northern New Mexico.

Estevan the Moor (ess-TEH-vahn)

(circa 1510-1539) The first black man to set foot in the American Southwest. Estevan, a Moroccan, was enslaved by the Portuguese when he was a teenager and was later sold to the Spanish. He converted to Christianity and, in 1527, accompanied his Spanish master on an ill-fated expedition to the New World.

Estevan and three Spaniards, including Alvar Nuñez Cabeza de Vaca, survived a shipwreck near what is now Galveston, Texas. They endured years in Indian captivity before they finally escaped and walked overland to Mexico. The Spanish viceroy listened attentively as the men passed on stories they had heard of the mythical Seven Cities of Cibola.

In 1539, Estevan accompanied a small party from Mexico on a reconnaissance of what is now western New Mexico. He was acting as a scout when he sent back word that he had discovered a great city, but he was killed by Zunis before he could return with details. The circumstances of Estevan's death are unclear: some say he was killed because he demanded turquoise and women; others believe it was because he wore owl feathers and the Zunis considered the bird a bad omen. The rest of the party returned to Mexico and, based on Estevan's incomplete report, confirmed the existence of cities of great wealth. Coronado's much larger exploratory expedition was launched the next year.

Evangelo's

Iconic Santa Fe bar. Evangelo Klonis left Greece as a stowaway at age 17, having sewed himself into a bag of coal that was loaded onto a freighter bound for California. By 1936, he was living in Santa Fe and running the Mayflower Café on the Plaza. Klonis enlisted in the army at the outbreak of World War II and earned United States citizenship and considerable celebrity during the war. A *Life* magazine photographer took a picture of him in combat, and the photo of his

Famous World War II photograph of
Evangelo Klonis

grizzled visage later appeared on the cover of *Life* and on a U.S. postage stamp.

Evangelo Klonis returned to Santa Fe and opened his namesake bar in 1970. He died in 1989, and the business is now owned by his son, Nick. The photos of Evangelo hanging on its walls make the bar a perpetual memorial to its founder.

Evangelo's Cocktail Lounge is on West San Francisco Street, at its intersection with Galisteo Street.

Every calculation based on experience elsewhere fails in New Mexico

Governor Lew Wallace's expression of frustration. In 1878, President Rutherford B. Hayes appointed Wallace governor of the New Mexico Territory and tasked him with breaking up the Santa Fe Ring and ending the Lincoln County War. Wallace was unable to do either. He happily left the Territory when he was appointed ambassador to the Ottoman Empire in 1881.

- F -

Fairview Cemetery

Historic Santa Fe cemetery. Fairview was founded in 1883 for non-Catholic burials and today contains about 3,700 graves, including those of three New Mexico governors and 10 Santa Fe mayors. Thomas B. Catron and other purported members of the Santa Fe Ring are interred there, as are members of Santa Fe's pioneer Jewish families. The 40-acre cemetery includes a caretaker's house and three mausoleums.

The graveyard has been plagued by prairie dogs for decades and, more recently, by homeless people camping on its grounds. Fairview Cemetery is on Cerrillos Road, immediately south of the School for the Deaf.

Fairview Cemetery

fajita (fah-HEE-tah)

Strips of grilled steak or chicken wrapped in a tortilla along with onions, peppers, and other side dishes. The name derives from *fajar*, "to wrap."

fandango (fan-DANG-o)

Old word for a dance or shindig. Historian Marc Simmons notes that American traders who came to Santa Fe in the 1820s and 1830s were scandalized by what they saw at public fandangos – the soldiers were slovenly, the priests drank too much, and the women rouged their cheeks and smoked cornhusk cigarillos.

Fanta Se (FAN-tuh SAY)

Word-play combination of "Santa Fe" and "fantasy." The term implies that Santa Fe is disconnected from the real world. It is true that many people come to Santa Fe ready to spend their money and energy exploring alternatives, particularly alternative medicine. It has been said that if Sedona, Arizona, is the New Age capital of America, then Santa Fe, with its cottage industry of bodyworkers, psychics, and herbalists, is the alternative healing capital.

Farmers Market, Santa Fe

Market for fresh, locally grown food. Vendors set up booths in and around the market building in the Railyard on Saturday and Tuesday mornings and on Thursday afternoons. As many as 160 farmers and 5,000 buyers attend the market at the peak of the growing season. The Santa Fe Farmers Market has been judged one of the best in the country.

Farmington

The principal city in New Mexico's Four Corners region and, with a population of 45,877, New Mexico's sixth most populous city. Farmington's principal industries are oil, gas, and coal extraction.

The city is adjacent to the Navajo Nation but, unlike Gallup, Farmington does not benefit economically from trading in Indian arts and crafts. In fact, the city has a reputation for racism against Indians.

In 1975, three Anglo high school students who were convicted of murdering three Navajo men received short sentences in a juvenile facility. The incident is recounted by author Rodney Barker in a 1988 book titled *Broken Circle*. In 2010, three Anglo men were arrested for using a hot coat hanger to brand a mentally challenged Navajo man with a swastika. The perpetrators' attorney immediately said, "This is not a *Broken Circle*-type incident."

farolito (fair-o-LEE-toe)

"Little lantern," a Christmas decoration made from a brown-paper bag weighted with sand and lit from within by a candle. Some businesses use an electric light in a hard-plastic bag to achieve the same glowing effect.

In Albuquerque, the paper-bag lantern is called a *luminaria*, but in Santa Fe, *luminaria* means "bonfire." The proper terminology has long been disputed. In 1969, the New Mexico House of Representatives passed a memorial allowing either term. The Senate countered by resolving that "the little lanterns of paper bags and candles ... should, historically and linguistically, be 'farolitos' and not 'luminarias'." The debate continues.

Farolitos at La Fonda in the 1930s

Farolito Walk

Christmas Eve tradition in which revelers walk down Canyon Road, Acequia Madre, and other Eastside streets singing Christmas carols, admiring the glowing farolitos, and warming themselves at curbside luminarias. The Farolito Walk has become increasingly boisterous, and some Eastside residents advocate curtailing or even eliminating the tradition.

Fashion Outlets of Santa Fe

The official name of the outlet mall at the intersection of I-25 and Cerrillos Road. The open-air, 122,000-square-foot shopping center's tenants are almost exclusively name-brand outlet stores.

Santa Fe Factory Outlets, as it was originally known, opened in 1993, at about the same time as the New Mexico Outlet Center (most recently known as ¡Traditions!), which is about halfway between Santa Fe and Albuquerque. Both malls have struggled financially, probably because shopping for bargains on designer clothing is a low priority for most visitors to Northern New Mexico.

faux adobe (foe uh-DOE-be), also fauxdobe (foe-DOE-be)

Faux, or fake, adobe; a term used to describe a building designed to look as though it were built with authentic adobe bricks. Most of the structures in Santa Fe are faux adobe, built with conventional wood or metal frames and then covered with adobe-colored stucco.

Disguising a building to conform with architectural fashion is an old practice in Santa Fe. In the 1890s, when red brick was in fashion, some authentic adobe buildings were painted over with fake bricks. The Oliver P. Hovey House on the corner of Griffin Street and Grant Avenue is the city's last surviving example of a faux-brick building.

feast days

Celebration days for New Mexico's pueblos. As part of their effort to convert the Indians to Catholicism, Spanish priests assigned a patron saint to each pueblo and saw to it that a feast was held on the annual saint's day. Feast days are still observed and are generally open to the public. The celebrations usually include ceremonial dancing and food.

Friends, family, and visitors from outside the pueblo may be invited into a private home for a meal. Visitors are cautioned to observe pueblo etiquette on feast days, as on all other occasions.

Patron saints and feast days for the Eight Northern Pueblos are as follows.

Pueblo	Saint	Date
Nambé	San Francisco	October 4
Ohkay Owingeh	San Juan	June 24
Picuris	San Lorenzo	August 10
Pojoaque	Our Lady of Guadalupe	December 12
San Ildefonso	San Ildefonso	January 23
Santa Clara	Santa Clara	August 12
Taos	San Geronimo	September 30
Tesuque	San Diego	November 12

Federal Courthouse

A noteworthy Santa Fe building. In 1850, Congress appropriated limited funds for the construction of a stone Greek Revival building to serve as the Territorial capitol, but construction was halted when the money ran out after only one and a half stories had been built. The roofless

Federal Courthouse

building remained ignored and unfinished for almost 40 years, until it was finally completed in 1889, too late to serve as the Territorial capitol. Today, the Santiago E. Campos Federal Courthouse (it was named for Campos, a federal judge, in 2007) represents one of the best unaltered examples of a 19th-century public building in the Southwest.

The Federal Courthouse is in the federal oval, next to the Joseph M. Montoya Federal Building. An obelisk honoring frontiersman Kit Carson stands near the main entrance.

federal oval

The federally owned property within the oval defined by the stone wall and wrought iron fence surrounding the Federal Courthouse and the Joseph M. Montoya Federal Building (which houses Santa Fe's main post office). The property is bounded by Paseo de Peralta and Federal Place on the north and south, and by Washington and Grant avenues on the east and west. An equestrian statue of Don Pedro de Peralta stands at the western end of the oval.

Fenn, Forrest

(1931-) Retired art dealer, author, and amateur archaeologist. A Texas native, Fenn spent 20 years as an Air Force pilot. He flew combat missions over Vietnam and earned a Silver Star, among other decorations, before retiring from the Air Force in 1972. He moved to Santa Fe and opened an art gallery soon after.

Fenn had great influence on Santa Fe's art scene. He encouraged sculptor Glenna Goodacre at the start of her career and gave Linda Durham and Nedra Matteucci their first jobs in the gallery business. He was also an aggressive and creative merchandiser. In 1986, *People* magazine profiled him in an article titled "Rivals Scorn His Santa Fe Gallery, but Forrest Fenn Baskets the Cash."

Fenn sold his gallery to Nedra Matteucci and retired in 1988. He has since written eight books, including biographies of artists Joseph Henry Sharp and Nicolai Fechin. His memoir, *The Thrill of the Chase*, was published in 2010. An amateur archaeologist, Fenn collects artifacts from San Lazaro, an abandoned pueblo on land he owns in the Galisteo Basin.

fetish

Small stone carving of an animal used as a talisman in Pueblo culture. Each animal fetish is believed to provide a specific power or protection to the person who possesses it. Bear fetishes, which are said to impart strength, are the most common.

Fiesta de Santa Fe (fee-ESS-tuh deh SAHN-tah FAY)

City-wide festivities held the weekend after Labor Day, America's oldest community celebration. Fiesta (Hispanic Santa Feans often use the plural "fiestas") began in 1712 as a commemoration of Don Diego de Vargas's 1692 reconquest of New Mexico after the Pueblo Revolt of 1680.

Fiesta's modern incarnation includes largely Hispanic religious and historical elements like La Conquistadora's procession, La Entrada, and the candlelight walk to the Cross of the Martyrs. It also includes more frivolous elements that were added by Anglo artists: the Fiesta Melodrama, the burning of Zozobra, the Pet Parade, and the Historical/Hysterical Parade.

Related activities begin months before Fiesta weekend. In early summer, the Fiesta Council selects a local Hispanic man and woman to play Don Diego de Vargas and *La Reina de la Fiesta*, "The Fiesta Queen." In July and August, Fiesta royalty make visitations to area churches. The Fiesta Melodrama, a send-up of Santa Fe politics and current events, begins its run at the Santa Fe Playhouse in late August.

Fiesta weekend officially begins the Thursday night after Labor Day with the burning of Zozobra, a 50-foot-tall effigy of Old Man Gloom, at the Fort Marcy Recreation Complex. On Friday, De Vargas, the Fiesta Queen, and their attendants march past the Plaza in La Entrada. Saturday's events include the morning Pet Parade and, in the evening, the *Gran Baile*, "Grand Ball." Fiesta ends on Sunday with the Historical/Hysterical Parade in the afternoon and a candlelight procession from St. Francis Cathedral to the Cross of the Martyrs in the evening.

Fiesta Melodrama

A spoof of Santa Fe politics and current events performed at the Santa Fe Playhouse. The play usually opens in late August and runs through

Fiesta weekend. Melodramas featuring stereotypical characters, simplistic plots, and exaggerated emotions were popular in the West in the 19th century.

Fine-'n'-you?

A Norteño's contracted response to "How are you?" The response may be contracted, but Northern New Mexicans do appreciate it when people take time for social niceties. Gringos from fast-paced big cities who get frustrated with contractors and salespeople may find that things happen faster when they themselves slow down.

First Presbyterian Church

One of downtown Santa Fe's three landmark churches. First Presbyterian dates to 1867 and is the oldest Protestant congregation in New Mexico. The current Spanish Pueblo-style building was designed by John Gaw Meem and dedicated in 1939. It underwent extensive renovation between 2006 and 2008, including the installation of an $800,000 pipe organ.

First Presbyterian participates in ecumenical events with Holy Faith Episcopal Church and St. Francis Cathedral, the other big, downtown churches. First Presbyterian is at the intersection of Griffin Street and Grant Avenue.

Five & Dime General Store

Variety store on the Santa Fe Plaza on West San Francisco Street. For over 60 years, the site was occupied by an F.W. Woolworth's store that locals and tourists alike appreciated for its Frito pies and low prices on things like straw hats, handkerchiefs, and film. When Woolworth's announced in 1997 that it was closing all of its stores, a group of local investors started a company called UTBW (Used To Be Woolworth's) and opened the Five & Dime in the old Woolworth's space. The UTBW group has since opened six more stores in other cities.

flaco/a (FLAH-co/cuh)

"Skinny." Doña Sebastiana, the skeletal personification of Death in New Mexico folklore, is also known as *La Flaca*, "The Skinny One."

flea markets

Santa Fe boasts two open-air flea markets. The original is located near the Opera on US 84/285, seven miles north of Santa Fe. Formerly known as Trader Jack's, the market is now operated by Tesuque Pueblo. A second market, called The Flea at the Downs, is located at The Downs at Santa Fe. The old racetrack is owned by Pojoaque Pueblo, which leases space to the flea market.

Folk Art Market

See INTERNATIONAL FOLK ART MARKET, SANTA FE.

Folk Art Museum

See MUSEUM OF INTERNATIONAL FOLK ART.

Fonda, Jane

(1937-) Oscar-winning actress (*Klute, Coming Home*), political activist, exercise guru, and owner of a Pecos-area ranch. In 2000, Fonda and her then-husband, Ted Turner, bought 2,200 acres of what had been the Forked Lightning Ranch. When the couple split a year later, she retained the property and now lives there part time.

Fonda has been active in Pecos River cleanup efforts. Although she is not often seen in Santa Fe, she has appeared at the Lensic with Eve Ensler, author of *The Vagina Monologues*, and has spoken at Santa Fe's Upaya Zen Center.

Ford, Tom

(1961-) Graduate of Santa Fe Prep, fashion designer, film director, and owner of a Santa Fe mega-mansion. Ford's parents relocated from Houston to Santa Fe when he was 11. After graduating from Santa Fe Prep in 1979, Ford moved to New York, where he acted in TV commercials, earned a degree in architecture, and hung out at Studio 54.

After college, he followed his interest in fashion and landed a job at Gucci, a company that had been struggling financially. He became wealthy when he reinvigorated that company, and even wealthier when he created his own Tom Ford brand. In 2005, he formed a film production company and, in 2009, directed the well-reviewed film, *A Single Man*.

Ford and his longtime partner, Richard Buckley, split their time between homes in London, Los Angeles, and New Mexico. He owns both a 16,000-square-foot mansion on a ridge on Santa Fe's Eastside and a ranch near Galisteo. (Ford told the *Los Angeles Times* that he dresses differently for each home. On his ranch, he wears brown cowboy boots, rather than black, because he thinks dust looks better on brown boots.)

Forked Lightning Ranch

Pecos-area ranch with a colorful history. The ranch's first owner was a self-styled cowboy from St. Louis named Clarence Van Nostrand. Van Nostrand never worked as a cowboy but was fascinated by the Wild West. He changed his name to Tex Austin and became a successful rodeo promoter.

In 1925, Austin bought up 5,500 acres of land near Pecos and hired architect John Gaw Meem to design the main house for the dude ranch that he operated on the property. Austin's Forked Lightning Ranch failed in the Great Depression, and he committed suicide in 1938.

In 1941, the Forked Lightning Ranch was acquired by Texas oilman E.E. "Buddy" Fogelson, who enlarged the spread to 13,000 acres. It became a center of social activity when he married actress Greer Garson in 1949. Fogelson died in 1987. A few years later, his widow sold the original 5,500 acres, including the ranch house, to The Conservation Fund, which donated it to the National Park Service.

In 1996, actor Val Kilmer acquired 5,300 acres of the property, which he called the Pecos River Ranch. In 2011, he sold all but 141 acres to Benjamin A. Strickling, a Texas oil and gas executive. In 2000, media mogul Ted Turner and his wife, Jane Fonda, acquired another part of the ranch, which Fonda kept when the couple split a year later. She retains the name and the cattle brand of the original Forked Lightning Ranch.

Fort Marcy

The first American military fort in New Mexico. In 1846, soon after occupying Santa Fe in the Mexican-American War, General Stephen Watts Kearny ordered a fort built atop a hill a few hundred yards northeast of the Plaza. Fort Marcy (named for Secretary of War William Marcy) was used to store gunpowder, but barracks were not built and the fort never housed troops. The adobe fort eventually disintegrated, and little evidence of it remains today.

The Fort Marcy site is east of Washington Avenue, behind the Cross of the Martyrs.

Fort Union National Monument

Ruins of the old fort that once guarded the Santa Fe Trail. In its time, Fort Union was the biggest military installation in the Southwest. It was manned from 1851 until 1891, when the Santa Fe Railway made the Trail obsolete.

Some of the ruins at
Fort Union National Monument

Fort Union National Monument is 94 miles northeast of Santa Fe, eight miles north of the town of Watrous. Ruts from the wagon trains are clearly visible from the ruins of the fort.

Four Corners

Specifically, the point where New Mexico, Arizona, Utah, and Colorado meet, the only place in the United States where it is possible to stand in four states at once. More generally, the term refers to the surrounding area, which in New Mexico includes part of the Navajo Nation, the city of Farmington, and most of San Juan County.

A stone marker on the Santa Fe Plaza that was commissioned by the Daughters of the American Revolution in 1910 to mark the end of the Santa Fe Trail erroneously places the Four Corners in

Erroneous Four Corners Marker

northeast, rather than northwest, New Mexico. On the marker's map, the state lines of Kansas, Oklahoma, Colorado, and New Mexico converge. In reality, the Kansas and New Mexico state lines never meet.

Frank Ortiz Dog Park

Santa Fe's first and largest off-leash dog park. The 140-acre park is just north of the Casa Solana neighborhood, at the intersection of Camino de las Crucitas and Buckman Road. Once part of the city landfill, the large field and adjacent ridge were set aside for the dog park in 1999. A memorial to the World War II Japanese internment camp is in the park on a ridge overlooking the Casa Solana neighborhood.

Many old-time Santa Feans appreciate the dog park as one of the few remaining places where city residents mingle easily, without regard to financial or social status.

There is a smaller, fenced-in dog park on Caja del Rio Road, near the Santa Fe Animal Shelter.

Fray Angélico Chávez History Library (FRY ahn-HELL-ee-co CHA-vez)

Research institution in downtown Santa Fe in what was once the city library. The Washington Avenue facility, named for Fray Angélico Chávez, is an adjunct to the New Mexico History Museum. (See also CHÁVEZ, FRAY ANGÉLICO.)

Fred Harvey Company

Restaurant and hotel company that catered to passengers on the Santa Fe Railway. Founder Fred Harvey, a former station agent, perceived a need for decent food and accommodations for the thousands of people who began traveling through the Southwest on the new rail line. To serve this need, he built and ran hotels called Harvey Houses, many of them designed by architect Mary Jane Colter. La Fonda, Santa Fe's oldest hotel, was a Harvey House from 1926 until 1968.

Harvey hired attractive young women, called Harvey Girls, to work as waitresses in his restaurants. (*The Harvey Girls*, a 1946 movie starring Judy Garland, characterized the young women as a civilizing influence on the Southwest.) The company's Indian Detours program provided auto transportation that allowed tourists to visit Indian pueblos and reservations.

frijoles (free-HO-lays)

"Beans." Frijoles are a staple of New Mexican food.

Frijoles Canyon's Anasazi ruins are the main attraction at Bandelier National Monument.

Frito pie

Iconic Santa Fe lunch. A Frito pie is created by opening a bag of Fritos, pouring a mixture of ground hamburger and red chile sauce (similar to what they call "chili" in Texas) over the chips, and topping it all with grated cheese. Frito pies were introduced to Santa Fe in the 1960s at the old Woolworth's lunch counter on the Plaza. The Five & Dime General Store carries on the Woolworth's tradition, selling over 30,000 Frito pies each year.

frybread

Symbolic Indian food. Frybread is deep-fried dough – similar to a glazed doughnut without the glaze or the hole in the middle. Indians first made frybread from the low-quality commodity ingredients provided to them by the United States government. Indian health activists point out that if frybread is symbolic of anything, it most represents the obesity and diabetes associated with a poor diet.

"Frybread Power" T-shirts, made popular by the 1998 movie *Smoke Signals*, are sold at the Institute of American Indian Arts Museum shop.

Fuchs, Klaus (FYOOKS)

(1911-1988) Los Alamos scientist who divulged America's atomic bomb secrets.

Fuchs was a 22-year-old German Communist who fled to England in 1933 as the Nazis came to power. After earning a Ph.D. in physics, he was recruited by the British to help in their nuclear research. He immediately began passing classified information to the Soviet Union.

Fuchs was in Los Alamos, on loan to the Manhattan Project, in 1945. He and his KGB contact, a New York-based courier named Harry Gold, scheduled their most important meeting for June 2, 1945, in Santa Fe. They synchronized their watches to the Spitz Clock (which then stood on the south side of the Plaza) and rendezvoused at exactly 4:00 p.m. on the Castillo Street Bridge. (The bridge, which no longer exists, was at that time just east of the current intersection of East Alameda Street and Paseo de Peralta.) Fuchs handed over America's most sensitive secrets at that meeting.

The CIA discovered Fuchs's war-time activities in 1950. Charged with espionage and threatened with the death penalty, he gave up the name of his courier, Harry Gold. Gold in turn named David and Ruth Greenglass, a couple who had spied for the Soviets during the war, and David Greenglass gave up his sister and brother-in-law, Ethel and Julius Rosenberg. The Rosenbergs refused to talk and were electrocuted in June 1953.

Klaus Fuchs served nine years in a British prison. He moved to East Germany after his release and worked there as a nuclear physicist until his death in 1988.

Fuller Lodge

Large, log-cabin building in the heart of Los Alamos. The National Historic Landmark was designed by John Gaw Meem in 1928 for the Los Alamos Ranch School. It is named for Edward Fuller, an early benefactor of the school. Today, Fuller Lodge houses the Los Alamos Historical Museum and the Art Center.

Fuller Lodge

- G -

gabacho (guh-BAH-cho)

Pejorative term for a white person. *Gabacho* originated in Mexico as a term for the French, who invaded Mexico in the 1860s. It was probably adopted from the French word *gavache*, which means "bumpkin" or "boor." Today, it is used by Mexicans and Mexican-Americans to mean any white person.

Gabacho is generally thought to be more derogatory than *gringo*, but just how derogatory is subject to interpretation. Gustavo Arellano writes a syndicated humor column called "Ask a Mexican" in which he answers questions from Anglos about Hispanic culture. Arellano often begins his responses with "Dear Gabacho" or "Dear Confused Gabacho."

Galisteo (gal-ih-STAY-o)

A community and a creek, both named for Galicia in Spain. The village of Galisteo is near the site of an old pueblo whose people migrated to Santo Domingo Pueblo (now known as Kewa Pueblo) in 1794.

Though it appears to be a sleepy little village, Galisteo is home to a surprising number of internationally known artists, writers, and other creative types. Potter Priscilla Hoback, New Age icon Chris Griscom, food writer Deborah Madison, artists Bruce Nauman and Susan Rothenberg, art critic Lucy Lippard, designer Tom Ford, playwright Bernard Pomerance, and many other accomplished people live in or near Galisteo. The village is on NM 41, 22 miles south of Santa Fe.

People who own surface rights in the Galisteo Basin were upset in 2007 when an oil company leased the mineral rights to 65,000 acres and planned to drill for oil. The company dropped its plans when the price of oil plummeted, but it is likely that those plans will be resurrected when oil prices rise. (See also SPLIT ESTATE.)

Gallegos (guy-AY-gos)

Prominent Hispanic surname derived from Galicia in Spain.

Padre Jose Manuel Gallegos was a Catholic priest who was defrocked by Bishop Jean Baptiste Lamy in 1852 because he refused to recognize Lamy's authority. Gallegos later served as the Territorial delegate to the United States Congress and as Speaker of the Territorial House of Representatives. His house on Washington Avenue is now occupied by the Santacafé restaurant.

Former Santa Fe Municipal Court Judge Fran Gallegos was known for her pink hat program, which required DUI offenders to perform public service while wearing bright pink baseball caps. Ms. Gallegos became a hairdresser after resigning from the bench.

gallery openings

Friday-night ritual. Art galleries along Canyon Road and elsewhere around Santa Fe have long offered their hospitality to potential customers and casual strollers alike. Until the practice was restricted, free wine and beer were plentiful at openings. The party atmosphere has been tempered somewhat by the restrictions, but the events are still popular.

A list of gallery openings can be found in *Pasatiempo*, the arts and entertainment supplement distributed in the Friday edition of *The New Mexican*.

Gallup

Western New Mexico city best known as a Navajo trading center. Because it is adjacent to the 17.5-million-acre Navajo Nation, Gallup, population 21,678, is in many ways a border town. It is a major hub for Indian arts and crafts and, because the Navajo do not allow the sale of alcohol on the reservation, it is a place where many Indians go to drink. According to Ian Frazier's *On The Rez*, Gallup's drunk tank holds 500 people, making it the largest jail cell in the country.

Gallup is on I-40, 197 miles west of Santa Fe.

Garcia Street Books

Independent bookstore on Santa Fe's Eastside. The decades-old store was acquired by Rick Palmer and Adam Gates in 2012. The store is on Garcia Street, next door to Downtown Subscription.

Gathering of Nations

North America's largest Indian powwow. The event, which began in 1984, is held in Albuquerque on the last weekend in April.

Gell-Mann, Murray (ghel-MAHN)

Murray Gell-Mann

(1929-) Nobel Prize-winning particle physicist and one of the founders of the Santa Fe Institute. In 1969, Gell-Mann won the Nobel Prize for describing subatomic particles, which he named "quarks" after a line in James Joyce's *Finnegan's Wake*. After moving to Santa Fe (where his license plate reads QUARKS), Gell-Mann's interest shifted from the micro to the macro. In 1984, he, George Cowan, and others founded the Santa Fe Institute, which focuses on the study of complex adaptive systems.

Strange Beauty, the 1999 account of Gell-Mann's life and contribution to physics, was written by Santa Fe resident George Johnson.

genízaro (heh-NEE-sah-ro)

A detribalized Indian. Slave-taking and slave-trading were common in New Mexico in the Spanish Colonial Period, and many Indian slaves were acquired by the Spanish. These people soon lost their tribal identities, and their descendants struggled to make their way between the Indian and Spanish cultures, neither of which fully accepted them. Genízaros are seldom discussed today, perhaps because they do not fit neatly into New Mexico's idealized tricultural model.

Genoveva Chavez Community Center

Genoveva Chavez Community Center (hen-o-VEH-vuh CHA-vez)

Santa Fe's biggest recreation center. The facility, which opened in 2000, serves the city's growing Southside. Its indoor amenities include an ice rink, an Olympic-sized swimming pool, a water slide, a basketball court, racquetball courts, a short track, and fitness equipment and classes.

The center is named for the late Genoveva Chavez, a gregarious Santa Fean known for her mariachi singing. GC3, as it is sometimes called, is on Rodeo Road, next to the Rodeo Grounds.

gente (HEN-tay)

"People." The city of Santa Fe has designated the Saturday before Memorial Day as *El Dia de la Gente*, "The People's Day."

Georgia O'Keeffe Museum

Museum dedicated to the work of artist Georgia O'Keeffe. Founded by philanthropists Anne and John Marion in 1997, it is currently the most-visited art museum in New Mexico.

The O'Keeffe Museum is in downtown Santa Fe on Johnson Street. The nearby Georgia O'Keeffe Museum Research Center focuses on American Modernism.

Gerald Peters Gallery

Gerald Peters Gallery

Entrepreneur Gerald Peters's enormous Spanish Pueblo-style art gallery. When the 32,000-square-foot gallery opened in 1998, some Santa Feans mocked its immensity by referring to it as the "Ninth Northern Pueblo." (See EIGHT NORTHERN INDIAN PUEBLOS.) The building is on Paseo de Peralta, between Acequia Madre Street and Canyon Road.

Geronimo

(circa 1829-1909) The Southwest's most famous Indian. The Chiricahua Apache was born in what is now Catron County, New Mexico. He began raiding settlements in Mexico, Arizona, and New Mexico after his wife and children were killed by Mexican soldiers in 1858, and he remained at war for 28 years. His surrender to the United States Army in 1886 marked the end of Indian hostilities in the Southwest.

Geronimo was held prisoner at Fort Sill, Oklahoma, until his death in 1909. He was buried at Fort Sill, but there has long been speculation that his skull was disinterred and taken to Yale University by members of the secret Skull and Bones Society.

Geronimo restaurant

Fine dining restaurant on Canyon Road. Geronimo was opened by Cliff Skoglund in 1990. In 2008, it was taken over by longtime chef Eric DiStefano and others when Skoglund left town under a financial cloud. (DiStefano also has an interest in the Coyote Café.) The restaurant, which serves "Global French Asian cuisine," is named for Geronimo ("Jerome" in English) Lopez, the original owner of the building it now occupies, not for the Apache warrior. Geronimo is on Canyon Road, just west of Camino del Monte Sol.

Ghost Ranch

One-time dude ranch now owned by the Presbyterian Church. The 21,000-acre property was donated to the church in 1955. It is used for classes, seminars, and spiritual retreats and has accommodations for overnight stays as well as day visits. Hikers are welcome on its many excellent trails.

Ghost Ranch is closely associated with artist Georgia O'Keeffe, who owned a house and seven acres on the property. She spent her winters in Abiquiu and her summers on the ranch. The Ghost Ranch logo, a sun-bleached cow's skull, was created by O'Keeffe.

The name is a loose translation of *Rancho de los Brujos*, "Ranch of the Witches." Ghost Ranch is on US 84, 61 miles northwest of Santa Fe and 13 miles north of Abiquiu.

The Presbyterian Church also maintains an in-town branch of Ghost Ranch. The property is in Santa Fe on the corner of Paseo de Peralta and Old Taos Highway. The enormous animal sculptures on the lawn make it easy to find.

Gila National Forest (HEE-luh)

National forest in southwest New Mexico. The vast, 3.3-million-acre preserve encompasses the Gila Wilderness, the first designated wilderness in the United States. The forest is named for the Gila River, which heads in New Mexico and flows into Arizona. The river's name may be a Spanish contraction of *tsihl*, an Apache word for "mountain."

Gilbert, Eddie

(1922-) The businessman who reinvented himself in Santa Fe. Many people come to remote New Mexico to start over, but few succeed as well as Eddie Gilbert.

Born Edward M. Ginsberg in New York City, Eddie dropped out of Cornell to serve in World War II. After the war, he changed his last name to Gilbert and entered the world of finance. His intelligence and drive made him very wealthy, and, by the late 1950s, he was an international jetsetter. But his ambition outstripped the rules.

Facing embezzlement charges in 1962, Gilbert fled to Brazil for five months before returning to stand trial. He was convicted and sentenced to two years in Sing Sing. He returned to high finance after his release, and, some years later, once again ran afoul of the law. Convicted of stock manipulation in 1981, he was incarcerated for another two years.

Gilbert came to Santa Fe in 1991 at the urging of his wife, Peaches. He established the BGK Group, a real estate investment company that made him a multimillionaire yet again. By the 2000s, he was a respected businessman and philanthropist. He and Peaches have generously supported charities like the Santa Fe Animal Shelter, the Santa Fe Youth Symphony, and the National Dance Institute. Gilbert sold his business in 2010. Later that year, outgoing Governor Bill Richardson rewarded him for his generous political contributions by granting him a pardon for his past misdeeds. (A New Mexico governor cannot pardon crimes committed outside the state, so the act was more symbolic than substantive.)

Boy Wonder of Wall Street: The Life and Times of Financier Eddie Gilbert, by Richard Whittingham, tells the Eddie Gilbert story through 2003.

GLBT (gay, lesbian, bisexual, transgender)

Santa Fe has always been welcoming to people who do not easily fit in elsewhere, and that includes GLBTs. There are no statistics, but the feeling among longtime city residents is that there were more lesbians than gay men in Santa Fe in the first half of the 20th century, but that gay men came to the city in greater numbers after John Crosby opened the Santa Fe Opera in 1957.

In any case, Santa Fe is now regarded as a particularly gay-friendly city. RainbowVision, which opened in 2006, was the nation's first full-service retirement community for GLBTs. Santa Fe has also been identified as having more single-sex households, per capita, than any city in the country except San Francisco. And, in 2011, *The Advocate* published an unscientific survey that named Santa Fe the "second gayest" city in the country.

Santa Fe is not known for its transgenders, but the town of Trinidad, Colorado, which is off I-25 just eight miles north of the New Mexico state line, is known as the "Sex Change Capital of the World."

Glorieta (glore-ee-EH-tuh)

Northern New Mexico village that was once a stop on the Santa Fe Trail. Glorieta, whose name may mean "forested crossroads," expanded in 1879 with the arrival of the Santa Fe Railway. Today, it is home to the Glorieta Baptist Conference Center.

The village is 18 miles southeast of Santa Fe via I-25 north. (The highway swings south just east of Santa Fe.)

Glorieta Pass, Battle of

Decisive Civil War battle called the "Gettysburg of the West." In early 1862, invading Confederates marched up the Rio Grande from El Paso, captured Santa Fe, and continued on toward Fort Union. They were challenged by Union troops 10 miles southeast of Santa Fe in the Battle of Glorieta Pass.

It appeared that the Confederates were winning the battle until Major John M. Chivington led his Colorado Volunteers behind enemy lines and destroyed Confederate supplies stored in Apache Canyon. Realizing that they could advance no farther, the Confederates gave up their invasion of New Mexico and retreated back to El Paso, taking with them Southern hopes for conquest of the West.

Major Chivington, the hero of Glorieta Pass, disgraced himself two years later when he led his men in the infamous attack on peaceful Cheyenne Indians in Colorado's Sand Creek Massacre.

goathead

Hated fruit of the puncturevine plant. The seeds of the low-growing, yellow-flowered annual are protected by burs with spines that look something like a goat's horns. Goatheads regularly puncture dogs' paws, the soles of tennis shoes, and bicycle tires. They are so hated by bicyclists that a Santa Fe-area cycling club once held a picnic at which members joyously whacked a goathead-shaped piñata.

Goatheads first appeared in California in 1903, probably after being brought into the United States in the wool of sheep imported from the Mediterranean region. The worst infestations are in New Mexico, Arizona, California, Nevada, Oregon, and Texas.

Goldberg, Natalie

(1948-) Author and teacher. Goldberg is known for combining the practice of Zen with the practice of writing. She is the author of ten books, including *Writing Down the Bones: Freeing the Writer Within* (1986). Originally from Long Island, Goldberg now lives in Santa Fe. She frequently leads writing seminars at the Mabel Dodge Luhan house in Taos.

Golden

Old mining town on the Turquoise Trail. A few adobe houses were built on the town site in the early 19th century when gold was first discovered in the nearby Ortiz Mountains. The community took the name Golden in anticipation of riches to come, but the quantity of ore was limited and mining operations ceased in 1884.

The town has long since returned to its sleepy, pre-gold-rush state. Unlike Cerrillos and Madrid, the other old mining towns along the Turquoise Trail, Golden does not attract many tourists. It is 38 miles south of Santa Fe on NM 14.

Glenna Goodacre's
"Tug O War,"
part of the Capitol Art Collection

Goodacre, Glenna

(1939-) Nationally known Santa Fe sculptor. Goodacre designed the Vietnam Women's Memorial on the Mall in Washington, D.C., and the Sacagawea one-dollar coin.

Glenna's daughter, Jill, a former Victoria's Secret model, is married to singer Harry Connick, Jr.

gordo/a (GORE-doe/duh)

"Fat" or "plump." *Cerro Gordo*, "Fat Hill," is on Santa Fe's Eastside.

Gorman, R.C.

(1931-2005) Rudolph Carl Gorman, universally known as R.C. Gorman, a Navajo artist famous for his paintings and sculptures of Indian women. *The New York Times* once dubbed Gorman the "Picasso of American art." He is also credited with founding the first Indian-owned art gallery, which he opened in Taos in 1968.

In 1997, the FBI looked into allegations that Gorman had engaged in improper sexual relations with children. It was concluded that he likely had, but charges were not filed because the statute of limitations had run out on the only provable cases.

Governor's Mansion

Home to New Mexico's governors since 1955. The modified Territorial-style house sits on 30 acres at 1 Mansion Drive, which is approximately a mile and a quarter north of the Plaza, off Bishop's Lodge Road. The 12,000-square-foot house is divided between public and private spaces.

The Governor's Mansion was particularly busy during Bill Richardson's tenure. He hosted guests as diverse as Bill Clinton, a delegation from North Korea, and numerous movie stars, including Harrison Ford and Calista Flockhart, who were married in the mansion.

grande (*GRAHN-day)

"Big," "great," or "grand."

*Anglos may pronounce the *grande* in Rio Grande in a single syllable, as in "I'm an old cowhand, from the Rio Grande." In all other cases, *grande* must be pronounced in the two-syllable Spanish style.

Grants

City about halfway between Albuquerque and Gallup, on the northern end of the lava-flow badlands known as El Malpais. The city, population 9,182, is named for the Grant brothers, who operated a railroad construction camp on the site in the 1880s.

Grants, the county seat of Cibola County, is on I-40, 79 miles west of Albuquerque, 140 miles southwest of Santa Fe.

Great River: The Rio Grande in North American History

Paul Horgan's two-volume history of New Mexico's defining river. *Great River* won the Pulitzer Prize for history in 1955. (Horgan won another Pulitzer in 1976 for *Lamy of Santa Fe*.)

Gregg, Josiah

(1806-1850) Explorer, journalist, medical doctor, and author. Gregg was intelligent and curious. He learned Spanish as a trader on the Santa Fe Trail and used his intimate knowledge of New Mexico to write *Commerce of the Prairies*, published in 1844. The two-volume book describes the culture and people of Santa Fe and Northern New Mexico as Gregg witnessed them from 1831 to 1840.

Gregg later earned a medical degree and worked as a correspondent and guide during the Mexican-American War. He joined the California gold rush in 1849 and is credited with discovering Humboldt Bay. Weakened by malnutrition and exhaustion, Gregg died in 1850 when he fell off his horse while attempting to ride out from a snowbound mining camp.

gringo/a

An English-speaking white person from outside the region, a white foreigner. The word probably derives from *griego*, the Spanish word for "Greek."

Gringo is sometimes construed as mildly derogatory. In the redistricting process for the New Mexico House of Representatives, one party accused the other of "gringo-mandering" a Santa Fe district to ensure the reelection of an Anglo representative. An editorialist at *The New Mexican* deemed it an insult, writing that "gringo is just as surely a slur as *mojado* [wetback]." Since then, however, the paper has run a column called *Pregúntele al gringo*, "Ask a Gringo," as a regular feature in *La Voz*, its Spanish-language section. Most people would agree that *gringo* is not as derogatory as *gabacho*, which is another word used to describe Anglos.

Griscom, Chris (GRISS-come)

(1942-) New Age icon and founder of the Light Institute in Galisteo. Griscom's teachings focus on past-life regression. The blond mother of six, who wears all-white robes, was once Shirley MacLaine's New Age mentor.

guacamole (gwah-cuh-MO-lay)

An avocado-based relish or dip. The word is a combination of *aguacate*, "avocado," and *mole*, "sauce." Guacamole is a staple of New Mexican cuisine, in part because it provides a cooling counter-effect to hot chiles.

Guad (GWAD)

Irreverent shorthand for Our Lady of Guadalupe. The word has been seen on bumper stickers reading "In Guad We Trust."

Guadalupe, Our Lady of
(gwah-duh-LOO-pay)

Apparition of the Virgin Mary seen by a Mexican Indian in 1531. The "Mother of the Americas" is a familiar icon in Mexico and the American Southwest. Her image is printed on T-shirts and baseball caps, painted on lowriders, and tattooed on innumerable

Our Lady of Guadalupe

New Mexicans. Guadalupe County, Guadalupe Street, the Guadalupe Café, and the Santuario de Guadalupe are named for her.

A controversy erupted around Our Lady in 2001 when an image of the Virgin wearing what looked like a rose-covered bikini was included in an exhibit at Santa Fe's Museum of International Folk Art. Los Angeles-based artist Alma López's depiction offended some local Catholics, who complained to the New Mexico Office of Cultural Affairs and to their state legislators. The exhibition ended early because of the protests.

In response to the controversy, a nonprofit organization began raising money to build a shrine in honor of Guadalupe. In 2008, a 12-foot-tall bronze statue of Our Lady was installed on the grounds of the Santuario de Guadalupe.

guapo (GWAH-po)

"Handsome." Some linguists believe that *wop*, the slur for Italians, derives from the Spanish word *guapo*. Italian laborers who came to work in Spain's vineyards in the late 19th and early 20th century were admired by the Spanish women, but the Spanish men found the Italians insufficiently macho and ridiculed them as *los guapos*, "the pretty boys."

guero/a (WHERE-o/ah)

"Blonde," or a white person. *Pinche guero* is an epithet that can be translated as "whitey" – or worse. *Guero loco* means "crazy white boy."

Gurulé (guh-roo-LAY)

One of New Mexico's most interesting surnames. Jacques Grolet was a French explorer who was captured by the Spanish in what is now Texas. In 1690, he was shipped to Spain, where he was imprisoned for two years before being released on the condition that he accept Spanish citizenship and return to the New World.

Grolet accepted the conditions, changed his name to Santiago Gurulé, and sailed for Mexico. He eventually settled in the New Mexico town of Bernalillo, where he married Elena Gallegos in 1699. Their many descendants carry on his adopted name.

Gusty Winds May Exist

The New Mexico Department of Transportation's oddly philosophical weather warning. Commuters between Albuquerque and Santa Fe are familiar with the warning sign near the arroyo at the San Felipe exit off I-25.

- H -

H-Board

See HISTORIC DESIGN REVIEW BOARD.

Häagen-Dazs

See PLAZA BAKERY.

hacienda (hah-see-EN-duh)

House, outbuildings, and land owned by a wealthy patrón. A hacienda can be a large landholding or an in-town estate like El Zaguán, which at one time boasted 24 rooms, a private chapel, corrals, cornfields, and an orchard.

Hackman, Gene

(1930-) Oscar-winning actor (*The French Connection*) and Santa Fe-area resident. Hackman has co-authored three novels with his Santa Fe neighbor, underwater archaeologist Daniel Lenihan, and has his artwork on display at Jinja, a Santa Fe restaurant he once co-owned.

Hackman used to be active in Santa Fe affairs – he served on the board and gave the keynote speech at the opening of the Georgia O'Keeffe Museum in 1997 – but he has been less involved in recent years. His wife, Betsy, is co-owner of Pandora's, an upscale linens store in the Sanbusco shopping center.

Hahn, Dave

(1961-) World-famous mountain guide and Taos ski patroller. Hahn was the first non-Sherpa to summit Mt. Everest 10 times. In the summer, when not on Everest, he guides expeditions up Mt. Rainier in Washington, up Denali (Mt. McKinley) in Alaska, and across the Shackleton Traverse in Antarctica. In the winter, he lives in Taos and works as a ski patroller and EMT at Taos Ski Valley. Hahn has contributed to *Outside* magazine, among other publications.

Handey, Jack

(1949-) Nationally known humorist who got his start in Santa Fe. Handey, who grew up and attended college in El Paso, was working as a reporter for *The New Mexican* in 1972 when he became friendly with his Canyon Road neighbor, comedian Steve Martin. Martin later hired Handey to write on his TV specials and recommended him to *Saturday Night Live* producer Lorne Michaels, who hired him as a writer. Handey is best known for *Deep Thoughts by Jack Handey*, but he also created *Toonces, The Driving Cat, Unfrozen Caveman Lawyer*, and many other classic SNL bits.

Handey and his wife, Marta Chavez Handey, moved from Manhattan back to Santa Fe in 2003. He published *What I'd Say to the Martians and Other Veiled Threats* in 2008. His frequent essays appear in *Playboy, The New Yorker*, and *Outside* magazine. The Handeys are active supporters of The Wildlife Center.

hantavirus (HAHN-tuh-vie-russ)

Deadly pulmonary disease. People contract hantavirus by inhaling dried particles of rodent fecal matter, often during spring cleanup of sheds and cabins that have been closed for the winter. Over 15 percent of all known cases in the United States have occurred in New Mexico, with the larger Four Corners region accounting for around 40 percent. Hantavirus is fatal in one out of three cases.

Haozous, Bob (HOWZ-us)

(1943-) Well-known Indian sculptor. Haozous, who lives and works in Santa Fe, is the son of the late Allan Houser, who was also a famous Indian artist.

Harry's Roadhouse

Locals' restaurant that serves sandwiches, burgers, and regional favorites in what was once an old gas station. Harry Shapiro and his wife,

Peyton Young, moved to Santa Fe from Philadelphia and opened Harry's in 1992. The Roadhouse's regular clientele include people who drive down from Santa Fe as well as those who live in the Eldorado subdivision or elsewhere on the southeast side of town. Historian and regular customer Hampton Sides wrote the foreword to the cookbook that Shapiro and Young published in 2006. Harry's Roadhouse is on Old Las Vegas Highway, about five miles south of the Santa Fe Plaza.

Harvey Company

See FRED HARVEY COMPANY.

Haussamen, Heath (HOUSE-uh-men)

Heath Haussamen

(1978-) Political blogger based in Las Cruces. Haussamen graduated from Santa Fe's St. Michael's High School and New Mexico State University before embarking on a career in journalism.

Haussamen started his nonpartisan web site in 2006. His site and its rival, *New Mexico Politics with Joe Monahan*, were judged to be among the best political blogs in the nation by *The Washington Post*'s Chris Cillizza. Haussamen's web address is <u>nmpolitics.net</u>.

healership

Too-cute term for the myriad counseling, self-realization, and body-work practices in Santa Fe. The term was seen in an ad for a financial consulting firm that promised to "help grow your healership."

Hearne, Bill

(1949-) Santa Fe's best-known country musician. For most of his career, Bill, a guitar player, performed with his wife, Bonnie, who played piano and harmonized on vocals. The couple met in Austin, Texas, in 1968. Although Bonnie has been blind since birth and Bill is so visually impaired as to be considered legally blind, they quickly established themselves at the center of the Austin music scene. Lyle Lovett, who attended their gigs, cites them as an influence on his music.

The Hearnes eventually moved to Santa Fe. They played regularly at La Fonda until health problems forced Bonnie to retire in 2003. Bill still performs at the hotel with the Bill Hearne Trio.

heishi necklace (HE-she)

A string of carefully cut, polished beads made from seashells (*heishi* means "shell"), turquoise, and other materials. Heishi necklaces are one of the oldest Indian jewelry forms. There is evidence that prehistoric Pueblo Indians obtained shells through trade networks that reached to distant coastal tribes. Kewa (formerly Santo Domingo) Pueblo and San Felipe Pueblo are known for their heishi necklaces.

hermano/a (air-MA-no/nuh)

"Brother" and "sister." In some contexts, *hermano* can refer to a member of the *Hermanos Penitentes*, "Brotherhood of Penitents," a secretive, Catholic lay organization.

Hermit's Peak

Mountain in the Sangre de Cristo range named for an Italian religious recluse. After decades of wandering through Europe and the Americas,

Tourists atop Hermit's Peak, circa 1898

62-year-old Giovanni Maria de Agostini arrived in Las Vegas, New Mexico, in 1863. He took up residence in a damp cave a few hundred feet below the summit of what was then known as *El Cerro de Tecolote*, "Owl Mountain," 16 miles northwest of Las Vegas, where he subsisted on water and corn meal that he bought with money earned from the sale of small wooden carvings. The ascetic hermit prayed constantly and ministered to the sick, and many of the people living around his mountain believed him to be a saint.

After four years in Northern New Mexico, Agostini wandered south to the Organ Mountains, near Las Cruces. He was murdered there by persons unknown in 1868. Agostini's Las Vegas mountain was renamed Hermit's Peak (or Hermit Peak) in his honor, and, for decades, locals made pilgrimages to his cave.

One of Santa Fe author Michael McGarrity's crime novels is set near and titled *Hermit's Peak*.

Heron Lake

Reservoir created in 1971 to hold water diverted to the Rio Chama by the San Juan-Chama diversion project. Though there are herons at the lake, it was named for local landowner and surveyor K.A. Heron. The no-wake, 5,900-acre lake is used for boating and fishing, and the surrounding Heron Lake State Park includes campsites along its shoreline.

Heron Lake is 106 miles northwest of Santa Fe via US 84 north.

Hewett, Edgar Lee

(1865-1946) Educator, archaeologist, anthropologist, and seminal figure in the creation of Santa Fe-style architecture. Hewett came to New Mexico upon his appointment as founding president of the New Mexico Normal School, now known as Highlands University. He later earned a doctorate in archaeology and dedicated himself to preserving and archiving Southwestern Indian artifacts. In 1907, he co-founded and served as the first director of what is now called the School for Advanced Research. In 1909, he became the first director of the Museum of New Mexico.

Hewett made many contributions to Santa Fe. He was instrumental in the revival of the city's unique architecture, spearheading the design and construction of the Museum of Fine Art (now the New Mexico Museum of Art), where his ashes are interred. He encouraged Maria Martinez to recreate black-on-black pottery and he resurrected Santa Fe's dormant Fiesta celebration, which included an embryonic Indian Market.

Hewett was not universally loved. Senator Bronson Cutting thought he was quick to take credit that rightfully belonged to others, and poet Witter Bynner found

Edgar Lee Hewett

him pompous. Bynner and his friends initiated Pasatiempo, a whimsical counter-Fiesta, in 1924 when Hewett began charging admission to the official celebration.

high desert

Misleading term for Santa Fe's climate. At 7,000 feet, the city is certainly high, but its average annual precipitation is around 14 inches. Most sources place the upper limit for a desert at 10 inches.

High Road to Taos

The slower, more scenic mountain route from Santa Fe to Taos. Because it is a New Mexico Scenic Byway, the High Road to Taos is usually capitalized. The low road to Taos is not.

Both routes follow US 84/285 from Santa Fe to Pojoaque. The High Road then turns onto NM 503 and runs east through Nambé, north on NM 98 through Chimayó, and east on NM 76. It follows NM 76 through the old villages of Truchas and Las Trampas before turning onto

NM 75, which runs through the village of Peñasco. The High Road then turns onto NM 518, which terminates at NM 68 (the low road) near Ranchos de Taos. From there, NM 68 leads to the town of Taos.

Most guide books suggest taking the High Road from Santa Fe to Taos and the low road on the way back. The High Road runs 76 miles and takes an hour and 50 minutes. The low road runs 70 miles and takes an hour and 20 minutes.

Highlands University, New Mexico

The only state university in Northern New Mexico. (Northern New Mexico College, formerly a community college, became a four-year school in 2005 but, because it does not grant graduate degrees, it is technically not a university.) Highlands was founded in Las Vegas, New Mexico, in 1893 as New Mexico Normal School, with Edgar Lee Hewett as its first president. Originally a teachers' college, the school today offers graduate and undergraduate degrees in the arts and sciences, business, education, and social work.

Because it draws primarily from Northern New Mexico, Highlands boasts a high percentage of Hispanic students. When Manny Aragon served as university president from 2004 to 2006, he attempted to extend this demographic to the faculty, but he ran into trouble when some Anglo professors sued, claiming that they were denied tenure or contract renewals based on their ethnicity. The cases were settled out of court.

hijole (EEE-ho-LAY)

Northern New Mexico's generic exclamation, sometimes translated as "Damn!" *Hijole* is often shortened to "eee!"

Hill, the

Dated nickname for Los Alamos. Los Alamos High School's sports teams are called the Hilltoppers.

Hillerman, Tony

(1925-2008) One of New Mexico's best-known novelists. Before attaining worldwide fame as an author, Hillerman won a Silver Star as an infantryman in World War II, worked as editor of *The New Mexican*, and taught for many years at the University of New Mexico. His best-selling crime novels are set on or near the Navajo reservation and feature policemen Joe Leaphorn and Jim Chee.

Hillerman's autobiography, *Seldom Disappointed*, was published in 2001. He is buried in Santa Fe National Cemetery. His daughter, Anne Hillerman, is a local freelance writer.

Hispanic

The usual term for a New Mexican of Spanish descent. Hispanic (sometimes styled "Hispano"), Indian, and Anglo are the three components of New Mexico's tricultural society.

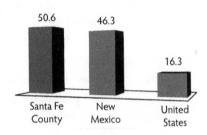

Hispanic
Percentage of Population

50.6 — Santa Fe County
46.3 — New Mexico
16.3 — United States

For most of New Mexico's Territorial Period, native Spanish-speakers were called "Mexicans" and English-speaking gringos were called "Americans." Mexicans became "Spanish-Americans" and Americans became "Anglo-Americans" in the early 20th century, when the New Mexico Territory was lobbying for statehood and political turmoil in old Mexico made association with that country less desirable. These terms later evolved into *Hispanic* and *Anglo*.

Because it means "pertaining to Spain," *Hispanic* was the perfect description for natives of Northern New Mexico who viewed the region as an isolated enclave of Spanish culture and themselves as more European than Latin American. The European connotation was diluted in 1980, however, when the United States Census Bureau began using *Hispanic* as the designation for any American with a Spanish-speaking heritage, and there is now no easy way to distinguish between a Hispanic whose family has been in New Mexico for centuries and a Hispanic who has recently arrived from somewhere else. Some native New Mexicans with long ties to the land call themselves *Norteños*, "Northerners," some refer to themselves as *Nuevomexicanos*, "New Mexicans," and still others call themselves *nativos*, "natives."

Hispanic New Mexicans also use other terms to describe themselves. Some, usually older people, prefer to be called Spanish rather than Hispanic. Some politically active people call themselves *Chicanos*, and some prefer *Latino*, which implies a solidarity with people from all over Latin America. Still others describe themselves as *Indo-Hispanic* or *mestizo*, terms that convey the idea of mixed Spanish and Indian blood. The term *Hispanic* is, however, accepted by most Northern New Mexicans, even those who also call themselves by another name.

Historic Design Review Board

Arbiters of Santa Fe's architecture, also known as the H-Board. In 1957, the city council passed a Historic Styles Ordinance that limits acceptable building styles in certain parts of the city. The powerful seven-member H-Board enforces the ordinance.

As might be expected, the board's decisions are often controversial. In 1984, Rosalea Murphy, late owner of the Pink Adobe restaurant, wanted to re-stucco her building in what she said was its original color. The H-Board denied her request and insisted on a more sedate shade. Actor Larry Hagman ran afoul of the board in 1995 when he wanted to add a second story to his Eastside home. The board denied his request, and he appealed to the city council. When the council denied his appeal, Hagman sued, claiming he was being discriminated against because he was a "wealthy, newcomer Anglo." He eventually dropped the lawsuit and left Santa Fe.

Historic Santa Fe Foundation

The offshoot of the Old Santa Fe Association created in 1961 to own and manage certain architectural landmarks. The nonprofit organization owns eight historic properties, including El Zaguán, where it makes its headquarters. Its properties are acknowledged with bronze plaques.

The Historic Santa Fe Foundation publishes the book *Old Santa Fe Today*, which describes the city's historic places.

Historical/Hysterical Parade in 1925

Historical/Hysterical Parade

The big parade on Fiesta Sunday, also called the *Desfile de la Gente*, the "People's Parade." The parade began in the 1920s as an elaborate spoof but is now a typical small-town affair with horseback riders, fire trucks, cheerleaders, and politicians.

hito/a (*HEE-toe/tah)

Term of endearment for a son or daughter. The word is a contraction of *hijo*, "son," and the diminutive *ito*. Professor Rubén Cobos notes in *A Dictionary of New Mexico and Southern Colorado Spanish* that Norteños have a particular affection for nouns in the diminutive form.

*The letter *h* is usually silent in Spanish, but this contraction is spelled with an *h* that is pronounced as if it were a *j*.

Hobbs

New Mexico city in the far southeastern corner of the state. Hobbs, population 34,122, is New Mexico's eighth most populous city. It is the largest community in Lea County, whose main industry is oil and natural gas extraction.

Hobbs, which is named for a storekeeper, is the birthplace of country singer Ryan Bingham, NFL quarterback Colt McCoy, and former New Mexico lieutenant governor Diane Denish. It is 311 miles southeast of Santa Fe via US 285 south.

hogan (HO-gahn)

Navajo structure. Traditional hogans are usually octagonal in shape, with a smoke hole in the center of the roof. Doorways face east to catch the sun's first rays.

Hogans are not seen around Santa Fe because most Navajos live far to the west in the Four Corners region. A replica of a hogan is on permanent display at the Museum of Indian Arts and Culture.

holy dirt

Dirt from the Santuario de Chimayó that is believed to have curative powers. The dirt is scooped from *el pocito*, "the little well," a hole in the earthen floor of a small room next to the chapel. Those who believe that they have been healed by the holy dirt leave cast-off crutches and written testimonials in the adjacent Prayer Room.

Holy Faith Episcopal Church

One of downtown Santa Fe's three landmark churches. Holy Faith's congregation has historically included some of the city's most influential Protestants, among them Senator Thomas B. Catron and architect John Gaw Meem.

The church was constructed in the late 19th century, contemporaneous with St. Francis Cathedral. The Star of David that appears in the interior stained glass window above Holy Faith's main entrance was intended as a thank-you to the Jewish Santa Feans who contributed to the church's building fund.

Holy Faith participates in ecumenical events with St. Francis Cathedral and First Presbyterian Church, the other big, downtown churches. Holy Faith is on East Palace Avenue, just east of Paseo de Peralta.

hondo/a (HAHN-doe/duh)

"Deep." Arroyo Hondo is a place name in both Santa Fe County and Taos County.

hoodoo (WHO-do)

Geologic formation caused by wind and water erosion. The hoodoos at Tent Rocks National Monument are a popular tourist attraction.

Hopi (HO-pee)

The largest Pueblo Indian tribe *not* located in New Mexico. The Hopi reservation is in Arizona, on land surrounded by the larger Navajo reservation. Like the Zuni, New Mexico's western-most Pueblo tribe, the Hopi are thought to be descended from the Mogollon rather than the Anasazi.

Hopper, Dennis

(1936-2010) Actor, artist, film director, and manic influence on the Taos hippie scene. Hopper first came to New Mexico to scout locations for the counterculture classic *Easy Rider*, and when he filmed the movie, he used Taos's New Buffalo community as the template for the commune scene. In 1970, after *Easy Rider*'s wild success, Hopper bought the Mabel Dodge Luhan house. He rented rooms to local hippies and visited the house off and on before selling it in 1977.

The Taos hippie years were marked by tension between local Hispanics and the mostly Anglo hippies. Hopper, who admitted to consuming prodigious quantities of drugs and alcohol in those years, made matters worse. An Anglo who lived in the Luhan house said that Hopper was "into this Wild West game, and when he was around there were guns and alcohol." A Hispanic Taoseño said, "Dennis thought he had made a great many friends in the valley because he had made Taos famous, but this was not true."

In 2009, the town of Taos sponsored a 40th anniversary celebration of the Summer of Love. Hopper, who was suffering from prostate cancer, participated in the festivities and displayed his art and photography at the Harwood Museum of Art. His funeral service was held one year later at the San Francisco de Asis Church in Ranchos de Taos. He is buried in the nearby Jesus Nazareno Cemetery.

Horgan, Paul

(1903-1995) Prolific author and recipient of two Pulitzer Prizes for his histories of New Mexico. *Great River: The Rio Grande in North American History* earned the award in 1955, and *Lamy of Santa Fe* won it in 1976.

Horgan moved with his tubercular father from Buffalo, New York, to Albuquerque at age 12. He attended New Mexico Military Institute in Roswell but left before earning a degree. Even so, he taught English literature at Wesleyan University and was awarded a total of 19 honorary degrees during his lifetime. Novelist Annie Dillard, who knew Horgan at Wesleyan, described him as "a man of great faith, a devout Catholic, a careful writer, and a loving teacher."

Horgan was a founding member of the Santa Fe Opera board of directors and served as its chairman for 10 years. Opera founder John Crosby said of him: "Much of what is now known as the tradition of the Santa Fe Opera is the consequence of the inspired counsel of Mr. Horgan."

horno (OR-no)

Beehive-shaped outdoor oven. Hornos were brought to New Mexico by the Spanish, but today they are more often associated with the Pueblo Indians.

Hornos

Hornos were a common sight in Northern New Mexico in the late 1800s, when gringo tourists first came to the Southwest. Visitors who saw dogs sleeping in the cooled-off ovens commented that New Mexicans must really love their pets to build them such wonderful adobe doghouses.

The surest way to see hornos today is to ride the Rail Runner Express.

Numerous backyard ovens can be seen from the train as it passes through the pueblos between Santa Fe and Albuquerque.

Horseman's Haven

Home of the hottest chile in Santa Fe. Rose and Louie Romero have served New Mexican food from their diner on Cerrillos Road since 1981. (They are fans of St. Michael's High School sports teams and named their place for the Horsemen.) Horseman's Haven is on Cerrillos Road, between Santa Fe Place and the Auto Park, six and a half miles south of the Plaza.

Houser, Allan

(1914-1994) Famous Indian artist. A Chiricahua Apache from Oklahoma, Houser changed his name from Haozous early in his career. He first came to Santa Fe in 1934 to study at the Santa Fe Indian School and later returned to teach at the Institute of American Indian Arts. Primarily a sculptor, Houser created some 700 major pieces and was honored with the National Medal of the Arts. His son, Bob Haozous, is also a well-known Santa Fe sculptor.

Allan Houser's
"When Friends Meet,"
part of the Capitol Art Collection

The Allan Houser Compound is 25 miles south of Santa Fe. Houser's sculptures are showcased on 10 acres of the 100-acre property. Tours can be arranged by reservation. The compound is off County Road 42, which intersects NM 14 about 12 miles south of I-25.

Howard, Edward Lee

(1951-2002) CIA agent who lived and worked in Santa Fe before defecting to the Soviet Union. Howard was recruited by the Agency in

1980. He received extensive training in covert intelligence gathering and counter-intelligence techniques, but was fired in 1983, just before his posting to Moscow, when it was discovered that he had lied about past drug use and petty theft. A native of Alamogordo, Howard moved his wife and son to Santa Fe, where he took a job with the state as a financial analyst. Drinking heavily and bitter over his termination by the CIA, he began providing information to the Soviets in 1984.

The CIA suspected that its erstwhile recruit was working for the other side. The FBI tapped his phone and put round-the-clock surveillance on his Eldorado home, but Howard employed the tradecraft he learned in his CIA training to elude his minders. On a September night in 1985, he and his wife, Mary, dined at a Canyon Road restaurant called Alphonse's (where Geronimo is now). Mary drove on the way home, and Howard dove out of the car as it rounded a curve. Mary raised a silhouette dummy in his place and continued driving as her husband walked to the Santa Fe bus station and boarded a bus to the Albuquerque airport. From there, Howard flew to New York and then on to Helsinki, where he requested asylum at the Soviet Embassy.

Edward Lee Howard died in Russia in 2002 from a broken neck suffered in a drunken fall down the stairs of his home. Some people think he was pushed.

huero (HWAIR-o)

See GUERO.

huevos (HWAY-vos)

"Eggs." Also slang for testicles.

huevos rancheros (ran-CHAIR-os)

A breakfast dish of eggs, cheese, and chile over corn tortillas.

Hyde Park Road

The road that runs from Santa Fe up into the Sangre de Cristo Mountains. The winding, sometimes-treacherous, 16-mile road climbs from the city's 7,000-foot elevation to the Ski Santa Fe parking lot at 10,350 feet.

Hyde Memorial State Park is eight miles up the road from Santa Fe. The park and the road are named for Benjamin Talbot Babbit Hyde, a Santa Fe educator and naturalist whose widow donated the property to the state after his death in 1933.

- I -

IAIA (each letter pronounced separately)

Shorthand for the Institute of American Indian Arts.

I AM Activity

Religious sect also known as the Saint Germain Foundation. The I AMs are among the earliest of the many out-of-the-mainstream religious seekers who have been drawn to Santa Fe.

The I AM Activity was started in 1930 by Guy W. Ballard, who claimed to have met Saint Germain while hiking on California's Mount Shasta. Ballard established the religious organization based on his status as an "accredited messenger of the ascended masters," whom he described as special beings who had evolved through multiple reincarnations. The Activity prospered, and Ballard became wealthy.

When Guy Ballard died in 1939, his widow, Edna, took over the organization. In 1942, after experiencing legal troubles in California, she and her followers moved to Santa Fe. At one time, as many as 600 I AM adherents lived in the area.

In *Turn Left at the Sleeping Dog*, Calla Hay, a reporter at *The New Mexican*, recalls how in 1951 the I AMs laid siege to the newspaper in response to a story critical of the organization. A 75-year-old former disciple who was confined in St. Vincent Hospital claimed that Edna Ballard had promised to take care of her needs, both worldly and other-worldly, in exchange for a donation of $12,000 in cash and $3,000 in jewels. When Ballard refused to pay her medical bills, the woman sued. The I AMs were unhappy with *The New Mexican*'s coverage of the suit and stormed the newspaper, demanding that Mrs. Ballard be allowed to approve any story before it appeared in print. Charges were filed, but the matter was ultimately settled out of court.

Edna Ballard and most of the I AMs eventually left the area. The handful of adherents still in Santa Fe maintain their sanctuary on Old Taos Highway, a block off Paseo de Peralta.

Imus, Don

(1940-) Nationally known radio personality and outspoken area resident. Imus once aimed his uncensored derision at Northern New Mexico. In a 2001 interview with *Santa Fean* magazine, he said, "I f***ing hate Santa Fe. Every yuppie chain-wearing, bead-sucking ass**** on the planet is there. Taos is a horror show as well. Too many people with f***ing long hair and earrings in Taos to suit me. Too many jerks from California."

Imus lost his radio and TV show in 2007 when he called the Rutgers women's basketball team "nappy-headed ho's." He apologized profusely and has since returned to the air.

He and his wife, Deirdre, run a 3,000-acre ranch for sick children in San Miguel County, near the village of Ribera.

Indian

The simplest of the many names for the first inhabitants of the Americas. "Native American" is used more frequently in other places, but "Indian" is more common in New Mexico. The late author Tony Hillerman used Indian exclusively, as does actor-activist Russell Means.

Indian
Percentage of Population

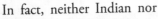

3.1	9.4	.9
Santa Fe County	New Mexico	United States

In fact, neither Indian nor Native American should be the first choice for describing a person. There is near-universal agreement that the best practice is to refer to people as being from, or members of, a particular tribe or pueblo. Well-meaning gringos who agonize over the issue may appreciate that many of the people being referred to do not take it so seriously. An old Indian joke goes:

New Mexico Tribes and Pueblos

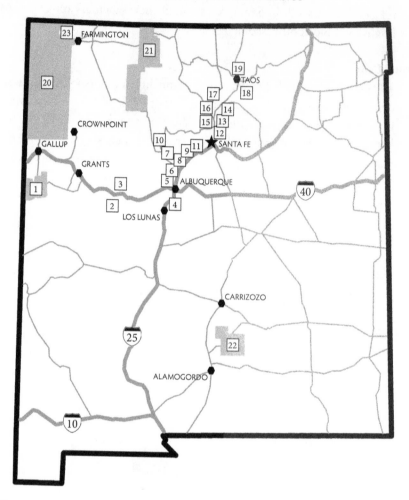

1 Zuni Pueblo	9 Kewa Pueblo	17 Ohkay Owingeh
2 Acoma Pueblo	10 Jemez Pueblo	18 Picuris Pueblo
3 Laguna Pueblo	11 Cochiti Pueblo	19 Taos Pueblo
4 Isleta Pueblo	12 Tesuque Pueblo	20 Navajo Nation
5 Sandia Pueblo	13 Pojoaque Pueblo	21 Jicarilla Apache Tribe
6 Santa Ana Pueblo	14 Nambé Pueblo	22 Mescalero Apache Tribe
7 Zia Pueblo	15 San Ildefonso Pueblo	23 Southern Ute Tribe
8 San Felipe Pueblo	16 Santa Clara Pueblo	

"Call us whatever you want. You white guys named us Indians because you thought you had landed in India. We're just glad you weren't looking for Turkey or the Virgin Islands."

Twenty-two separate Indian tribes are located in New Mexico: the 19 pueblos, the Jicarilla and Mescalero Apache tribes, and the Navajo Nation. (The Southern Ute reservation extends from Colorado into northwestern New Mexico, but that part of the reservation is largely uninhabited, and the Ute are not considered a New Mexico tribe.)

In addition to the Apache, Navajo, and Pueblo people born in the state, Indians from other tribes around the country have chosen to make their homes in or near Santa Fe. These include full- or part-time residents like actor Russell Means (Sioux), author N. Scott Momaday (Kiowa), actor Wes Studi (Cherokee), and activist Charlene Teters (Spokane).

There are four pueblos in Santa Fe County – Tesuque, Pojoaque, Nambé, and San Ildefonso – but they are not populous, and Indian people constitute a smaller percentage of the population of the county than they do of the state at large. However, the Indian artists and intellectuals who live in the area, the Indians who sell their jewelry under the portal of the Palace of the Governors, the annual Indian Market, and the resident Institute for American Indian Arts and Museum of Indian Arts and Culture all combine to give Indian people in Santa Fe a greater cultural presence than their numbers would suggest.

Indian casinos

Gaming establishments operated by New Mexico's Apache, Navajo, and Pueblo tribes in accordance with the federal Indian Gaming Regulatory Act.

The relatively recent proliferation of Indian casinos is tied to the evolution of tribal sovereignty. The tribes long argued that, as sovereign nations, they should be allowed to operate casinos on their own land, even if their reservations were in states that outlawed gambling. The states objected, but, in 1987, the United States Supreme Court sided with the Indians in *California v. Cabazon Band of Mission Indians*. Then, in 1988, Congress passed the Indian Gaming Regulatory Act, which allows tribes to operate casinos, but only after they negotiate compacts with the states. Most of the compacts, including New Mexico's, have provisions for sharing some percentage of gaming revenue with the state.

Casino income is unevenly distributed among New Mexico's tribes and pueblos. Those like Sandia Pueblo that are near cities have reaped great financial benefits. Others, like Picuris and Jemez pueblos, are so far from any population center that they have not bothered to build casinos.

Indian country

A legal term used to describe the geographical bounds of a self-governing Indian community. Indian country is usually thought of as a reservation or pueblo, but places like the Santa Fe Indian School are also considered Indian country. Indian people in Indian country are largely exempt from state laws and taxes but are subject to both tribal and federal laws and taxes.

Jurisdictional disputes are common. In 1997, part-time New Mexico resident Russell Means tested the tribal sovereignty of the Navajo Nation when he challenged its right to prosecute him for assaulting his then-father-in-law. Means conceded that he and his father-in-law are both Indians and that the alleged offense took place in Indian country but argued that he is exempt from Navajo law because he is an Oglala Sioux. The Navajo Nation Supreme Court and the United States federal courts ruled against Means, and the United States Supreme Court declined to hear his appeal.

Indian Detours

A touring option developed by the Fred Harvey Company that combined train travel with automobile tours. The first Detour took place in 1925 when passengers on the Santa Fe Railway disembarked from the train in Las Vegas, New Mexico, for an extended auto tour. The tour passed through many of Northern New Mexico's villages and pueblos before rejoining the train in Albuquerque.

The pueblos benefited from the program through increased sales of souvenirs, but, for the first time, they also experienced large numbers of inquisitive and occasionally inconsiderate tourists wandering through

Indian Detours car in Cordova

their villages. The Indian Detours program ceased operation during the Depression.

Indian Market

Santa Fe's biggest tourist draw, the world's largest gathering of creators and collectors of American Indian art. Anthropologist Edgar Lee Hewett put on an "Indian Fair" at the 1922 Fiesta, but the event struggled for years before finally taking off in the 1970s.

Indian Market is organized by the Southwestern Association for Indian Arts (SWAIA). The annual event is held on the Plaza on the weekend following the third Thursday in August.

Indian School

See SANTA FE INDIAN SCHOOL.

Indo-Hispanic

Term for a person of mixed Indian and Spanish blood. Mestizo, or "mixed race," has a similar meaning.

Info Mesa

Term for high-tech Santa Fe coined in a *Wired* magazine article about the city's burgeoning informatics industry. Santa Fe's high-tech potential springs from the city's proximity to Los Alamos National Laboratory, the Santa Fe Institute, and Albuquerque's Sandia National Laboratories.

Some people believe that the Santa Fe Info Mesa may one day become a technopolis to rival California's Silicon Valley. Others are less optimistic.

Institute of American Indian Arts (IAIA)

School for Indian artists. IAIA was established in 1962 at the instigation of Lloyd Kiva New, an Oklahoma Cherokee who became wealthy trading Indian art in Scottsdale, Arizona. New's stated purpose was to give young Indian artists a place to dabble in any style or medium that inspired them. Artists Fritz Scholder, Allan Houser, and Dan Namingha have all been associated with the institute, either as teachers or students.

The IAIA's Museum of Contemporary Native Arts is in downtown Santa Fe on Cathedral Place, across from St. Francis Cathedral. The IAIA student campus is south of town, off Rancho Viejo Boulevard.

International Folk Art Market, Santa Fe

Market for folk arts and crafts from around the globe. The two-day event, which was inaugurated in 2004, is already the largest international folk art market in the world. Unlike Spanish Market and Indian Market, which take place on the Plaza, the Folk Art Market takes place on Museum Hill. It is held on the second weekend in July.

Isleta Pueblo (is-LET-uh)

"Little Island" Pueblo. The Spanish gave the pueblo its name in 1540 because at that time its people were living on an island in the middle of the Rio Grande. Isleta was the only New Mexico pueblo that did not participate in the 1680 Pueblo Revolt.

In 1898, the Edison Company came to Isleta to film *Indian Day School*, the first moving picture shot in New Mexico. Today, the Tiwa-speaking pueblo operates the Isleta Gaming Palace and the Isleta Eagle Golf Course.

Isleta Pueblo is 73 miles south of Santa Fe via I-25.

Isotopes

Albuquerque's semiprofessional AAA baseball team. The Isotopes are the farm team for the Los Angeles Dodgers.

The name comes from an episode of *The Simpsons* in which fictional Springfield's hometown team, the Isotopes, is scheduled to move to Albuquerque – until the plan is foiled by Homer Simpson. The name is particularly appropriate given New Mexico's association with the Sandia and Los Alamos national laboratories.

-J-

jackalope

Mythical cross between a jackrabbit and an antelope, a creature created by a taxidermist. In Santa Fe, the antlered bunny is the logo for a six-and-a-half-acre shopping emporium on Cerrillos Road. Founded in 1976 by owner Darby McQuade, Jackalope offers goods imported from Mexico and elsewhere as well as locally produced craft items. The business has branch stores in Albuquerque and Los Angeles.

Jackalope

Jacona (hah-CONE-uh)

Diffuse community in Santa Fe County named for an old Tewa pueblo. Nearby Jaconita (hah-cone-EE-tuh) is a diminutive. Jacona is 19 miles from Santa Fe, one mile west of Pojoaque on NM 502.

Japanese internment camp

The Santa Fe camp that confined ethnic Japanese during World War II. The 80-acre camp, which operated from March 1942 to April 1946, was located in what is now the Casa Solana neighborhood.

While Japanese families were detained together in relocation camps elsewhere in the West, the Santa Fe internment camp housed only male prisoners. At its peak, the prisoner population was about 1,800. For most of the war, internees were allowed to work outside the camp, in Tesuque apple orchards or at a local golf course, but this practice came to an end when survivors of the Bataan Death March began returning home in March 1945 and anti-Japanese sentiment intensified.

In 1999, a Santa Fe city council meeting became heated when survivors of the Death March vehemently opposed a proposal to erect a memorial to the internment camp. Opposition was eventually overcome, and the memorial was installed in April 2002 in Frank Ortiz Park on a ridge overlooking Casa Solana.

Jaramillo (hah-rah-MEE-o)

New Mexico surname. Josefa Jaramillo of Taos married Kit Carson, and the Jaramillo family of Chimayó owns and operates the Rancho de Chimayó restaurant. But for Santa Feans, the name is most associated with former mayor Debbie Jaramillo.

Jaramillo, Debbie

(1952-) Santa Fe's controversial mayor from 1994 to 1998. Jaramillo, who criticized the marketing mentality of her predecessor, Sam Pick, was elected on a platform of "Santa Fe for Santa Feans." Convinced that her hometown was being overrun by wealthy Anglos, she said, "These are conquerors who did not need arms to take over the town. They have come instead with their big money and their higher education." Many Santa Feans, both Anglo and Hispanic, agreed that the city needed to control growth but were put off by Jaramillo's confrontational style. She was defeated in her 1998 reelection bid by Larry Delgado.

Debbie Jaramillo

Debbie's brother, Ike Pino, who once served as her city manager, became the New Mexico representative for the Arizona company that created Rancho Viejo, a sprawling housing development south of Santa Fe. Her son, Angelo Jaramillo, is an actor and author. In 2006, he published a book of fiction titled *The Darker: Tales of a City Different* that revisits his mother's central theme. *Publisher's Weekly* describes the book as "... a grim portrait of disenfranchised native New Mexicans."

Jemez Mountains (*HAY-mez, HEH-mez)

Mountains west of Santa Fe, across the Rio Grande. The mountain range and its many hot springs were formed by volcanic upheavals. The Valles Caldera, "Caldera Valleys," are in the center of the range. On the mountains' east side, the Pajarito Plateau encompasses Los Alamos, White Rock, and Bandelier National Monument.

The Jemez Mountains, which are named for Jemez Pueblo, have been cursed with forest fires since the turn of the 21st century. The Cerro Grande fire of 2000 burned 47,000 acres and 280 homes. The Las Conchas fire of 2011 burned 156,000 acres and 63 homes.

*Anglos often say HAY-mez. Spanish speakers say HEH-mez.

Jemez Pueblo

The only remaining Towa-speaking pueblo. In 1838, the people of Pecos Pueblo, who were also Towa speakers, abandoned Pecos and joined Jemez, where their descendants can be found today. *Jemez* is a Towa word of uncertain origin.

Jemez Pueblo has not benefited from Indian gaming because it is too far from any large population center to support a casino. The pueblo's leaders have entered into a partnership with Santa Fe entrepreneur Gerald Peters to build a casino near Anthony, in the southern part of the state, far from the pueblo's location in Northern New Mexico. Off-reservation casinos are rare, however, and thus far Jemez has not been successful in obtaining the requisite licenses.

Jemez Pueblo is on the southwest side of the Jemez Mountains, on NM 4. It is about 70 miles from Santa Fe via I-25 south and US 550 north.

Jemez Springs

Northern New Mexico community named for Jemez Pueblo and nearby hot springs. The village, population 250, is a popular place for relaxing weekend getaways. Jemez Springs is also home to the Servants of Paraclete, a religious order that at one time treated Catholic priests who molested children.

Jemez Springs is 72 miles from Santa Fe via US 84/285, NM 502, and NM 4.

Bernard Seligman, Zadoc Staab, and Lehman Spiegelberg with Kiowa Indian scouts on the Santa Fe Trail

Jews in New Mexico, A History of the

Henry J. Tobias's 1990 study of the Jewish presence in New Mexico. In the late 19th century, Santa Fe merchant families like the Spiegelbergs, Staabs, and Seligmans were among the state's commercial and civic leaders.

When President and Mrs. Rutherford B. Hayes visited Santa Fe in 1880, they stayed in the home of Lehman Spiegelberg. (The Spiegelberg Shop at the New Mexico History Museum is named for this family.) Abraham Staab was a friend of Archbishop Lamy and contributed generously to the construction of St. Francis Cathedral. The Staab house on East Palace Avenue is now part of La Posada, and the ghost of Abraham's wife, Julia, is said to haunt the hotel.

Santa Fe's Jewish population declined when commercial opportunities moved elsewhere after the Santa Fe Railway bypassed the city in 1880, but the founding merchant families continued to be influential. Arthur Seligman, who clerked at his father's store in the 1880s and 1890s, served as mayor of Santa Fe from 1910 to 1912 and as governor of New Mexico from 1931 to 1933.

Arthur Seligman

A History of the Jews in New Mexico focuses on the Territorial Period and the early 20th century. In 2008, Tobias published a follow-up book titled *Jews in New Mexico Since World War II*.

Jicarilla Apache Nation (hick-uh-REE-uh)

One of the two Apache tribes with reservations in New Mexico (the Mescalero being the other). The Jicarilla, whose name means "little basket," benefit from oil and gas extraction on their 843,000-acre reservation.

Most of the Jicarillas live in the town of Dulce, which is 131 miles northwest of Santa Fe and five miles south of the Colorado border.

jito/a (HE-toe/tuh)

See HITO.

Johnny

Nickname for a St. John's College student or graduate. Notable Johnnies include *Santa Fe Reporter* editor Andy Dudzik, environmentalist Sam Hitt, writer Duncan North, and entrepreneur Gerald Peters.

Johnson, Gary

(1953-) New Mexico's Republican governor from 1995 to 2003. Johnson made his fortune with Big J Enterprises, a construction company he founded while attending the University of New Mexico in the mid-1970s.

Johnson was a political novice when he won the gubernatorial election over incumbent Democrat Bruce King in 1994. He was easily reelected in 1998. Johnson's tenure as governor was characterized by extreme in-

Gary Johnson

dependence from both the New Mexico Legislature and his own party. His campaign for the decriminalization of marijuana gave him national exposure, including an interview in *Playboy*, but put him at odds with virtually every other politician in New Mexico.

After leaving the governor's mansion in 2003, Johnson retired from politics to concentrate on other adventures, including a successful climb up Mt. Everest. He eventually returned to the fray, frequently appearing on news programs as a spokesman for libertarian causes. Johnson campaigned for the Republican and the Libertarian nominations for the 2012 presidential election. The ex-governor lives in Taos.

Johnson, George

(1952-) Prominent science writer and Santa Fe resident. Johnson writes regularly for *The New York Times* and is the author of eight books, including *Strange Beauty: Murray Gell-Mann and the Revolution in 20th-Century Physics* and *The Ten Most Beautiful Experiments*, which he discussed on television with Stephen Colbert on *The Colbert Report*. Johnson addresses local issues in an intermittent "online journal" called the *Santa Fe Review*.

Jornada del Muerto (hor-NAH-duh del MWAIR-toe)

A deadly stretch of desert in southeast New Mexico. For most of its length, El Camino Real followed the Rio Grande. It became difficult to follow the river north of Las Cruces, however, so the trail veered to the east, and travelers had to trek across arid land for about 90 miles before getting back to the Rio Grande. The detour was fraught with danger.

The Place Names of New Mexico attributes the name of the desert detour to a German trader who was arrested for sorcery in 1670. After escaping from jail near present-day Albuquerque, the man tried to make his way to Mexico but died in the desert, either from thirst or at the hands of hostile Indians. His pursuers named the area where they found his bones *Jornada del Muerto*, "Dead Man's Journey."

Journal Santa Fe

The *Albuquerque Journal*'s Santa Fe edition. The Tuesday-through-Saturday *Journal Santa Fe* offers a different perspective from that of Santa Fe's hometown newspaper, *The New Mexican*. The *Journal* leans Republican while *The New Mexican* leans Democratic, so the papers usually disagree on politics, but their views are also influenced by their respective locations.

Because the *Journal*'s parent company is based in Albuquerque, it does not hesitate to focus on negative stories about Santa Fe. For instance, when the FBI released crime statistics for 2009, and the Santa Fe area once again scored badly, *The New Mexican*'s headline read "Judge to Expand Use of GPS Monitoring." The *Journal*'s headline read "Burglars Plunder the City Different."

The *Journal Santa Fe*'s offices are on the corner of Cerrillos Road and Montezuma Avenue.

juniper

Northern New Mexico's pernicious early-spring allergen. Juniper trees are everywhere – Northern New Mexico's terrain is technically known as piñon-juniper woodlands – and it is impossible to escape their pollen.

just off the bus

Former Mayor Debbie Jaramillo's dismissive description of newcomers to Santa Fe. She first leveled the charge at City Councilman Cris Moore when he questioned her decision to appoint her brother-in-law chief of police.

- K -

kachina (kuh-CHEE-nuh)

A carved and costumed doll representing a Pueblo deity. The dolls were created by the Hopi and Zuni to teach their children about the tribes' various gods. They are now made by other Pueblo tribes and the Navajo. Kachinas of varying degrees of craftsmanship are sold to tourists as souvenirs and to collectors as works of art.

Kasha-Katuwe

See TENT ROCKS NATIONAL MONUMENT.

Kaune's (KAH-nee's)

Iconic grocery store on the southeast corner of Old Santa Fe Trail and Paseo de Peralta. The Eastside crowd shops at Kaune's Neighborhood Market for caviar, imported cookies, and kosher foods.

Kachina

Itinerant grocery peddler Henry S. Kaune established the first of several markets in 1896. The sole remaining Kaune's is now owned by Cheryl Pick Sommer, daughter of former mayor Sam Pick.

The Kaune neighborhood, an Allen Stamm development officially named Casa Linda, derives its nickname from Kaune Elementary School. The school (which was closed in a 2010 consolidation) was named for Henry Kaune's son, Alfred, a longtime member of the Santa Fe school board.

Kearny, Stephen Watts (KEER-nee)

(1794-1848) American general who led the 1846 invasion of New Mexico in the Mexican-American War. Ulysses S. Grant, who served under Kearny in the 1840s, called him "one of the ablest officers of the day."

Kearny took pains to assure the people of New Mexico that they would not suffer under American rule. Though he was a Protestant, he attended a Catholic mass as a show of respect to New Mexico's predominant religion. He instructed lawyers under his command to draw up a set of laws based on American and Mexican legal precedents. The Kearny Code, as it was called, was printed in Spanish and English and distributed to the people of New Mexico. The relatively peaceful transition to American rule can be credited to Kearny's humane and sensible policies.

Santa Fe's Kearny Avenue (sometimes misspelled "Kearney") is named for the general.

Keresan (CARE-uh-sun)

A family of languages spoken by Pueblo Indians. Different dialects of Keres (CARE-us) are spoken at Acoma, Cochiti, Kewa (formerly Santo Domingo), Laguna, San Felipe, Santa Ana, and Zia pueblos.

New Mexico's other pueblos speak one of the Tanoan languages (Tewa, Tiwa, and Towa) or Zunian.

Kewa Pueblo (KAY-wah)

The Indian community formerly known as Santo Domingo Pueblo. Due to its proximity to the Cerrillos turquoise mines, the pueblo has always been known for its jewelry, particularly its heishi necklaces. More recently, it has become known for its cheap pueblo gas.

Kewa Pueblo is off I-25, 25 miles south of Santa Fe.

Khalsa (KALL-suh)

The surname adopted by New Mexico Sikhs. The Punjabi word is of Arabic derivation and means "pure." Khalsa is the most common "Anglo" (neither American Indian nor Hispanic) surname in the Española phone book.

Kilmer, Val

(1959-) Movie star and, since 1983, Santa Fe-area resident. Kilmer once owned a Pecos River ranch that had been part of the Forked Lightning Ranch owned by actress Greer Garson and her husband, oilman Buddy Fogelson. In 2011, he sold most of the property to a couple from Midland, Texas, but has retained 141 acres for a personal residence.

The actor has a reputation for being difficult. After directing him in *The Island of Dr. Moreau*, John Frankenheimer vowed never to work with him again. The veteran director said, "If I were making *The Val Kilmer Story*, I wouldn't cast Val Kilmer."

Kilmer once flirted with running for governor of New Mexico, but his public statements about the state came back to haunt him. In a 2003 *Rolling Stone* magazine interview, Kilmer said that "eighty percent of the people in my county are drunk" and that he carries a gun because San Miguel County is "the homicide capital of the Southwest."

Kilmer actively supports the Santa Fe Film Festival and The Wildlife Center.

King, Bruce

(1924-2009) New Mexico's affable, three-time Democratic governor. King served from 1971-75, from 1979-83, and from 1991-95. He was defeated in his 1994 reelection bid by Republican upstart Gary Johnson.

Between stints in the Governor's Mansion, King lived in southern Santa Fe County on a large ranch outside the small community of Stanley. His autobiography, *Cowboy in the Roundhouse*, was published in 1998.

Bruce and Alice King

A master of the malapropism, King once described a particularly thorny issue as a "box of Pandoras."

King, Gary

(1954-) New Mexico's attorney general. The son of former governor Bruce King, Gary holds a Ph.D. in chemistry as well as a law degree. The

Democrat served in the New Mexico Legislature for 12 years before he was elected attorney general in 2006.

Kirtland Air Force Base

Air Force base in southeast Albuquerque. The 52,000-acre base effectively surrounds Sandia National Laboratories, and its personnel collaborate with Sandia on the development of high-tech weapons, including an airborne laser that is to be a part of America's strategic missile defense. Air Force units also maintain the approximately 2,000 nuclear warheads that are stored on the base. Kirtland is one of New Mexico's largest employers.

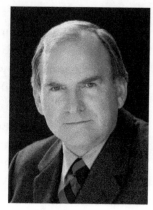

Gary King

kiva (KEY-vuh)

Pueblo Indian ceremonial space. Kivas are usually circular and at least partially underground.

kiva fireplace

Rounded, corner fireplace in a Santa Fe-style building, sometimes called a beehive fireplace because of its shape. Though its name suggests a Pueblo heritage, the kiva fireplace was a Spanish contribution.

Kokopelli (ko-ko-PELL-ee)

Oversold image of a humpbacked flute player. Kokopelli originated as a petroglyph representing fertility.

koshare (ko-SHAR-ay)

The "sacred clown" in Pueblo culture.

Koshare kachina

Koshares make fun of their own people and mock the spectators at Pueblo dances and feast days. They may pantomime a white woman seeing an Indian for the first time or they may mimic a child throwing a tantrum. Koshares paint their bodies in black and white stripes, and watermelons are a standard prop in their performances. Like most humorists, koshares are respected within their culture.

- L -

La Bajada Hill (bah-HAH-duh)

Steep hill on I-25, 19 miles south of Santa Fe. La Bajada, whose name means "The Descent," was at one time much more daunting than it is today. The old route five miles northwest of the current interstate had 23 hairpin turns and was so steep that Model T's had to climb it in reverse, the only gear low enough to make the grade.

La Bajada marks the southern boundary of Northern New Mexico. Historically, the land below the rise was known as the Rio Abajo, "Lower River," and the land above it was known as the Rio Arriba, "Upper River." The Rio Arriba region is now called Northern New Mexico.

La Casa Sena

"The Sena House," the anchor restaurant in Santa Fe's historic Sena Plaza. Entrepreneur Gerald Peters opened La Casa Sena in 1983. The restaurant offers two options: the main dining room, including courtyard seating; and La Cantina, where staff take frequent breaks from waiting tables to belt out show tunes. Both the main dining room and La Cantina serve "American Southwestern Cuisine." La Casa Sena is in Sena Plaza on Palace Avenue, just east of the Plaza.

La Choza (CHO-suh)

One of the places locals go for New Mexican food. La Choza, which means "The Shed," is the younger sister of an older downtown restaurant on Palace Avenue. The Carswell family opened its downtown restaurant, The Shed, in 1953. They opened La Choza 30 years later. Both establishments specialize in New Mexican food, but La Choza tends to be cheaper because it is outside the downtown area frequented by tourists. La Choza is on Alarid Street, one block off Cerrillos Road.

La Cienega (see-EN-eh-guh)

Northern New Mexico community whose name means "marsh." La Cienega, population 3,819, is associated with the nearby Las Golondrinas living history museum and the defunct horse racetrack, The Downs at Santa Fe. La Cienega is 11 miles southwest of Santa Fe.

La Conquistadora (con-key-stuh-DOR-uh)

"Our Lady of the Conquest," the statue of the Virgin Mary that Don Diego de Vargas credited with helping in the reconquest of New Mexico after the 1680 Pueblo Revolt. The 29-inch-tall icon was brought to Santa Fe from Mexico in 1625. The fleeing Spanish rescued it from a burning church during the 1680 uprising and took it with them to El Paso del Norte. De Vargas brought the statue back to Santa Fe in the reconquista of 1692.

La Conquistadora has played a role in the Fiesta de Santa Fe since the first celebration in 1712. In late June or early July of each year, the crowned and costumed statue is carried from its chapel in St. Francis Cathedral to Rosario Chapel, on the grounds of Rosario Cemetery, where it remains for one week.

In 1992, Archbishop Robert Sanchez renamed the statue "Our Lady of Peace" in response to Indian complaints that the old name glorified cultural domination.

Caballeros de Vargas
and
La Conquistadora

La Cueva (CWAY-vuh)

Northern New Mexico village whose name means "The Cave." La Cueva is in Mora County, five miles southeast of the town of Mora. It is 89 miles northeast of Santa Fe via I-25 north and NM 518 west.

La Farge, John Pen

(1951-) Son of Oliver La Farge and the author of *Turn Left at the Sleeping Dog*. Pen La Farge is a well-known Santa Fe preservationist. He has served on the boards of the Historic Santa Fe Foundation and the Old Santa Fe Association.

La Farge, Oliver

(1901-1963) Anthropologist and prolific author. A Harvard graduate, La Farge lived in Santa Fe off and on in the late 1920s and early 1930s and made the city his permanent home after World War II. He was a serious student of American Indian culture. His novel *Laughing Boy*, the story of a Navajo, won the 1930 Pulitzer Prize for fiction.

Oliver and Consuelo
La Farge

La Farge wrote both fiction and nonfiction, and was a columnist for *The New Mexican*. In 1959, he published *Santa Fe: The Autobiography of a Southwestern Town*, which is a compilation of stories from the newspaper. Some of his own columns were reprinted in *The Man with the Calabash Pipe*, published in 1966.

Oliver La Farge had a son and a daughter from his first marriage. His son, Peter La Farge (1931-1965), was a singer and songwriter who appeared with Bob Dylan in Greenwich Village in the 1960s. Peter wrote *The Ballad of Ira Hayes*, which was recorded by Johnny Cash. Oliver's second marriage, to native New Mexican Consuelo Baca, produced John Pen La Farge.

La Farge was a colonel in the Army Air Corps in World War II and is buried in Santa Fe National Cemetery. The Oliver La Farge Branch Library on Llano Street is named for him.

La Fonda

"The Hotel," Santa Fe's oldest and best-known lodging establishment. La Fonda is famous for its rich history and award-winning Spanish Pueblo-style architecture. According to Spanish Colonial records, there has been an inn at the southeast corner of the Plaza since 1610. Over the centuries, guests of the various establishments on the site have included Spanish conquistadors, General Stephen Watts Kearny, frontiersman Kit Carson, Governor Lew Wallace, scientist J. Robert Oppenheimer, and movie stars too numerous to mention. (Contrary to popular belief, however, Billy the Kid never washed dishes there.)

The current facility, built in 1922 and enlarged to 167 rooms in 1927, owes its look to architect John Gaw Meem and designer Mary Jane Colter. The hotel was operated by the Fred Harvey Company from 1926 to 1968. The Ballen family has owned it since then.

Confused tourists have been known to ask for directions to the "Jane Fonda Hotel." A more common error is to refer to the establishment as "the La Fonda hotel," which, literally translated, means "the the hotel hotel."

La Llorona (yo-RO-nuh)

"The Weeping Woman" in Latin American folklore, a ghostly apparition that haunts arroyos and acequias. One of the many stories of La Llorona's origin is that she was an Aztec princess who had a son by conquistador Hernán Cortés. According to legend, Cortés informed her that he was taking the child and returning to Spain without her, so she killed the boy and herself, and her restless soul now wanders the earth in search of the child. When La Llorona encounters mortals in her nightly travels, she lets out a blood-curdling scream and then disappears. Borrachos, "drunkards," who sometimes sleep in arroyos, have described their frightening encounters with the wailing apparition. Santa Fe parents have long used the specter of La Llorona to persuade their children to come home at dusk.

The myth of La Llorona is closely related to the true story of Malinche, the Indian woman who served as Cortés's interpreter and who gave birth to his child.

La Posada (po-SAH-duh)

"The Inn," a luxurious Santa Fe spa and hotel occupying six acres on the southeast corner of Paseo de Peralta and East Palace Avenue. The main building encompasses what was once the home of merchant Abraham Staab. La Posada is said to be haunted by the ghost of Abraham's wife, Julia, who died in the house in 1896.

La Puebla (PWEB-luh)

Northern New Mexico community two miles east of Española. *Puebla* means "town," though it is unknown why the place uses the feminine form rather than *pueblo*, the more common masculine form.

La Puebla is 25 miles northeast of Santa Fe via US 84/285 and NM 88.

La Raza (RAH-suh)

Short for *La Raza Cosmica*, "The Cosmic Race." The term refers to the mixture of Old World and New World blood inherited by most Mexicans. Like Chicano, La Raza is a self-referencing expression that indicates an ethnic and political consciousness not necessarily shared by all Hispanics.

La Villa Rivera (VEE-uh rih-VAIR-uh)

See Old St. Vincent Hospital.

La Voz de Nuevo México (VOSE deh new-AY-vo MEH-hee-co)

"The Voice of New Mexico," *The New Mexican*'s Spanish-language section. *La Voz* appears in the paper's Monday edition.

Lab, the

Shorthand for Los Alamos National Laboratory. In Albuquerque, "the Labs" refers to the Sandia National Laboratories.

Laboratory of Anthropology

Research facility founded by John D. Rockefeller in 1927 to study the Southwest's indigenous cultures. In 1947, the Laboratory became part of the Museum of New Mexico system. In 1987, the Museum of Indian Arts and Culture was opened adjacent to the Laboratory to exhibit its extensive collection. The Laboratory of Anthropology is part of the complex on Museum Hill.

Laguna Pueblo (lah-GOO-nuh)

A large pueblo with land in four counties. *Laguna* means "lake." The pueblo was named for a natural lake that existed in Coronado's time but that has since dried up.

The Keresan-speaking pueblo is 111 miles southwest of Santa Fe via I-25 south, I-40 west, and NM 117 north.

lambe (LAHM-bay)

"Flatterer" or "bootlicker." A Northern New Mexico state legislator was so obsequious to the governor that his detractors called him "the lambe from Nambé."

Lamy (LAY-me)

Rail junction south of Santa Fe. In 1880, the Santa Fe Railway opted to bypass its namesake. Santa Fe's disappointed leaders, including Archbishop Lamy, successfully lobbied for a spur line that would bring the train into the city.

The main line and the spur met in the middle of a large tract of land that Lamy held in trust for the Catholic Church. The rail junction was named in his honor.

Today, the community consists of a smattering of houses, a couple of historic buildings, and the train depot, which is still used by Amtrak and the Santa Fe Southern Railway. Lamy is 21 miles south of the Santa Fe Plaza via I-25 north and US 285 south.

Lamy, Jean Baptiste (*LAY-me)

(1814-1888) Catholic bishop, one of the most influential figures in the history of Santa Fe and Northern New Mexico. Born and educated in France, Lamy served as a priest in Ohio before being made a bishop and accepting an assignment to the newly formed Territory of New Mexico.

Lamy's sophisticated European sensibilities were offended by what he found when he arrived in Santa Fe in 1851: many of the priests were married, the Hermanos Penitentes were reenacting the Crucifixion in bloody detail, and churches were decorated with primitive santos. He embarked on a lifelong mission to reform not just the Church, but New Mexico society at large. Lamy's efforts were not universally welcomed, however. He met with resistance from local clergy, most notably Padre Antonio José Martinez, with

Jean Baptiste Lamy

whom he carried on a long-running feud. A fictionalized account of their dispute is described in Willa Cather's *Death Comes for the Archbishop*.

Lamy took personal charge of the construction of St. Francis Cathedral (where he is buried), and he invited Catholics from various orders to come to New Mexico to help him with other aspects of his mission. The Christian Brothers started the school for boys that evolved into St. Michael's High School and the College of Santa Fe (now called the Santa Fe University of Art and Design); the Sisters of Charity established St. Vincent Hospital; and the Sisters of Loretto founded a school for girls, Loretto Academy, and raised the funds for Loretto Chapel.

In 1875, New Mexico became an archdiocese and Lamy was promoted to archbishop. Archbishop Lamy has the rare distinction of being the subject of highly acclaimed works of both fiction and nonfiction. *TIME* magazine counts *Death Comes for the Archbishop* as one of the All-TIME Best 100 English-language novels, and the nonfiction *Lamy of Santa Fe*, by Paul Horgan, won a Pulitzer Prize for history in 1976.

*The name, which is French, is properly pronounced lah-MEE, although most people say LAY-mee for both the man and the town named for him.

land grants

Awards of land made by New Mexico governors in the Spanish Colonial Period and the Mexican Period. In the Spanish Colonial Period, communal land grants were typically made to families or groups of families as a way of populating Northern New Mexico's frontier areas to create a bulwark against Indian raiding parties. The villages of Truchas and Las Trampas were settled in this way.

In the Mexican Period, large land grants were made to individuals. In 1841, Governor Manuel Armijo granted over 1.7 million acres in northeast New Mexico to a trader named Charles Beaubien. This tract later became known as the Maxwell Land Grant.

After the Mexican-American War, the communal land grants became the subject of contention. Although the 1848 Treaty of Guadalupe Hidalgo was crafted to protect the property rights of native New Mexicans, unscrupulous Anglo lawyers and surveyors managed to acquire vast tracts of communally owned land. In the 1960s, Hispanic resentment over the loss of this land was expressed in the sometimes-violent Alianza movement.

New Mexico now recognizes a number of land grants as political subdivisions of the state, but the issue remains contentious. A bipartisan committee of the New Mexico Legislature regularly hears testimony from people seeking compensation for land that was granted to their ancestors but that has long since been lost.

Land of Enchantment

New Mexico's nickname. New Mexico was known as the "Sunshine State" until 1935, when *New Mexico Magazine* began using the nickname "Land of Enchantment." It first appeared on New Mexico license plates in 1941. It is also the title of the official state ballad by Taos songwriter Michael Martin Murphey.

Land of Disenchantment is the title of University of New Mexico professor Michael L. Trujillo's 2009 ethnographic study of the people of the Española Valley. Trujillo's view contrasts with the idealized vision of Norteños that is presented by some anthropologists – and all tourist brochures.

"Land of Entrapment" is a variation. Some say it means that once they get to New Mexico, people never want to leave. Cynics say that it costs so much to live in New Mexico, particularly in Santa Fe, that people cannot afford to leave.

Land of Mañana

"Land of Tomorrow," a dig at the legendary capacity of New Mexicans for procrastination. Gringos newly arrived from places where efficiency is highly valued sometimes have a hard time adjusting to New Mexico's relaxed pace.

LANL (LAN-ull)

Shorthand for Los Alamos National Laboratory. The acronym is heard more often than the full name.

Lannan Foundation

Santa Fe-based charitable foundation. Lannan moved its headquarters from Los Angeles to Santa Fe in 1997. It is now New Mexico's largest private foundation.

The Lannan Foundation's most visible local contribution is its sponsorship of the Readings and Conversations series. These periodic events, which are held at the Lensic, feature a writer reading from his or her work and answering questions posed by a peer. Novelist Annie Proulx praised the series in a *Pasatiempo* interview, saying that Lannan is "more interested in finding the good stuff than 'parading lit stars'." The Lensic is usually sold out for Readings and Conversations events.

Las Campanas (cahm-PA-nuss)

"The Bells," a ritzy development 10 miles northwest of Santa Fe. The 4,730-acre resort community has two 18-hole golf courses designed by Jack Nicklaus, an equestrian center with an indoor arena, four tennis courts, and sites for 1,700 homes. Arizonan Lyle Anderson, the "Father of Desert Golf," was the principal developer. Many of the houses in Las Campanas are second homes, occupied only occasionally by their wealthy owners.

During the drought of the early 2000s, when city residents were enduring water restrictions, some Santa Fe cars sported bumper stickers reading "I'll Stop Watering My Garden when Las Campanas Stops Watering Its Golf Courses."

Las Conchas fire (CON-chuss)

The largest fire in New Mexico history. The fire in the Jemez Mountains began in late June 2011 when a tree fell across a power line. By mid-July, dry conditions and high winds had driven the blaze to consume more than 156,000 acres. The fire is named for the place where it began. Las Conchas, whose name means "The Shells," is 20 miles west of Los Alamos.

The Las Conchas fire was much bigger than the 47,000-acre Cerro Grande fire, but it was not as destructive, at least in the short term. The Cerro Grande fire destroyed 280 homes near Los Alamos. The Las Conchas fire, which was generally confined to the forest, destroyed 63 homes. The fire's long-term effects cannot be immediately determined, however, because of the increased danger of flash floods in canyons that have been denuded of vegetation.

Las Cruces (CREW-sess)

New Mexico's second most populous city, after Albuquerque. Las Cruces was established in 1848, after the Mexican-American War, when Americans began pouring into southern New Mexico. The city, population 97,617, serves the commercial needs of the fertile Mesilla Valley and is home to New Mexico State University. It is also a popular retirement community.

Las Cruces, "The Crosses," was probably named for the crosses over the graves of the many people killed in Apache raids. The city is at the intersection of I-25 and I-10, 282 miles south of Santa Fe.

Las Golondrinas (go-lahn-DREE-nuss)

El Rancho de las Golondrinas, "The Ranch of the Swallows." Once the last paraje, or rest stop, on the Camino Real, the 200-acre ranch is now a living history museum featuring 33 authentically furnished buildings representing life in 18th- and 19th-century New Mexico.

Las Golondrinas is open to the public for self-guided tours from June through September. It is 15 miles south of Santa Fe, near the community of La Cienega.

Las Posadas (po-SAH-dahs)

"The Inns," a traditional nativity play in which actors portraying Mary and Joseph go from house to house seeking shelter. In Santa Fe, hundreds of celebrants follow the couple around the Plaza as they look for a place to stay. They are rebuffed by devils, who are in turn hissed and booed by the crowd, before finally being allowed into the courtyard of the Palace of the Governors.

Las Trampas (TRAHM-pus)

Northern New Mexico village on the High Road to Taos. The village, whose name means "The Traps," is named for the Rio de las Trampas, which flows through it. The 250-year-old San José de Gracia Church is the village's main attraction.

Las Trampas is on NM 76, 45 miles north of Santa Fe.

Las Vegas

The original Las Vegas. The New Mexico city had been a railroad boom town for more than 25 years when Las Vegas, Nevada, was laid out in 1905. Las Vegas, New Mexico, got its start in the 1820s as a stop on the Santa Fe Trail and prospered further when the Santa Fe Railway came through in 1879. The city, whose name means "The Meadows," is known for its Victorian architecture.

With a population of 13,753, Las Vegas is Northern New Mexico's second most populous city, after Santa Fe. It is the county seat of San Miguel County and home to Highlands University. United World College and Montezuma Castle are nearby. Numerous movies, including *Easy Rider* (1969), *Red Dawn* (1984), and *No Country for Old Men* (2007), have been filmed in the city. Las Vegas is 68 miles east of Santa Fe via I-25 north.

Las Vegas Optic

Las Vegas's hometown paper. The *Optic* was founded in 1879 and operated as a daily until 2009, when its distribution was limited to Mondays, Wednesdays, and Fridays. It is, like the *Los Alamos Monitor*, owned by Landmark Community Newspapers, a subsidiary of Landmark Media Enterprises based in Norfolk, Virginia. The *Optic* no longer endorses political candidates.

latilla (lah-TEE-uh)

A wooden pole, usually peeled, that is used in the construction of a Spanish Pueblo-style ceiling. Latillas are placed on top of, and perpendicular or diagonal to, the vigas that make up the ceiling's first layer.

Latillas laid diagonally over vigas

Latino/a

Broad term for a Spanish-speaking person who has a Latin American heritage. Most New Mexicans of Spanish descent refer to themselves as Hispanic.

Law, Lisa

(1943-) Photographer who chronicled the 1960s counterculture. Law started taking photographs in 1964 when she became acquainted with California's early folk and rock groups. She and her husband, Tom, moved to New Mexico in 1967. The couple lived in Santa Fe and on a farm in Truchas and were frequent visitors to the New Buffalo commune. In 1969, they attended Woodstock as part of the Hog Farm contingent.

In 1987, Law published *Flashing on the Sixties*, a collection of photographs of the hippies, activists, and musicians that she met in her travels among the counterculture.

Lawrence, D.H.

(1885-1930) English author of *Lady Chatterley's Lover* who came to New Mexico in 1922 at the invitation of Mabel Dodge Luhan. In the mid-1920s, Lawrence and his wife, Frieda von Richthofen (a cousin of

Germany's famed Red Baron), spent nearly two years at Kiowa Ranch, a property 13 miles north of Taos that was given to them by their hostess.

Lawrence died in France in 1930. Five years later, Frieda brought his ashes back to New Mexico and had them interred at the ranch. She was later buried next to him.

The D.H. Lawrence Ranch and Memorial, as Kiowa Ranch is now known, is owned by the University of New Mexico.

Legislature, New Mexico

New Mexico's bicameral legislative body. The Legislature is composed of 70 representatives and 42 senators, who receive no pay except for a per diem and mileage allowance when on official business.

The Legislature meets at the Roundhouse for 30 days in even-numbered years and for 60 days in odd-numbered years. Legislative sessions begin at noon on the third Tuesday in January.

Democrats have controlled the New Mexico Legislature for decades. Since 1933, they have held a majority in the House every year except one (1953). They have maintained a majority in the Senate over the same period except for the four years between 1985 and 1988. (The Senate was evenly split in 1985 and 1986, and Republicans held a one-seat majority in 1987 and 1988.)

Lensic Performing Arts Center (LEN-zick)

Santa Fe's premier performing arts center. The original movie theater, designed by the Boller brothers, was built on West San Francisco Street by Nathan Salmon and E. John Greer in 1931. In 2000, the pseudo-Moorish theater underwent a year-long, $8.2

Lensic Performing Arts Center

million renovation. It is now an 821-seat venue for the performing arts as well as for films, lectures, and literary events.

"Lensic" is an acronym created from the first initials of Greer's six grandchildren.

Lincoln County War

Outbreak of lawlessness from 1878 to 1881 in southeast New Mexico's Lincoln County. The war began as a dispute between rival factions of merchants and cattlemen and deteriorated into a virtual free-for-all among hired gunfighters, including Billy the Kid.

President Rutherford B. Hayes appointed Lew Wallace governor of the Territory and tasked him with ending the war, but Wallace was unable to do so. The Lincoln County War eventually wound down of its own accord.

lintel (LIN-tull)

A wooden bridge that supports the wall over a window or a doorway in an adobe building.

Little Texas

The southeast corner of New Mexico, including the cities of Carlsbad, Clovis, Hobbs, and Roswell. Ranching and oil and gas extraction are the area's main industries. As the nickname indicates, the region has more in common with neighboring Texas than with Northern New Mexico.

Living Treasures

Program honoring Santa Fe-area elders. Inaugurated in 1984 by Mary Lou Cook and others, Living Treasures honors people 70 years of age or older for their spirit and community service.

A 1997 book of photo essays titled *Living Treasures: Celebration of the Human Spirit* profiles the first honorees. A second volume titled *Living Treasures: Our Elders, Our Hearts* was published in 2009.

Living Wage Ordinance

Santa Fe's cutting-edge minimum-wage law. The original 2004 ordinance mandated an $8.50-an-hour minimum wage, applicable to all city businesses with 25 or more employees. In 2006, the rate was increased to $9.50 an hour. In 2008, the city council expanded the law to include all businesses, regardless of the number of employees, and tied future increases to the federal Consumer Price Index. In 2012, Santa Fe had the nation's highest minimum wage.

llano (YAH-no)

"Plain." The *Llano Estacado*, "Staked Plains," covers parts of northwestern Texas and eastern New Mexico. Llano Quemado, whose name means "Burned Plain," is a small community on NM 68, one-half mile south of Ranchos de Taos.

Localflavor Magazine

Free monthly magazine covering food and lifestyle topics in Santa Fe, Taos, and Albuquerque. The newsprint magazine was founded in 1994 by Christopher Kolon, who sold it to Patty and Peter Karlovitz in 1997. *Localflavor* is distributed throughout New Mexico.

Lone Butte (beaut)

The best-known butte formation in the Santa Fe area. Lone Butte is 17 miles south of the Plaza, near the intersection of NM 14 and Bonanza Creek Road.

Long Walk, The

New Mexico's own Trail of Tears. In January 1864, after their surrender to militia colonel Kit Carson, 8,500 Navajos were forced to join 500 Mescalero Apaches at the Bosque Redondo reservation in east-central New Mexico. The forced march from what is now eastern Arizona and western New Mexico to the reservation lasted 18 days and resulted in the deaths of over 200 men, women, and children. The Navajo refer to the sad trek as The Long Walk.

Loretto Chapel (lo-REH-toe)

Gothic-revival church in downtown Santa Fe. The chapel patterned after Sainte-Chapelle in Paris was commissioned by the Sisters of Loretto and dedicated in 1878. A mysterious stranger built its miraculous staircase three years later. The chapel is now privately owned but it is open to the public, including for weddings. Loretto Chapel is on Old Santa Fe Trail at its intersection with Water Street.

Los Alamos

The hilltop home of Los Alamos National Laboratory. The "city" of Los Alamos, which is not incorporated, has a population of 12,019. This makes it Northern New Mexico's third most populous community, after Santa Fe and Las Vegas. Los Alamos boasts the highest concentration of Ph.D.s of any place in the country.

"The Cottonwoods" is 35 miles north of Santa Fe via US 84/285 and NM 502.

Loretto Chapel

Los Alamos County

The wealthiest county west of the Mississippi. Los Alamos County is New Mexico's smallest county in area, and most of its 17,950 residents

Celebrating the creation of Los Alamos County in 1949

live in the city of Los Alamos or in the bedroom community of White Rock. The vast majority work for or are otherwise affiliated with Los Alamos National Laboratory. This accounts for the county's high median income, just over $100,000, which is the fifth-highest in the country and the highest in the West. (In New Mexico, Sandoval County is a distant second at $57,000; Santa Fe County is third at $53,000.)

Los Alamos Monitor

Los Alamos's hometown newspaper. The paper is delivered five days a week, every day except Saturday and Monday. The *Monitor* was established in 1963 by the McMahon family. Like the *Las Vegas Optic*, it is now owned by Landmark Community Newspapers, a subsidiary of Landmark Media Enterprises based in Norfolk, Virginia. The paper endorsed Gore, Kerry, and Obama in the recent presidential elections but has since ceased making political endorsements.

Los Alamos National Laboratory

America's prime nuclear weapons laboratory and the raison d'etre for the city of Los Alamos. The 27,000-acre research facility was established in the 1940s as part of the Manhattan Project, the World War II effort to develop the atomic bomb.

The early 2000s were a trial for the Lab. Wen Ho Lee was wrongly

Los Alamos National Laboratory

accused of espionage, the Cerro Grande fire destroyed 280 area homes, and Lab security became the butt of talk show jokes. Until June 2006, the Lab was operated for the United States Department of Energy by the University of California, but its management was put out to bid after the many problems. It is now managed by Los Alamos National Security LLC, a company formed by the University of California, Bechtel Corporation, and others.

Los Alamos National Laboratory (often shortened to LANL) continues to concentrate on nuclear weapons but also conducts research on computers, energy, biomedical science, and environmental protection. It is one of Northern New Mexico's largest employers.

Los Alamos Ranch School

Boys' school located on land now occupied by the city of Los Alamos. The institution, founded in 1917 by Ashley Pond, Jr., was displaced when its site was requisitioned for the Manhattan Project.

Contrary to popular belief, chief scientist J. Robert Oppenheimer did not attend the Ranch School. He selected Los Alamos as the site for secret atomic research because he was familiar with the area from previous visits to New Mexico. Beat poet William Burroughs, novelist Gore Vidal, and Santa Fe Opera founder John Crosby are alumni of the school.

Ashley Pond and Fuller Lodge, which was designed for the school by John Gaw Meem, are vestiges of the Los Alamos Ranch School.

Los Alamos Study Group

Albuquerque-based nuclear disarmament group. The nonprofit organization monitors events at the Lab and questions LANL's official statements.

Los Cinco Pintores (SINK-o pin-TORE-es)

"The Five Painters" – Jozef Bakos, Fremont Ellis, Walter Mruk, Willard Nash, and Will Shuster – who joined the Santa Fe art colony in the early 1920s. The artists exhibited their work together and lived near each other in primitive adobe houses that they built by hand. Their bemused neighbors on Camino del Monte Sol called them "the nuts in the huts."

Will Shuster, best known of the group, inaugurated the ritual burning of Zozobra as part of the 1924 Fiesta.

Los Luceros (loo-SAIR-os)

Northern New Mexico ranch and hacienda. The 148-acre property was once owned by Mary Cabot Wheelwright and is now owned by New Mexico's Cultural Affairs Department.

Film director Robert Redford has teamed with the state in a project at the ranch called "Milagro at Los Luceros." The program is designed to train New Mexico's Indian youth in film and art.

Los Luceros is 26 miles north of Santa Fe, one mile west of NM 68 (the low road to Taos).

Los Lunas (LOON-us)

The next to the last stop on the southbound Rail Runner Express. Los Lunas, population 14,835, is 24 miles south of Albuquerque.

People sometimes ask why the masculine *los* is used in front of the feminine *lunas*, which means "moons." The reason is that the village was named for the Luna family, and family names are considered masculine.

Los Lunas is off I-25, 87 miles south of Santa Fe.

low road to Taos

The quicker river route from Santa Fe to Taos. The High Road to Taos is capitalized because it is a New Mexico Scenic Byway. The low road is not.

From Española to Taos, the low road follows NM 68, which parallels the Rio Grande for most of its length. Most guidebooks suggest that visitors take the High Road on their way to Taos and the low road on their way back to Santa Fe. But there is something to be said for taking the reverse course – if everyone else is following the guidebooks' advice, then traffic may be lighter for those who take the low road to Taos and the High Road on the way back.

From Santa Fe, the 70-mile low road takes about one hour and 20 minutes, versus one hour and 50 minutes for the 76-mile High Road.

lowrider

A customized car that has been lowered from its factory specifications so that it rides closer to the ground. Some lowriders feature hydraulic lifts that raise each wheel independently.

Lowriders are a cultural phenomenon in Hispanic Northern New Mexico. Santa Fe author Carmella Padilla's 1999 book, *Low 'n' Slow: Lowriding in New Mexico*, includes photographs of cars and their owners. The city of Española proudly bills itself as the "Lowrider Capital of the World."

Luhan, Mabel Dodge (*LOO-hahn)

(1879-1962) Foremost promoter of the Taos art colony. Born into a wealthy family in Buffalo, New York, Mabel Ganson suffered a nervous breakdown at age 22 when her first husband was killed in a hunting accident. She and her second husband, Edwin Dodge, moved to a villa in Florence, Italy, where Mabel dressed in Renaissance garb and hosted a salon for writers and artists. She left Dodge and moved her salon to Greenwich Village, where she met her third husband, post-impressionist artist Maurice Sterne.

Weary of the New York social scene, the Sternes moved to Taos in 1918. Soon after their arrival, Mabel met and fell in love with Tony Lujan, a Pueblo Indian living the traditional life at Taos Pueblo. Mabel and Tony left their spouses and moved in together. They married in 1923 and remained together until Mabel's death in 1962.

Mabel Dodge Luhan

Mabel Dodge Luhan (she changed the spelling of Tony's surname to make it easier for her Anglo friends to pronounce) spent her considerable energy bringing artists and intellectuals to New Mexico. She is credited with introducing writer Willa Cather, artist Georgia O'Keeffe, psychologist Carl Jung, photographer Ansel Adams, and numerous other creative types to the Land of Enchantment. Her greatest coup was the English writer D.H. Lawrence and his wife, Frieda, whom she convinced to stay by giving them a ranch. Luhan was a complex character, and her guests were not always charmed. Her wheedling manipulations led Lawrence to call her "a stout white crow, a cooing raven of misfortune."

Actor Dennis Hopper owned the Mabel Dodge Luhan house from 1970 to 1977, during the tumultuous Taos hippie years. Today, the house serves as a conference center and boutique hotel.

*Mabel's last name is always pronounced in the Anglo fashion, LOO-hahn, with the accent on the first syllable.

Luján, Ben Ray (*loo-HAHN)

(1972-) Northern New Mexico's Democratic congressman. Luján was elected in November 2008 to occupy the Third Congressional District seat vacated by Tom Udall, who was elected to the United States Senate. Ben Ray is the son of Speaker of the New Mexico House of Representatives Ben Luján. Before running for Congress, Ben Ray served as chairman of the state's Public Regulation Commission.

Ben Ray Luján

*Anglos often say LOO-hahn, but the accent indicates that the emphasis is on the second syllable.

luminaria (loo-min-AH-ree-uh)

Term for a bonfire or a lantern, depending on where you are. In Santa Fe, *luminaria* refers to a bonfire. In Albuquerque and the rest of the country, the word refers to the candle-in-a-bag lantern that Santa Feans call a "farolito."

- M -

Macaione, Tommy (mass-ee-O-nee)

(1907-1992) Artist and eccentric local character. Macaione moved from Connecticut to Santa Fe in 1952, and for the next 40 years he supported himself by selling his paintings of flowers and streetscapes. Macaione was challenged in matters of hygiene and housekeeping. In his old age, he kept as many as 80 dogs and cats in his house and sometimes traded paintings for pet food.

A bronze statue of "El Diferente" stands in Macaione Park, at the intersection of Paseo de Peralta and Hillside Avenue.

MacGraw, Ali

(1938-) Oscar-nominated actress (*Love Story*) and Tesuque resident. MacGraw moved from Malibu to Northern New Mexico in 1994 and immediately became involved in local causes. Among other good works, she has lent her name and time to the Santa Fe Rape Crisis Center and the Santa Fe Animal Shelter, contributed a costume to La Conquistadora, and narrated a film about the life of Stewart Udall. She received a New Mexico Governor's Award for Excellence in the Arts in 2008.

Ali MacGraw

MacGraw's manifest appreciation for Northern New Mexico belies the perception among some old-time Santa Feans that immigrants from California, particularly those from the entertainment industry, are not as interested in local culture as people from other places. (See CALIFORNICATION.)

MacLaine, Shirley

(1934-) Oscar-winning actress (*Terms of Endearment*), author, and New Age seeker who maintains homes in Abiquiu and Santa Fe. Mac-Laine's well-documented spiritual quest includes past-life regression sessions with Chris Griscom. The Galisteo healer is mentioned in Mac-Laine's 1986 book, *Dancing in the Light.*

The actress raised the ire of local conservationists in 1993 when she attempted to build a home on Atalaya Mountain. Opposition from Dale Ball, Stewart Udall, and the Trust for Public Land ultimately quashed the project, but the incident has not been forgotten. Science writer George Johnson refers to the still-visible scar of a road that was bulldozed up the mountain in advance of construction as "Shirley MacLaine Boulevard."

MacLaine briefly served as chair of the New Mexico Film Commission in 2003. She has appeared at the Santa Fe Film Festival as both a presenter and an honoree.

Madrid (*MAD-rid)

Old mining town now devoted to galleries and shops. Madrid was a mining town from the mid-1800s until the 1950s, when the demand for coal dried up and it became a virtual ghost town. It remained essentially uninhabited until resettled by hippies and artists in the 1970s. Today, Madrid is a popular stop for tourists and day-trippers from Santa Fe and Albuquerque. The Mine Shaft Tavern is the town's principal eating and drinking establishment.

Madrid is 24 miles south of Santa Fe on NM 14 (the Turquoise Trail).

*Note the difference in pronunciation between MAD-rid and the more usual muh-DRID.

Magoffin, Susan (muh-GOFF-in)

(1827-1855) Author of a journal describing her journey down the Santa Fe Trail. Magoffin left Independence, Missouri, in June of 1846 as the 18-year-old bride of trader Sam Magoffin. Her impressions of the people and places she encountered en route and in Santa Fe offer valuable insights into the period, particularly since her trip coincided with the march into New Mexico of the American army under General Stephen

Watts Kearny. Magoffin died at age 28 after giving birth to her second child.

Malinche (muh-LIN-chay)

(circa 1500-1529) Indian woman who served as an interpreter for conquistador Hernán Cortés in his conquest of Mexico. Malinche is often described as Cortés's mistress, but, given that she was his prisoner, "mistress" may not be the right term. In any event, she is known to have borne a child by him.

Malinche has multiple symbolic meanings. In the Matachines dance, she represents the reconciliation of the Aztec and Spanish cultures. In other contexts, she is seen as a traitor to her people. Soon after the New Mexico Legislature banned cockfighting, opponents of the ban organized a "Malinche Cockfighting Derby" in honor of a state legislator whom they felt had betrayed her Hispanic culture by voting against the bloody sport. Malinche is also seen, perhaps most accurately, as a tragic figure caught between two cultures and lacking the free agency to make a choice between them.

malpais (mal-pie-EESE)

"Badlands." In New Mexico, the term applies to uninhabitable land that is overrun with ancient lava flows. El Malpais National Monument, off I-40 near Grants, is the most accessible example of such terrain.

mañana (mahn-YAH-nuh)

"Tomorrow," or, as the old joke goes, "In Spain, mañana means tomorrow... in New Mexico, it just means later."

mano (MAH-no)

Literally "hand," although in Northern New Mexico the word is often used as a shortened version of *hermano*, "brother." *Manito*, "little brother," is a combination of *mano* and the diminutive *ito*.

Maria's

Old-time Santa Fe restaurant known for its extensive margarita menu. Maria's, which serves New Mexican food, was founded in 1952 by Gilbert and Maria Lopez. It has been owned and operated by Al and Laurie Lucero since 1985. In 1999, Al Lucero published *The Great Margarita Book*, with a foreword by Robert Redford. Redford wrote of Maria's, "I am glad it's there. I'm glad I've tasted their margaritas, and I hope not too many people find out about it." Maria's New Mexican Kitchen is on West Cordova Road, half a block east of St. Francis Drive.

mariachi (mah-ree-AH-chee)

Music genre that originated in Guadalajara, Mexico, or the musicians who play it. A typical mariachi band consists of a half dozen or more sombrero-wearing musicians playing guitars (including an oversized guitar called a *guitaron*), trumpets, and violins in a fast, syncopated style. In addition to the sombrero, the mariachi costume includes a short jacket and snug trousers decorated with silver studs.

The origin of the word *mariachi* is unclear. Some sources, noting that mariachi bands have always played at weddings, believe that the word may derive from the French word for "marriage." A more credible guess is that it is a Spanish adaption of a Coca Indian word.

Mariachi is a popular music form in Santa Fe, with local and visiting groups appearing frequently on the Plaza bandstand.

Marian Hall

See Old St. Vincent Hospital.

Marion, Anne

(1938-) Santa Fe's foremost art patron. Texan Anne Windfohr Marion inherited the Burnett Oil and Tandy Corporation fortunes, and heads the Burnett Foundation, which uses its considerable assets to fund art and education in Texas and New Mexico. In 1988, she married John L. Marion, who was at that time chairman of Sotheby's. The couple lives in Santa Fe part-time.

The millions of dollars that the Marions have donated locally have reshaped the Santa Fe art scene. They were primarily responsible for the creation of the Georgia O'Keeffe Museum, SITE Santa Fe, the Santa Fe Art Institute, and the Marion Center for Photographic Arts.

Martinez

The most common Hispanic surname in New Mexico. There has been no official statewide count, but a sportswriter for *The New Mexican* once did a word search of surnames. He concluded that in his five years of covering high school and college sports in Northern New Mexico, he had encountered the name Martinez 362 times, more than twice as often as runner-up Chávez, at 172 times.

Taos social diva Mabel Dodge Luhan credited Padre Antonio José Martinez for the prevalence of the name in Northern New Mexico. Long after his death, she wrote of him: "He did not believe in celibacy and a great many women loved him and apparently they all called their offspring Martinez, so his descendants of that name are to be found at all cardinal points of the valley." Robert Julyan offers a more likely explanation in *The Place Names of New Mexico*. He names Herman Martín Serrano, who accompanied Oñate on the 1598 expedition to New Mexico, as the progenitor of the many Martinezes in Northern New Mexico. Martinez means "son of Martin," and, according to Julyan, by the 19th century, many of Herman's descendants had dropped Serrano and adopted Martinez as their surname.

Martinez, Maria

(circa 1889-1980) San Ildefonso artist associated with black-on-black pottery. Martinez made red-and-white pottery before she and her husband, Julian, resurrected the black-on-black technique in the 1920s. Her signed pieces rank among the most valuable Indian art.

Maria Martinez

Martinez, Padre Antonio José

(1793-1867) Catholic priest, educator, and arch-nemesis of Archbishop Jean Baptiste Lamy. Martinez was ordained in 1822 and assigned to a parish in Taos, where he started New Mexico's first primary school.

During the Mexican-American War, Kit Carson accused Martinez of fomenting the Taos Revolt against the new American government. The accusation was never proved, however, and Martinez went on to become the first president of New Mexico's Territorial Legislature. The priest is best known for his resistance to Archbishop Lamy's efforts to reform the Catholic Church in New Mexico. A fictionalized account of their feud is found in Willa Cather's *Death Comes for the Archbishop*.

Padre Antonio José
Martinez

Padre Martinez is buried in Taos's Kit Carson Park. A statue of him stands in the Taos plaza.

Martinez, Susana (*sue-SAH-nuh)

(1959-) New Mexico's – and the nation's – first female Hispanic governor. Republican Martinez took office in 2011 after a hard-fought campaign against Democrat Diane Denish, who served as lieutenant governor under Bill Richardson.

Martinez was born and raised in El Paso. Her parents started a security business when she was a teenager, and she worked as a guard while attending college at the University of Texas at El Paso. She moved to Las Cruces soon after graduating from law school at the University of Oklahoma. Martinez was elected district attorney for the 3rd Judicial District in Doña Ana County in 1996 and served in that office until her run for governor in 2010. Her husband,

Susana Martinez

"First Gentleman" Chuck Franco, is retired from the Doña Ana County Sheriff's Department.

*Note the pronunciation of the governor's first name. In Spanish, the second syllable is pronounced SAH, as opposed to the English ZA.

Maryol family

Santa Fe food dynasty. The family started in the food service business in 1930 when Greek immigrant Tony Maryol set up an ice cream stand on the Plaza. His children started three classic Santa Fe restaurants: Georgia established Tomasita's in 1974; Jim and his wife, Ann, established Tia Sophia's in 1975; and Toni started Diego's in 1988.

The family's third generation now runs the family businesses. Georgia's son, George Gundrey, runs Tomasita's and the Atrisco Café, which he opened in the DeVargas Center space previously occupied by Diego's. Tia Sophia's is now owned and managed Jim and Ann's son, Nick Maryol. Nick's younger brother, Alex, is a well-known blues guitarist.

Matachines, Los (mah-tuh-CHEE-ness)

Ritual dance of uncertain origin and inexact meaning. The Matachines dance is said to have been brought to Spain by the Moors, and then to Mexico by the Spanish. Its original meaning is unknown, though most agree that the New World version of the dance is a metaphor for the Catholic conquest of the pagan Aztecs.

Characters include *El Monarca*, "The King," who is said to represent the Aztec king Montezuma, and Malinche, the virginal maiden who offers her hand and Christianity to El Monarca. (The Malinche character is named for and represents the real Indian consort of conquistador Hernán Cortés.) *El Toro*, "The Bull," interferes with the offering, and *El Abuelo* "The Grandfather," provides comic relief. El Monarca's

Matachines dancer

attendants, Los Matachines, wear a veiled headdress that looks like a bishop's miter.

The Matachines dance is performed in Hispanic villages and Indian pueblos up and down the Rio Grande. Many pueblos stage the dance in late December as part of their Christmas celebrations.

matanza (ma-TAHN-zuh)

"Slaughter," "barbecue," or "feast." When Governor Gary Johnson's tax bill was defeated in the Legislature, he promised a matanza of the pork bill that appropriates money for legislators' pet projects.

Matteucci, Nedra (muh-TOO-chee, NEE-druh)

(1950-) One of Santa Fe's best known and most successful art dealers. The daughter of Judge William T. Smith of Dexter, New Mexico, Matteucci attended the University of New Mexico in Albuquerque, where she met her husband, Richard. In 1983, she took a job with Forrest Fenn, Santa Fe's most prominent gallery owner at that time. She and her husband eventually bought the Fenn Galleries.

The Morning Star Gallery on Canyon Road specializes in Native American art, and the Nedra Matteucci Galleries on Paseo de Peralta specialize in historical Western art, including works from the early Taos art colony. Matteucci has served on the boards of the Georgia O'Keeffe Museum and the Santa Fe Opera.

Maxwell Land Grant

The largest land grant in New Mexico history. In 1841, Governor Manuel Armijo awarded more than 1.7 million acres in northeast New Mexico to a trader named Charles Beaubien. Ostensibly, the grant was given to help populate an outlying area, but there is some evidence that Armijo received compensation for his largesse. The grant became known as the Maxwell Land Grant when it came under the control of Lucien Maxwell, Beaubien's son-in-law and a friend of Kit Carson.

Ted Turner's Vermejo Park Ranch was once part of the Maxwell Land Grant. The 578,000-acre ranch is the largest privately owned, contiguous tract of land in the United States.

mayordomo (my-or-DOE-mo)

Superintendent, or ditch boss, of a local acequia. The mayordomo is responsible for distributing water from the acequia and for organizing the parciantes, those who draw water from the ditch, in the annual cleaning of the acequia. The mayordomo's importance is illuminated in an 1891 New Mexico law, still on the books, that disqualifies from the position "persons of ill-health, of a notable malady, or who are demented or of unsound mind, or who are lame either in one leg or both or one arm or both ...."

Mayordomo: Chronicle of an Acequia in Northern New Mexico (1988) is Dixon author Stanley Crawford's account of his tenure as a mayordomo.

McCarthy, Cormac

(1933-) Pulitzer Prize-winning novelist and writer in residence at the Santa Fe Institute. McCarthy met Nobel Prize-winning physicist Murray Gell-Mann at a 1989 dinner for recipients of MacArthur genius grants and visited the Santa Fe Institute at Gell-Mann's invitation. McCarthy appreciated the intellectual company at SFI and made frequent visits to the institute from his home in El Paso. In 1999, he moved to Tesuque to be closer to SFI.

Already a critically acclaimed and widely read novelist, McCarthy became even better known after moving to Northern New Mexico. His novel *The Road* won the 2007 Pulitzer Prize for fiction, and, in 2008, the movie adaptation of his book *No Country for Old Men* (much of which was filmed in New Mexico) won four Academy Awards, including the Oscar for best picture.

McCord, Richard

(1941-) Santa Fe author. McCord moved from New York City to Santa Fe in 1971 and founded the *Santa Fe Reporter* three years later. He edited and co-published the alternative paper for 14 years before selling it to Rockefeller heiress Hope Aldrich. In 1996, he published *The Chain Gang: One Newspaper Versus the Gannett Empire*, the story of the Gannett chain's underhanded attempts to acquire the *Reporter*.

In 2003, McCord published a collection of essays titled *The Other State, New Mexico, USA*. One of his essays describes how he met John Erlichman, the Nixon confidante who gained notoriety for his part in the Watergate scandal. Erlichman moved to Santa Fe in 1975 and gave the *Reporter* his first post-Watergate interview soon thereafter.

McCune Charitable Foundation

Santa Fe-based charitable fund. The foundation was established in 1989 from the estate of Marshall McCune, heir to a Pittsburgh banking and oil fortune. It accepts grant requests for a wide range of community-based New Mexico projects.

(Santa Fe's McCune Charitable Foundation is not the same thing as the much larger McCune Foundation, which was established in the will of Marshall's brother, Charles, and is based in Pittsburgh.)

McGarrity, Michael

(1939-) Former Santa Fe County deputy sheriff and best-selling crime novelist. McGarrity's many novels take place in modern New Mexico and feature a fictional lawman named Kevin Kerney.

McKinney, Robert

(1910-2001) Longtime publisher of *The Santa Fe New Mexican* and founder of *The Taos News*. Originally from Amarillo, Texas, McKinney acquired his wealth by investing in the stock of bankrupt railroads in the 1930s. He bought *The New Mexican* in 1949 and founded *The Taos News* in 1959. In 1976, he sold *The New Mexican* to the Gannett Company but later sued the media giant and regained control of the paper.

McKinney read Latin and Greek, composed poetry (*The New York Times* declared his book of poetry one of the 10 best of 1947), and served as ambassador to Switzerland in the Kennedy administration. In New Mexico, he was instrumental in developing the San Juan-Chama Diversion Project and in persuading St. John's College to open a branch in Santa Fe.

McKinney's daughter, Robin McKinney Martin, has run the newspapers since his death.

Means, Russell

(1939-) Controversial Indian activist and actor. An Oglala Sioux, Means was an early member of the American Indian Movement and a leader at the 1973 siege of Wounded Knee. He has since been active in Libertarian Party politics.

Means has appeared in many movies. He is perhaps best known for his role as the Daniel Day-Lewis character's adoptive Indian father in *The Last of the Mohicans*. Means lives part-time in the San Miguel County village of San Jose.

Meem, John Gaw

(1894-1983) The person most responsible for popularizing Santa Fe-style architecture. Meem came to Santa Fe's Sunmount Sanatorium in 1920 as a tuberculosis patient and quickly developed a passion for the area's indigenous adobe buildings. His main contributions as an architect were the adaptation of the old Spanish-Pueblo style to new buildings and the revival of Territorial style.

Meem's Santa Fe commissions include the Laboratory of Anthropology, Cristo Rey Church, and numerous public schools. He also designed many of the buildings on the UNM campus in Albuquerque and, in a departure from adobe, the log-built Fuller Lodge in Los Alamos.

Meem donated much of the land for St. John's College. The college library is named for him.

menudo (meh-NEW-doe)

Soup made with tripe (scraped and boiled cow stomach), posole, and red chiles. (Also, inexplicably, the name of the puerile Puerto Rican rock group that gave singer Ricky Martin his start in 1984.)

mesa (MAY-suh)

"Table" or "tableland." In geologic terms, a mesa is a broad, flat-topped elevation with one or more steep sides. San Ildefonso Pueblo's Black Mesa is a dramatic local example.

The difference between a mesa and a butte is best explained by ranchers: "If you can graze a few cattle on it, it's a mesa. If not, it's a butte."

Mesa Verde National Park (MAY-suh VAIR-dee)

Park in southwestern Colorado that contains more than 600 cliff dwellings and other evidence of prehistoric Anasazi culture. The cliff dwellings were occupied from about 600 A.D. to about 1300 A.D., when their inhabitants moved south into New Mexico and Arizona and formed the pueblo communities that exist to this day. (The National Park Service no longer uses the term "Anasazi." It refers to Mesa Verde's original inhabitants as "Ancestral Puebloans.")

Mesa Verde, "Green Mesa," National Park is 296 miles from Santa Fe via US 550.

Mescalero Apache Tribe (mess-cuh-LAIR-o)

One of two Apache tribes living on reservations in New Mexico. (The Jicarilla tribe is the other.) The Spanish named the Mescaleros for the mescal agave plant that was gathered and eaten by their nomadic ancestors. The Mescaleros live on a 460,600-acre reservation near Ruidoso in south-central New Mexico.

The Mescalero reservation is also home to many people who consider themselves Chiricahua Apaches. After Geronimo's capture in 1886, the Chiricahuas were imprisoned at Fort Sill, Oklahoma. When they were released in 1913, many of them moved from Fort Sill to the Mescalero reservation.

The financial success of the Mescaleros predates Indian gaming and is largely due to the efforts of their late president, Wendell Chino. Chino famously said, "Zunis make pottery, Navajos make rugs, and Apaches make money." He was responsible for the construction, in 1975, of the tribe's Inn of the Mountain Gods, a resort featuring a 253-room hotel and an 18-hole golf course. Casino gaming was added later.

Of New Mexico's 22 tribes and pueblos, only a few reservations are in the southern half of the state. The Mescalero reservation is by far the largest.

Mesilla Valley (meh-SEE-uh)

The largest irrigated area in New Mexico. The fertile valley of the Rio Grande that stretches from just north of Las Cruces to the Texas border is known for the cotton, chile, and pecans grown there.

Mesilla is a diminutive of *mesa*, which means "table" or "tableland." The valley is named for the tableland above the Rio Grande flood plain.

mestizo/a (mess-TEE-zo/zuh)

A person of mixed Spanish and Indian blood. Indo-Hispanic is an academic way of saying the same thing.

Mexican gray wolf

See WOLF, MEXICAN GRAY.

Mexican-American War

1846-1848 war in which the United States invaded Mexico and annexed much of its northern territory. The acquisition of the present-day states of California, Nevada, and Utah, and parts of Arizona, Colorado, New Mexico, and Wyoming, was officially recognized in the Treaty of Guadalupe Hidalgo. (The balance of what is now the state of New Mexico was acquired in the 1853 Gadsden Purchase.)

Many Americans, including Abraham Lincoln, protested the war at the time. Others, like General William Tecumseh Sherman, regretted it later. Sherman, who detested the climate and people of the Southwest, said that the United States should again declare war on Mexico – and force it to take back New Mexico.

Although there was fierce fighting in Mexico itself, the invasion and occupation of New Mexico were relatively peaceful. There were a number of reasons for this. First, many New Mexicans were disenchanted with the government of Mexico, which was both far away and politically unstable. Second, New Mexico Governor Manuel Armijo offered no resistance to the invading American army. He is said to have taken a bribe from the Americans, and, whether or not this is true, he did order his troops to abandon their defensive positions in Apache Canyon before any fighting took place. Finally, and perhaps most importantly, American General Stephen Watts Kearny took pains to assure Nuevomexicanos that their property rights and religion would be respected under American rule.

Mexican Period

1821 to 1846, when New Mexico was a province of the newly independent nation of Mexico. For New Mexico, the significant effect of independence from Spain was the opening of previously outlawed trade with the United States along the Santa Fe Trail. The Mexican Period ended with the Mexican-American War.

Hispanic New Mexicans do not necessarily relate to the country of Mexico. For those whose ancestors came to Northern New Mexico in the 16th or 17th century, the relatively short 25-year Mexican Period is a mere blip compared to the region's 223 years as part of New Spain and 166 years as part of the United States.

MIAC (MY-ack)

Acronym for the Museum of Indian Arts and Culture.

micaceous pottery (my-KAY-shuss)

Glittering pueblo pottery made with clay containing flecks of mica.

mijo/a (ME-ho/ha)

A contraction of *mi*, "my," and *hijo*, "son" or *hija*, "daughter." *Mijo* is a term of affection that is most often used by an older person when speaking to a child.

milagro (mee-LAH-grow)

"Miracle," also, a trinket made of silver or pot metal that was originally designed to be pinned to the robes of a Catholic saint in a church or shrine. Molded in the shape of an eye, leg, arm, torso, or other body part, the milagro was used to indicate to the healing saint the location of the supplicant's distress. Today, milagros are most often sold as tourist souvenirs.

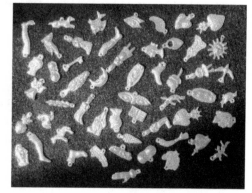

Milagros

Milagro Beanfield War, The

Taos author John Nichols's best-known book. The lighthearted story revolves around the mythical Northern New Mexico village of Milagro and the struggle between its traditional villagers and water- and land-grabbing developers. The book was published in 1974.

Director Robert Redford's movie version was filmed in the village of Truchas in 1988. Some Norteños were taken aback by the odd mixture of disparate Spanish accents and the inauthentic costumes (nobody in New Mexico wears a sombrero), but the film was generally praised for its depiction of local culture.

Miller, Mark

(1949-) The "father of contemporary Southwest cooking." A former anthropology student at Berkeley, Miller opened the Coyote Café in Santa Fe in 1987. He has since started many other restaurants, including the Red Sage at Pojoaque Pueblo's Buffalo Thunder Resort. Miller has written numerous cookbooks and has lectured around the world. Although he no longer owns a restaurant in Santa Fe, many of the chefs in the city trained under him at the Coyote Café, so his influence will be felt for years to come.

Mirabal, Robert (MEER-uh-ball)

(1966-) Indian musician from Taos Pueblo. The long-haired flutist and singer has produced numerous CDs, won two Grammys, written a book of poetry, and appeared on TV in an episode of *Walker, Texas Ranger*.

miraculous staircase

Legend coiled around a spiral staircase. When the Loretto Chapel was completed in 1878, it lacked a staircase to its elevated choir loft. According to the legend, the Sisters of Loretto prayed about the

Miraculous staircase

missing staircase to St. Joseph, patron saint of carpenters, and a white-bearded stranger soon knocked on their door asking for work. The mysterious carpenter built a masterfully crafted spiral staircase and left without identifying himself or asking for pay, leading some of the sisters to conclude that their benefactor was St. Joseph himself. The fact that the staircase was fashioned without nails or any visible support added to the mystery. *Ripley's Believe It or Not!* picked up the story in the late 1930s, and it has been a Santa Fe staple ever since.

Local historian Mary Jean Straw Cook has identified the mysterious carpenter as an itinerant eccentric named François-Jean "Frenchy" Rochas. Rochas was found murdered in a remote cabin in Dog Canyon, south of Alamogordo, in 1894.

mitote (mih-TOE-tay)

"Buzz" or "gossip." *The New Mexican* runs a weekly column called "El Mitote" that notes celebrity sightings and other local gossip.

Mogollon (mug-ee-OWN)

Prehistoric Indian culture that once thrived in southwest New Mexico, western Arizona, and northern Mexico. The culture dates from about 150 A.D. to about 1300 A.D., when, like the Anasazi, the Mogollon left their homes for unknown reasons. It is believed that the Hopi and Zuni tribes are descended from the Mogollon.

Archaeologists named the ancient culture for southwest New Mexico's Mogollon Mountains. The mountains were probably named for Juan Ignacio de Flores Mogollón, governor of New Mexico from 1712 to 1715.

mojado/a (mo-HA-doe/duh)

"Wet." The word is sometimes used by Norteños to mean "wetback," a slur for an undocumented immigrant. Hispanics whose families have been in New Mexico for centuries are not always welcoming to newcomers from south of the border.

It is a fact, however, that the greatest contribution to Northern New Mexico's unique Hispanic culture was made by an immigrant from Mexico. Professor Rubén Cobos was born in Mexico and lived in San Antonio, Texas, before moving to Albuquerque. His *Dictionary of New Mexico and Southern Colorado Spanish* preserves the unique language and, by extension, the culture of Hispanic Northern New Mexico.

mole (MO-lay)

Generic name for many different sauces used in Mexican cuisine. The word is sometimes used in combined form, as in *guacamole*. In the United States, *mole* most often refers to mole poblano, a chile sauce that includes Mexican chocolate among its ingredients.

Momaday, N. Scott (MOM-uh-day)

(1934) Author Navarre Scott Momaday, usually referred to as N. Scott Momaday. The writer is credited with introducing Native American literature to mainstream America. He was born into the Kiowa tribe in Oklahoma, but his parents were educators who taught on various reservations, and he lived among New Mexico's Navajo, Apache, and Pueblo Indians as a child. He graduated from the University of New Mexico and earned a Ph.D. in

N. Scott Momaday
on the cover of the *Santa Fe Reporter*

English literature from Stanford. In 1969, he won the Pulitzer Prize for fiction for *House Made of Dawn*, a novel set in Jemez Pueblo.

Momaday moved to Santa Fe after retiring from the University of Arizona. He has lectured at St. John's College and the Institute of American Indian Arts.

Monahan, Joe

(1954-) New Mexico's first political blogger. Monahan was born in Pennsylvania and moved to New Mexico in the early 1970s. He lives in Albuquerque, where he operates a public relations business and maintains *New Mexico Politics with Joe Monahan*, the nonpartisan blog he started in 2003.

Joe Monahan

Monahan relies on anonymous insiders he calls "alligators" to keep him posted on who is running for what office and who is being investigated. In a survey by *The Washington Post*'s Chris Cillizza, Monahan's site and Heath Haussamen's *NMPolitics.net* were both listed among the best political blogs in the nation. Monahan's blog address is joemonahansnewmexico.blogspot.com.

monsoon season

The beginning of July through the end of August, when southerly winds bring much-needed rain. New Mexico is on the northern fringe of a large-scale summer weather pattern called the Mexican monsoon. In a typical year, 30 to 40 percent of Northern New Mexico's precipitation falls in the monsoon season. Rodeo de Santa Fe, once held in July, was moved to late June to avoid the inevitable rains.

Santa Fe's Average Precipitation by Month
(in inches)

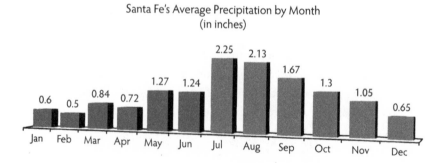

Jan	Feb	Mar	Apr	May	Jun	Jul	Aug	Sep	Oct	Nov	Dec
0.6	0.5	0.84	0.72	1.27	1.24	2.25	2.13	1.67	1.3	1.05	0.65

Montezuma Castle

Montezuma Castle

One-time luxury hotel near Las Vegas, New Mexico, now owned by United World College. The resort flourished in the 1880s and 1890s when a spur rail line delivered guests to the hotel from the Santa Fe Railway station in Las Vegas. The hotel closed in 1903.

The ornate building was subsequently owned by the Baptist Church and then by the Catholic Church. In 1981, it was acquired by the Armand Hammer Foundation, which uses it as part of the United World College campus. The castle underwent a $10.5 million renovation in 2000 and 2001.

Montezuma Castle is five miles northwest of Las Vegas and is open for guided tours on certain Saturdays. The nearby hot springs are a popular attraction.

Montoya, Josefina (mahn-TOY-uh)

(1815-) Fictional character created by the American Girl Doll Company. Josefina is part of the Historical Character series, in which each doll comes with a narrative. Josefina's story is that she is a Hispanic girl living on a New Mexico ranch between 1824 and 1826. She makes the acquaintance of American traders, who are just beginning to appear in New Mexico, and her dream is to become a curandera, or folk healer, like her godmother.

Las Golondrinas, which was once a working ranch and is now a living history museum south of Santa Fe, offers a "Josefina tour" that explains what daily life would have been like for a New Mexican girl in the 1820s.

Mora County (MORE-uh)

Northern New Mexico county, one of the poorest in the state. The Mora Valley is one of the most beautiful in New Mexico, but it does not get many visitors, mostly because Mora County is off the usual tourist route between Santa Fe and Taos. *Mora* means "mulberry."

The town of Mora, the county seat, is 94 miles northeast of Santa Fe via I-25 north and NM 518 west.

morada (more-AH-duh)

Penitente chapel, a small, usually windowless adobe building that serves as a meeting place for the secretive *Hermanos Penitentes*, "Brotherhood of Penitents." The public can view an example of a morada at Las Golondrinas.

Mormon Battalion Monument

Mormon Battalion Monument

Stone monument commemorating Mormon volunteers in the Mexican-American War. The 25-foot-tall stone pillar topped with a bronze wagon wheel is halfway between Santa Fe and Albuquerque, just south of the defunct ¡Traditions! shopping center at the Budaghers exit off I-25.

The approximately 500 Mormons who enlisted in the United States Army during the Mexican-American War were organized into the Mormon Battalion. Though it did not see combat, the unit is credited with one of the longest marches in United States military history, marching from Council Bluffs, Iowa, in

July 1846 and arriving in San Diego, California, in July 1847. The battalion passed through Santa Fe in October 1846.

Like the obelisk in the center of the Santa Fe Plaza, the Mormon Battalion Monument has undergone an unauthorized alteration. The monument originally noted that the volunteers "marched through a wilderness where nothing but savages and wild beasts are found." At some point, the politically incorrect word "savages" was chiseled out, just as it has been removed from the obelisk on the Plaza. The same mystery sculptor may be responsible for both alterations.

mountain lion

Feline predator, also called catamount, cougar, puma, and panther. *Guinness World Records* credits the mountain lion with the most names of any animal. The cat has so many names because it is found in almost every country in the Americas.

Mountain lions are common in New Mexico, though encounters with humans are rare. There was a human fatality in 1974, and another in 2008, when a mountain lion attacked and killed a man in Pinos Altos, in southern New Mexico. In 2010, a 150-pound cat that had been wandering around Santa Fe was captured and released into the wild.

Mountain Man Trade Fair and Rendezvous

Santa Fe's annual celebration of the mountain-man lifestyle. The mid-August event, which features demonstrations of frontier clothing, weapons, and skills by modern re-enactors, is held in the courtyard behind the Palace of the Governors.

The mountain-man phenomenon was closely tied to big-city fashion trends. Beaver hats were so popular in the United States and Europe between 1825 and 1845 that fur companies struggled to meet the demand, and a hardy man could make good money running beaver traps in the streams of the Rocky Mountains.

Mountain men met at a designated place each spring to trade or sell their furs. The village of Taos was such a rendezvous spot for trappers working the southern Rockies. The men who gathered there traded with the Indians and each other, flirted with the local belles, and consumed vast quantities of a locally produced whiskey called "Taos Lightning." When beaver hats went out of vogue, some of the trappers, like Kit Carson, married Taos girls and settled in the area.

The annual Santa Fe Mountain Man Trade Fair began in 1985 as a way to add an Anglo event to the summer celebrations of Indian Market and Spanish Market.

movida (mo-VEE-duh)

A secret or underhanded move. When Highlands University President Manny Aragon was accused of favoring Hispanics for faculty positions, he defended his actions by saying, "When non-minority individuals find a good professor, it's networking. If Hispanics find someone good, it's a movida, an under-the-table deal."

Murphey, Michael Martin

(1945-) Singer-songwriter and Taos resident. Murphey composed *Land of Enchantment*, New Mexico's state ballad. A native of Dallas, he had his biggest hit, *Wildfire*, in 1975. He moved to Taos in 1978.

Murphey is always referred to by all three names. He began using his middle name when he appeared in a movie in 1981 and wanted to avoid confusion with another actor named Michael Murphy.

Murphy, Rosalea (ROSE-uh-lee)

(1912-2000) Founder and longtime proprietor of the legendary Pink Adobe restaurant. A native of New Orleans, Murphy moved to Santa Fe and opened the Pink Adobe in 1944. She added the adjacent Dragon Room bar in 1978.

Murphy painted, wrote cookbooks, and maintained an imposing presence in the Dragon Room. In her later years, she held court at a corner table with her dogs Gina Lollobrigida and Don Juan seated on the bench on either side of her. She dressed in brightly colored blouses, hand-tooled cowboys boots, and her signature "R" and "M" silver earrings. Murphy claimed to have thrown Georgia O'Keeffe out of the Dragon Room simply because she disliked O'Keeffe and her paintings.

Rosalea's daughter, Priscilla Hoback, is a well-known potter. She and her son, Joe Hoback, now run the Pink Adobe and the Dragon Room.

Museum Hill

The museum complex off Camino Lejo on Santa Fe's Eastside. State-run facilities on the hill include the Museum of International Folk Art, the Museum of Indian Arts and Culture, and the Laboratory of Anthropology. These institutions are clustered around Milner Plaza, which is named for Charles and Edwina Milner, who donated much of the money for the plaza. The International Folk Art Market is held on Museum Hill on the second weekend of July.

The nearby Wheelwright Museum and Museum of Spanish Colonial Art are privately run but are considered part of the Museum Hill complex.

Museum of Indian Arts and Culture (MIAC)

One of the four primary institutions in the Museum of New Mexico system. The Museum Hill facility displays over 1,300 items in a permanent exhibit called *Here, Now & Always.*

MIAC is affiliated with the adjacent Laboratory of Anthropology. The museum was established in 1987 as an exhibition space for the Lab's extensive collection of Southwest Native American material culture.

Museum of International Folk Art

One of the four primary institutions in the Museum of New Mexico system. Opened in 1953, the Museum Hill facility now contains more than 135,000 artifacts, which makes it the largest collection of international folk art in the world. The International Folk Art Market is affiliated with the museum.

Museum of New Mexico

The state of New Mexico's museum system. The system's four primary institutions are in Santa Fe. The New Mexico History Museum (which includes the adjacent Palace of the Governors and the Fray Angélico Chávez History Library) and the New Mexico Museum of Art are downtown on Palace Avenue. The Museum of International Folk Art and the Museum of Indian Arts and Culture are on Museum Hill. All four museums offer free admission to everyone on Friday evenings and to New Mexico residents (with ID) on Sundays.

The museum system also includes various monuments scattered throughout the state. Among these are the Jemez State Monument near Jemez Springs, the Coronado State Monument in Bernalillo, and the Fort Sumner State Monument in Fort Sumner.

The Museum of New Mexico was founded in 1909 by anthropologist Edgar Lee Hewett to prevent the dispersal of Indian artifacts to eastern museums.

Museum of Spanish Colonial Art

Repository for the Spanish Colonial Arts Society's collection of retablos, bultos, tinwork, straw appliqué, and other traditional Hispanic art. The collection is displayed in a 5,000-square-foot house on Museum Hill that was designed and built by John Gaw Meem in the 1930s.

mystery sculptor

Anonymous workman who made an unauthorized alteration to the obelisk in the center of the Santa Fe Plaza. The obelisk was erected in 1868 as a memorial to the Territory's Civil War dead and "the heroes who have fallen in various battles with savage Indians." In 1974, a long-haired, coveralls-wearing man, whom bystanders mistakenly assumed to be a city employee, chiseled out the politically incorrect word *savage*.

The same word has also been removed from the Mormon Battalion Monument near the defunct ¡Traditions! shopping center. The same mystery sculptor may be responsible for both alterations.

Myth of Santa Fe, The

University of New Mexico professor Chris Wilson's 1997 book about Santa Fe's architectural and cultural history. Wilson's thesis is that Santa Fe's success in marketing itself as a tourist destination has resulted in a contrived conformity in local architecture. He also laments the commodification of complex local cultures into the more saleable tricultural model.

- N -

Nambé Pueblo (nom-BAY)

One of the Eight Indian Northern Pueblos. Nambé is known for its lake and waterfall. It is not affiliated with Nambé Mills, makers of Nambé Ware. The Tewa-speaking pueblo is 20 miles north of Santa Fe, off NM 503.

Nambé Ware

Shiny cookware, serving dishes, and decorative items made of a unique, eight-metal alloy. Nambé Ware resembles silver, can be used for oven baking or stove-top cooking, and never needs polishing. The alloy was created in 1953 by Martin Eden, a former metallurgist with Los Alamos National Laboratory. He and others formed a company called Nambé Mills (not affiliated with Nambé Pueblo) to manufacture and market the new product. The company later added crystal items to its inventory.

For many years, the Nambé Mills foundry at Cooks Road and Agua Fria Street was the only significant manufacturing operation in Santa Fe, but that changed when the company began outsourcing its castings to China and India. Nambé LLC, as it is now known, maintains retail outlets in downtown Santa Fe on Paseo de Peralta and on San Francisco Street. The company is owned by John Hillenbrand of Hillenbrand Industries, the Indiana bed and casket maker.

National Dance Institute of New Mexico (NDI-NM)

One of Santa Fe's most successful nonprofits, the largest arts education organization in New Mexico. NDI-NM's goal is to motivate New Mexico schoolchildren through dance.

Ballet dancer Jacques d'Amboise founded the nonprofit National Dance Institute in New York City in 1976 and brought the program to Santa Fe in 1990. In 1994, Catherine Oppenheimer, a teacher with the

New York operation, relocated to Santa Fe to expand the program into the National Dance Institute of New Mexico.

NDI-NM has been wildly successful at fundraising. In 2001, the Santa Fe School Board signed a 50-year lease that granted the organization three and a half acres on Alto Street, on Santa Fe's Westside, for the token rent of one dollar a year. In 2003, after a successful capital campaign, NDI-NM opened The Dance Barns, a 33,000-square-foot facility with two small studios and two larger studios that open to a 500-seat theater. First Lady Laura Bush flew in to attend the opening.

Catherine Oppenheimer met and married entrepreneur Garrett Thornburg after moving to Santa Fe. Thornburg serves as NDI-NM's treasurer, overseeing assets in excess of $20 million.

Native American

One of the formal names for the first inhabitants of the Americas. In New Mexico, "Indian" is used more frequently than "Native American." The term Native American is problematic because, technically, anyone born in America is a native American. Some writers overcome this problem by using Native with a capital N to signify that the person referred to is an Indian. (See INDIAN.)

Nauman, Bruce

(1941-) Internationally known conceptual artist and Galisteo horse rancher. Nauman has lived on a 750-acre ranch near Galisteo since 1979. In 1995, *Time Magazine*'s Robert Hughes wrote, "Nauman, beyond much dispute, is the most influential American artist of his generation." Nauman is married to painter Susan Rothenberg.

Navajo

The most populous of New Mexico's three Indian groups. (The others are the Apache and the Pueblo Indians.)

Like the Apaches, the Navajo are Athabascans who migrated to the Southwest between 1300 A.D. and 1500 A.D. Both groups raided the indigenous Pueblo Indians, but, unlike the Apaches, the Navajo adopted many Pueblo ways, including the practice of agriculture. The word "Navajo" is derived from the Tewa *nava hu*, "place of large cultivated fields." (The Navajo call themselves *Diné*, "The People.")

The Navajo population, which was reduced to about 9,000 in 1880, now numbers between 275,000 and 300,000. Roughly 175,000 tribal members live on the Navajo Nation's 17.5-million-acre reservation, which is mostly in Arizona and New Mexico's Four Corners region.

Navajo code talker

World War II radioman. Navajo soldiers and marines were recruited to transmit messages in their native language to foil enemy eavesdroppers. The 2002 movie *Windtalkers* dramatizes the code talker experience.

Navajo Nation

The political entity that governs the Navajo tribe and its 17.5-million-acre reservation. The Navajo Nation is divided into 110 chapters, 51 of which are either in New Mexico or straddle the New Mexico-Arizona border.

NDI-NM

See NATIONAL DANCE INSTITUTE OF NEW MEXICO.

New Buffalo commune

The first and best known of the many Taos hippie communes. The community was founded in 1967 on land purchased by poet Rick Klein near the village of Arroyo Hondo, 10 miles north of Taos. New Buffalo became a destination for counterculture types after 1969 when the movie *Easy Rider* featured a scene based on the commune.

The idealism of the early years inevitably wore off. As Klein later said, "The '60s were visionary, the '70s were the time of hard work, and the early '80s were a time of wine, heroin, and shotguns." Klein and his wife, Terry, later operated a bed and breakfast on the New Buffalo site.

New Mexican food

The dishes most associated with New Mexico. New Mexican food is much like Mexican food in that it is usually made up of some combination of tortillas, beans, and meat. The difference is that New Mexican food is often smothered in red or green chile, or both, and includes regional favorites like blue corn tortillas, posole, and sopaipillas.

New Mexican, The Santa Fe

The Santa Fe New Mexican vendor Awesome Valdez

Santa Fe's daily newspaper. First published in 1849, *The New Mexican* is one of the oldest papers in the West. Its current ownership began with the late Robert McKinney's acquisition of the paper in 1949. In 1976, he sold it to the Gannett Company, publishers of *USA Today*, but regained control in 1989. *The New Mexican* is now owned by his daughter, Robin McKinney Martin, who lives in the Santa Fe area.

The paper is well-regarded. Santa Fean George Johnson, author of eight books and a regular contributor to *The New York Times*, says of *The New Mexican*, "... there is probably not a town this size in the country with a better newspaper. In fact, I can't think of a town five, maybe ten, times this size with as good a daily, and that is because of the staff." *The New Mexican* endorsed Al Gore for president in 2000, John Kerry in 2004, and Barack Obama in 2008.

The New Mexican's editorial offices are on Marcy Street. In addition to the usual methods of distribution, the paper is sold by vendors, some flamboyantly outfitted, who stand in the medians near busy intersections.

New Mexico

The Land of Enchantment, a large, poor, often-overlooked Southwestern state. New Mexico is the nation's fifth-largest state in area. It is 45th in population density, with most of its 2,059,179 residents living along the Rio Grande corridor in the principal cities of Albuquerque, Las Cruces, Rio Rancho, and Santa Fe.

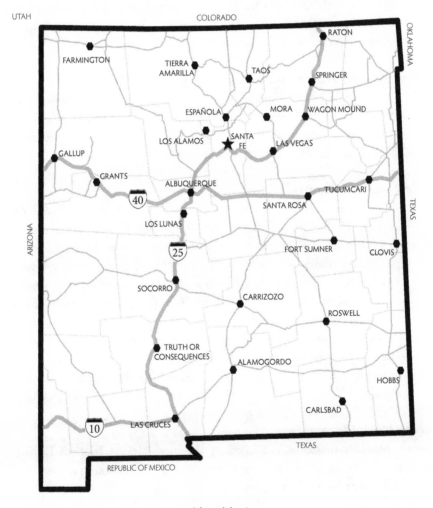

New Mexico

New Mexico's population includes a higher percentage of Hispanics (46.3 percent) than any other state, as well as a significant percentage of American Indians (8.5 percent). It is a poor state with many problems, a fact reflected in its perennially low placement in state rankings of social indicators. (See THANK GOD FOR MISSISSIPPI.)

Many Americans seem to be unaware of New Mexico, perhaps because it is eclipsed by Texas and Arizona. *New Mexico Magazine* runs a regular feature called "One of Our Fifty is Missing" in which readers submit amusing examples of how people elsewhere in the country have failed to recognize New Mexico as part of the United States.

New Mexico: A Biographical Dictionary 1540-1980

Multi-volume encyclopedia of the people of New Mexico. Author Don Bullis includes references to anyone he believes has had an impact on New Mexico. The first volume was published in 2007 and the second in 2008. Bullis plans to publish a third.

New Mexico History Museum

The newest addition to the four primary institutions in the Museum of New Mexico system. The 96,000-square-foot facility, which opened in May 2009, replaces the Palace of the Governors as the state's principal history museum. Named for former United States Senator Pete V. Domenici, the new building boasts a 210-seat auditorium, two smaller theaters, an education center, and the Spiegelberg Shop (named for one of Santa Fe's early merchant families).

The adjacent Palace of the Governors and Fray Angélico Chávez History Library are adjuncts to the museum. The History Museum's main entrance is on Lincoln Street, just behind the Palace of the Governors.

New Mexico Magazine

Monthly magazine published by the New Mexico Tourism Department. The magazine's first issue came out in 1924, making it the oldest state magazine in the country.

New Mexico Museum of Art

New Mexico Museum of Art

One of four primary institutions in the Museum of New Mexico system. The art museum's building dates to 1916 and represents one of the earliest revivals of Spanish Pueblo-style architecture. The museum also houses St. Francis Auditorium, a 450-seat venue for lectures and musical performances.

The New Mexico Museum of Art is on Palace Avenue, across Lincoln Avenue from the Palace of the Governors.

New Mexico music

Regional Hispanic music. Lyrics are usually in Spanish but often include English verses.

New Mexico music evolved from corridos, Spanish folk songs from the 16th and 17th centuries, that were later influenced by penitente hymns and Mexican ranchera and mariachi music. New Mexico music lacks the quick polka beat usually associated with the norteño style of northern Mexico and the tejano style of Texas.

New Mexico Politics with Joe Monahan

See MONAHAN, JOE.

New Mexico State University (NMSU)

New Mexico's second-largest institution of higher education, after the University of New Mexico. The land grant university serves the southern part of the state, with its main campus in Las Cruces and with branches in Alamogordo, Albuquerque, Carlsbad, and Grants. NMSU's Aggies sustain a fierce athletic rivalry with the University of New Mexico's Lobos.

New Mexico Territory

The land that later became the states of New Mexico and Arizona. In 1848, at the end of the Mexican-American War, Mexico ceded its northern provinces to the United States in the Treaty of Guadalupe Hidalgo. In 1850, the United States government named this land the New Mexico Territory. The Gadsden Purchase of 1853 added a strip of land along the Territory's southern border. The future state of New Mexico reached its current configuration when the Arizona Territory was separated from the New Mexico Territory in 1863.

nicho (NEE-cho)

A niche, or small cut-out, in an adobe wall. A nicho may be used to display a bulto, a pot, or some other work of art.

Nichols, John

(1940-) Taos resident and prolific writer. Nichols has authored 19 books and hundreds of essays. His first novel, *The Sterile Cuckoo*, was made into a 1969 movie starring Liza Minnelli. *The Milagro Beanfield War*, published in 1974, is the best known of his many works. A movie version of *Milagro*, directed by Robert Redford, was released in 1988.

Nichols moved from New York City to Taos in 1969. At that time, there was considerable tension between Anglo newcomers and native Taoseños, but Nichols, who is fluent in Spanish, became an advocate for Northern New Mexico's Hispanic culture. He described himself as "the propaganda arm for a group of quixotic Spanish-speaking septuagenarians locked in mortal combat with the United States government over the preservation of their water rights, their land, their culture, their very historical roots."

NM 14

New Mexico state route 14, a National Scenic Byway also known as the Turquoise Trail. The scenic road runs 47 miles south from Santa Fe through the old mining towns of Cerrillos, Madrid, and Golden before ending at I-40.

NMPolitics.net

See HAUSSAMEN, HEATH.

NMSU

See NEW MEXICO STATE UNIVERSITY.

Norteño (nor-TAIN-yo)

"Northerner," a native of El Norte, or Northern New Mexico. The term is usually applied to Hispanics rather than Anglos and Indians. (In Mexico, *norteño* refers to a person from northern Mexico, or to the style of music played there.)

Northern New Mexico

El Norte, "The North," the north-central part of New Mexico, where Pueblo Indians and descendants of the first Spanish settlers maintain their unique cultures. The area was originally known as the Rio Arriba, or "Upper River," region of the Rio Grande.

The word *culture* is often overused, but Northern New Mexico's Hispanic and Indian communities meet its strictest definition, which includes long ties to the land, a unique language, and a unique religion. The survival of these cultures in an increasingly homogenized society can be credited to the region's long isolation and to the communities' ongoing efforts to protect their traditions and values.

Northern New Mexico

Using the regional Spanish dialect as a guide, Northern New Mexico can be roughly defined by the "W" formed by I-25 to the south and east, US 550 to the west, and the Colorado border to the north. Though they are in "northern" New Mexico in the geographical sense, the cities of Clayton in the northeast and Farmington in the northwest are not culturally part of Northern New Mexico.

Northern New Mexico College

Longtime community college that became Northern New Mexico's second state-supported, four-year institution of higher education. (Highlands University, in Las Vegas, was the first.) The school has campuses in El Rito and Española.

Northern New Mexico-style architecture

Building style featuring adobe walls and a pitched roof, usually of metal. (Santa Fe-style buildings, which include both Spanish Pueblo and Territorial styles, have flat roofs.) Northern New Mexico style is closely associated with Santa Fe architect and homebuilder Betty Stewart. It is sometimes called "Betty Stewart style."

Nuevomexicano/a (new-AY-vo-meh-hee-CAHN-o/uh)

"New Mexican."

- O -

obelisk

Monument in the center of the Santa Fe Plaza, also called the Soldier's Monument. The pillar was erected in 1868 as a memorial to the Territory's Civil War dead and "the heroes who have fallen in various battles with savage Indians." In August 1974, the word "savage" was chiseled out by a mystery sculptor impersonating a city worker.

A smaller obelisk dedicated to frontiersman Kit Carson stands in front of the Federal Courthouse.

Ohkay Owingeh (O-kay o-WIN-gay)

Tewa-speaking Indian community formerly known as San Juan Pueblo, the largest of the Eight Northern Indian Pueblos.

The pueblo was the site of the first Spanish settlement in New Mexico. Don Juan de Oñate occupied it in 1598 and named it San Juan de los Caballeros – San Juan for St. John the Baptist and caballeros for the gentlemen on the expedition. Po'pay, the medicine man who led the 1680 Pueblo Revolt, was from San Juan Pueblo, though he was living in Taos Pueblo when he organized the uprising.

San Juan Pueblo reverted to its traditional name in 2005. *Ohkay Owingeh* means "Place of the Strong People." The Eight Northern Indian Pueblos Council is based at the pueblo. Ohkay Owingeh is 30 miles north of Santa Fe off NM 68.

ojo (O-ho)

"Eye." In the Southwest, *ojo* also means "spring."

Ojo Caliente (O-ho cah-lee-EN-tay)

Northern New Mexico community named for its mineral springs. Ojo Caliente, "Hot Spring," attracts visitors to its sodium, soda, lithia, iron, and arsenic mineral waters. The springs are part of a business that includes a restaurant, a gift shop, a massage clinic, and guest cottages. Ojo Caliente is 51 miles north of Santa Fe on US 285.

Ojo Sarco (SAR-co)

Northern New Mexico village on the High Road to Taos. Ojo Sarco, "Blue Spring" (*sarco* is a variant of *zarco*, which means "blue"), is on NM 76, 45 miles north of Santa Fe and one mile south of Las Trampas.

O'Keeffe, Georgia

(1887-1986) New Mexico's most celebrated artist. O'Keeffe first visited the state in 1917. She returned in 1929 at the invitation of Mabel Dodge Luhan, and, seduced by the light and the landscape, visited frequently over the following years. After the death of her husband, photographer Alfred Stieglitz, in 1949, she made New Mexico her permanent home. For 35 years, O'Keeffe alternated between her Abiquiu house and her seven-acre property on Ghost Ranch. She moved to Santa Fe in 1984, two years before her death at age 98.

O'Keeffe

Georgia O'Keeffe
on the cover of *New Mexico Magazine*

The Georgia O'Keeffe Museum opened in Santa Fe in July 1997.

Old St. Vincent Hospital

Downtown property that once housed St. Vincent Hospital. The hospital moved to St. Michael's Drive in 1977 and was renamed Christus St. Vincent Regional Medical Center in 2008.

The old St. Vincent facility on the corner of Palace Avenue and Paseo de Peralta was sold to the state and used as office space for many years.

The main hospital building was renamed La Villa Rivera, and the adjacent building, which had been used as a convent by the Sisters of Charity, was called Marian Hall.

In 2007, Drury Hotels, a Midwestern hotel chain, bought both buildings with the intention of converting them to hotels. The company's plans were approved by city authorities, including the H-Board, but the sluggish economy has delayed the project. (See also CHRISTUS ST. VINCENT REGIONAL MEDICAL CENTER.)

Old Santa Fe Association

Nonprofit organization founded in 1926 by John Gaw Meem and others to preserve Santa Fe's architectural and cultural heritage. The group was instrumental in the passage of the 1957 Historic Styles Ordinance, which empowers the Historic Design Review Board to control the architecture in certain sections of the city.

In 1961, the Historic Santa Fe Foundation was created as a separate entity to own and manage historic properties. This has allowed the Old Santa Fe Association to concentrate on its original mission of lobbying for preservation.

Oldest House in America

Old adobe house at 215 East DeVargas Street in Barrio de Analco. The house is said to have been built in 1646, but that is clearly an exaggeration as its vigas have been date-tested and are known to date from the mid-1700s.

Oñate, Don Juan de (own-YAH-tay)

(1552-1626) Spanish conqueror of New Mexico. Born in Mexico to a wealthy family, Oñate made his name as an Indian fighter on New Spain's northern frontier. In 1595, he was ordered by the Spanish crown to colonize the upper Rio Grande Valley, which had been explored by Coronado in 1540. Oñate led his expedition from El Paso del Norte in the spring of 1598. He and his men marched up the Rio Grande, stopping at Indian pueblos along the way, and established the first capital of Spanish New Mexico at the site of the present-day pueblo of Ohkay Owingeh.

Oñate developed a reputation for cruelty during his tenure as governor. In 1599, the people of Acoma Pueblo were subjugated after a fierce battle. When the pueblo surrendered, Oñate ordered its population enslaved and the amputation of one foot from each warrior over 25 years of age. In 1606, he was called back to Mexico City,

Don Juan de Oñate

where he was tried and convicted of cruelty to both colonists and Indians. He successfully appealed the conviction but is still a controversial character in New Mexico history. In 1999, protestors cut the right foot off of the equestrian statue of Oñate at the Oñate Monument and Visitor's Center near the village of Alcalde. In 2007, Indians from Acoma Pueblo protested the installation of an even larger equestrian statue of Oñate in El Paso.

Historian Marc Simmons's biography of Oñate is titled *The Last Conquistador: Juan de Oñate and the Settling of the Far Southwest*.

Oppenheimer, J. Robert

(1904-1967) Scientist in charge of the development of the atom bomb. In 1942, Oppenheimer chose Los Alamos as the laboratory site for the Manhattan Project. (Contrary to popular belief, Oppenheimer did not attend the Los Alamos Ranch School. He was familiar with Northern New Mexico from visits to a ranch on the Pecos River.)

When the first bomb was exploded at the Trinity Site in July 1945, Oppenheimer quoted a line from the *Bhagavad-Gita*: "Now I am become Death, the destroyer of worlds."

Ortiz Mountains (or-TEASE)

Mountain cluster 30 miles southeast of Santa Fe. The range is named for shepherd José Ortiz, whose 1828 discovery of gold flecks in the mountains precipitated the first gold rush west of the Mississippi.

The Ortiz Mountains are east of NM 14 (the Turquoise Trail), between Madrid and Golden.

Otowi Bridge

(*AH-tuh-wee)

Single-lane suspen-
sion bridge that crosses
the Rio Grande on the
road from Pojoaque to
Los Alamos. The old
bridge (a new one has
since been erected next
to the original) was
made famous in Peggy
Pond Church's 1959
book, *The House at

Otowi Bridge

Otowi Bridge: The Story of Edith Warner and Los Alamos. Edith Warner, a transplant from Pennsylvania, lived near the bridge from 1928 until her death in 1951. She ran a tearoom in her house and counted Indians from San Ildefonso Pueblo and scientists from Los Alamos among her friends and customers.

The Otowi gauge is an important measure of the flow of the Rio Grande below its confluence with the Rio Chama. The Otowi Station Book Store and Science Museum Shop is in Los Alamos next to the Bradbury Museum.

*Some people say O-tuh-wee, but AH-tuh-wee is more common. Peggy Pond Church thought the accent should be on the second syllable, but most people, including the staff at the Otowi Station Book Store, put the accent on the first.

outlet mall

See FASHION OUTLETS OF SANTA FE.

Outside magazine

Santa Fe's largest publishing concern. The magazine was founded by *Rolling Stone's* Jann Wenner in 1977 and sold to current owner Lawrence Burke two years later. *Outside* moved from Chicago to Santa Fe in 1994.

The monthly outdoor adventure magazine has a well-deserved reputation for good writing: *Into Thin Air* by Jon Krakauer and *The Perfect Storm* by Sebastian Junger both had their start as articles in the magazine. Frequent contributors include humorist Jack Handey and historian Hampton Sides, both of whom live in Santa Fe, and mountaineer Dave Hahn, who lives in Taos.

Outside is housed in a large Spanish Pueblo-style building on Market Street, between Sanbusco and the Railyard.

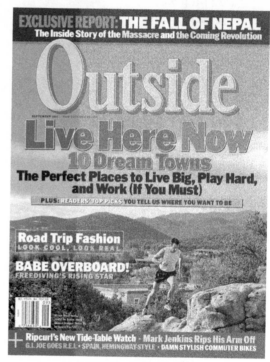

Outside magazine cover
featuring Santa Fe

owl

See TECOLOTE.

- P -

Padilla (puh-DEE-yuh)

Prominent New Mexico surname. Carmella Padilla is the author of *The Chile Chronicles: Tales of a New Mexico Harvest* and *Low 'n' Slow: Lowriding in New Mexico*. Los Padillas, named for its founding family, is a multi-generational Albuquerque street gang.

Pajarito Plateau (pah-ha-REE-toe)

Plateau on the east flank of the Jemez Mountains. Los Alamos, White Rock, and Bandelier National Monument are all on Pajarito, "Little Bird," Plateau. It was named by Edgar Lee Hewett.

Palace Avenue

One of Santa Fe's historic streets. Palace Avenue runs east for a mile and a half from Grant Avenue to its terminal intersection with Canyon Road. The one-block stretch that passes between the Plaza and the Palace of the Governors (for which the street is named) is pedestrian-only.

In World War II, Manhattan Project workers reported to a nondescript office at 109 East Palace Avenue, just east of the Plaza, where "gatekeeper" Dorothy McKibben issued them identification cards and directed them to Los Alamos. A 2005 book by Jennet Conant is titled *109 East Palace: Robert Oppenheimer and the Secret City of Los Alamos*.

Palace of the Governors

The oldest public building in continuous use in the United States, the center of Santa Fe tourist activity. The building on the north side of the Plaza is known for its long portal, where Indian artists sell handcrafted items to tourists.

The Palace was built in 1610, soon after Don Pedro de Peralta established Santa Fe as the capital of Spanish New Mexico. It served as the capitol of the colonial Spanish government until 1680, when rebellious Indians occupied it in the Pueblo Revolt. Don Diego de Vargas reclaimed the building for Spain in 1693, and it remained the colonial capitol for the next 128 years.

When Mexico gained freedom from Spain in 1821, the Palace became the provincial capitol of the Mexican government. Twenty-five years later, in 1846, during the Mexican-American War, it became the capitol of the United States Territory of New Mexico. Except for a few weeks in 1862 when it was occupied by invading Confederates, it served as the Territorial capitol until 1866, when a new building was erected.

The Palace of the Governors became the state's history museum in 1913. In 2009, it became an adjunct to the new and much larger New Mexico History Museum, which is adjacent to and behind the Palace.

Pancakes on the Plaza

The United Way's annual Fourth-of-July fundraiser. Over 500 volunteers assemble on the Plaza on the morning of the Fourth to serve pancakes to thousands of hungry celebrants. The event has been held since 1975. Santa Feans who rarely venture downtown do come to the Plaza for this event.

Paolo Soleri (POW-lo so-LAIR-ee)

Outdoor amphitheater on the grounds of the Santa Fe Indian School. The facility, which was designed by – and named for – Italian-American architect Paolo Soleri, was completed in 1965.

In 2008, the Santa Fe Indian School's governing body ordered the demolition of many old buildings on the campus. Paolo Soleri was slated for demolition but was spared when Indian School graduates whose commencement exercises had been held there and Santa Feans who had attended concerts at the venue successfully opposed its destruction.

paraje (puh-RAH-hay)

"Rest stop." In Spanish Colonial times, travelers on the Camino Real regularly camped at the same places. Some of these rest stops, like Belen and Bernalillo, eventually developed into towns.

parapet

On a Santa Fe-style building, that part of the exterior wall that extends above the flat roof. Water is channeled off the roof through canales, or rainspouts, that project through the parapet to the outside of the building.

The parapets of Territorial-style buildings are protected from the elements by two or three courses of red brick.

parciante (par-see-AHN-tay)

A person with water rights to an acequia. The parciantes are obligated to help with the annual spring cleaning of the acequia.

parroquia (puh-RO-key-uh)

"Parish church." St. Francis Cathedral was constructed around and over an existing parroquia, most of which was demolished and removed when the cathedral was completed. La Conquistadora's chapel is the sole vestige of the original parroquia.

pasatiempo (pah-suh-tee-EM-po)

"Pastime." *Pasatiempo* is the name of the arts and leisure insert in the Friday edition of *The New Mexican*. Santa Feans consult *Pasa* for movie reviews (where films are rated in chiles rather than stars), gallery openings, and other entertainment news.

Pasatiempo was also the name of the counter-Fiesta started in 1924 by Anglo artists and writers, including poet Witter Bynner and artist Will Shuster, who thought that the official Fiesta celebration overseen by Edgar Lee Hewett had become too serious and too commercial.

Paseo de Peralta (puh-SAY-o day per-ALL-tuh)

Santa Fe's horseshoe-shaped mini-beltway. "Paseo" wraps around downtown on the south, east, and north. It starts in the south at St. Francis Drive, runs east for a mile, swings north for half a mile, and then runs back west, re-intersecting St. Francis Drive a mile north of where it began. Downtown Santa Fe is loosely defined as the area bounded by Guadalupe Street on the west and Paseo de Peralta on the south, east, and north.

Because Paseo twice intersects both St. Francis Drive and Guadalupe Street, direction-givers should differentiate between the intersections.

Paseo de Peralta is named for Don Pedro de Peralta, the Spanish governor who founded Santa Fe.

Pasqual's

Small, downtown restaurant known for its breakfasts. The establishment is named for San Pasqual, the patron saint of kitchens and cooks. Katharine Kagel opened the 50-seat restaurant in 1979, and she still owns and operates it. Pasqual's is in downtown Santa Fe on the corner of Don Gaspar Avenue and Water Street, across the street from Doodlet's.

patrón (pah-TRONE)

"Boss" or "proprietor." At one time, *patrón* meant a wealthy landowner, but its current meaning is closer to the English word *patron* (PAY-trun), particularly in the political sense. Some critics say that New Mexico state government functions like a patrón system, with elected officials rewarding supporters with government jobs and contracts for public projects.

paz (pahz)

"Peace." The word is seen on an overpass above US 84/285 north of Santa Fe.

Peace Prayer Day

The Sikhs' annual community celebration. The June event draws people from all over the country to Española for a day of entertainment and prayers for peace. Peace Prayer Day was first held in 1986.

Pecos (*PAY-cose, PEH-cose)

Northern New Mexico village in San Miguel County. Pecos, population 1,392, is associated with the Pecos Benedictine Monastery, Pecos National Historical Park, and the old Forked Lightning Ranch, parts of which are now owned by movie stars Jane Fonda and Val Kilmer. *Pecos* is an Indian word of unknown origin.

The village is 23 miles southeast of Santa Fe via I-25 north (Pecos is southeast of Santa Fe, but the highway swings south before turning back north) and NM 50.

*Anglos say PAY-cose, while Hispanics say PEH-cose.

Pecos Benedictine Monastery

Monastery and retreat facility two miles north of the village of Pecos. The "double monastery" of the Our Lady of Guadalupe Abbey and the Olivetan Benedictine Sisters of Our Lady of Guadalupe Abbey houses both monks and nuns. The one-time dude ranch has been hosting retreats since the 1950s. Pecos Benedictine Monastery is 25 miles southeast of Santa Fe on NM 63.

Pecos National Historical Park

National park two miles south of the village of Pecos. The park encompasses the ruins of Pecos Pueblo, including what remains of its 17th-century Spanish Mission Church, and part of the Forked Lightning Ranch once owned by actress Greer Garson. Built in 1925, the Forked Lightning Ranch's main house was one of architect John Gaw Meem's first commissions. The park also includes a section of the Santa Fe Trail and two separate tracts of land associated with the Civil War Battle of Glorieta Pass.

The pueblo ruins portion of the park is open to the public for self-guided tours. The Forked Lightning Ranch and the Battle of Glorieta Pass sites require ranger-guided tours.

Pecos National Historical Park is on NM 63, 25 miles southeast of Santa Fe.

Pecos Pueblo

Abandoned pueblo southeast of Santa Fe. Once a major trade center with over 2,000 inhabitants, New Mexico's eastern-most pueblo both benefited and suffered from its location on the edge of the plains. The people of Pecos traded with the nomadic tribes to the east, but they were repeatedly attacked by those same tribes, and the pueblo gradually lost influence and population. In 1838, its last residents left Pecos and moved

to Jemez Pueblo, the only other Towa-speaking pueblo. Descendants of the Pecos refugees can still be found at Jemez.

The Pecos Pueblo ruins are now part of the Pecos National Historical Park.

Pecos River (*PAY-cose, PEH-cose)

New Mexico's second-longest river, after the Rio Grande. The Pecos heads in the Sangre de Cristo Mountains northeast of Santa Fe and meanders south through the eastern part of the state. It passes through or near Santa Rosa, Fort Sumner, Roswell, and Carlsbad before crossing into Texas, where it eventually drains into the Rio Grande.

The Pecos River is not usually referred to as the "Rio Pecos." Unlike the Rio Grande and the Rio Chama, which flow through Hispanic Northern New Mexico, the Pecos flows through the largely Anglo eastern part of the state, so it keeps its English appellation.

*The name sounds more like PAY-cuss or PECK-us when pronounced by cowboys in southeast New Mexico.

Pecos Wilderness

Northern New Mexico's high-country nature preserve. The wilderness area's 223,667 acres encompass lakes, waterfalls, grassy meadows, and some of the Sangre de Cristo Mountains' highest peaks, including Truchas Peak, the state's second-highest at 13,102 feet, and Santa Fe Baldy at 12,622 feet. The Pecos Wilderness is open to the public, though recreational use is limited to low-tech activities such as hiking, backpacking, and camping. Motorized vehicles and wheeled contrivances of any sort are prohibited.

The mountains were not always so protected. In the late 19th and early 20th centuries, uncontrolled hunting, grazing, and timbering killed off the native elk, sheep, grizzly bears, and wolves. Further depredation was avoided when the high country was designated a federally protected Primitive Area in 1933 and a Wilderness Area in 1964. Elk and Rocky Mountain bighorn sheep have been successfully reintroduced into the preserve.

Campers and hikers can access the Pecos Wilderness from various trailheads on its periphery, or they can drive 45 miles from Santa Fe and begin their hike from one of the vehicle-accessible campgrounds near Cowles, a settlement at the northern end of NM 63. The drive from Santa Fe takes about 70 minutes.

Hikers are advised to boil or filter water taken from streams in the Pecos Wilderness: the water may look pristine, but the intestinal parasite *giardia* is usually present. Those climbing to higher elevations in the summer should plan to be off the mountains early in the day to avoid afternoon thunderstorms.

Pedernal (peh-der-NALL)

Cerro Pedernal, the "Flint Hill" or "Flint Mountain," northwest of Abiquiu. The flat-topped prominence was the subject of many paintings

Pedernal

by Georgia O'Keeffe, who said, "God told me if I painted it enough, I could have it." After O'Keeffe died in 1986, there was brief talk of renaming the Pedernal in her honor, but the proposal was not adopted.

Peña Blanca (PAIN-yuh BLAHN-cuh)

A small community on NM 22 between Kewa Pueblo and Cochiti Pueblo. Peña Blanca, "White Rock," is 32 miles south of Santa Fe.

Peñasco (pen-YAH-sco)

Northern New Mexico village on the High Road to Taos. Peñasco, "Rocky Bluff," is actually a conglomeration of several small villages. It is 51 miles from Santa Fe.

pendejo/a (pen-DAY-ho/ha)

"Dummy" or "loser." The word derives from a slang word for a pubic hair.

penitente (pen-ih-TEN-tay)

A member of *Los Hermanos Penitentes*, "The Brotherhood of Penitents." The Catholic lay organization originated in the 17th and 18th centuries when there were too few ordained priests in New Mexico to sustain church ritual. While the volunteer penitentes filled the gap, their self-flagellation and other rites related to the Passion of Christ eventually brought them into disfavor with Church hierarchy. The Penitentes still exist but maintain a low profile, meeting in small adobe chapels called moradas. An example of a morada is open to the public at Las Golondrinas.

Penitentiary of New Mexico

Site of the most savage prison riot in United States history.

The first penitentiary in or near Santa Fe opened in 1885 near what is now the intersection of St. Francis Drive and Cordova Road. According to local legend, the city's leaders, when given a choice between a prison or a college, opted for the prison because it would provide more jobs. The Territorial Penitentiary incorporated a brick-making facility, and many homes in Santa Fe were constructed using its bricks. Santa Fe's Pen Road was named for the original prison.

Old Main complex at the Penitentiary of New Mexico

The current penitentiary, which was built in 1956 as a replacement for the aging original, is infamous for the riot that took place there in 1980. The bloody uprising in which captured guards were tortured and 33 suspected snitches were murdered and mutilated is considered the most savage prison riot in U.S. history.

The Penitentiary of New Mexico still houses state prisoners, although the Old Main complex where the riot took place is no longer used. The prison is 11 miles south of Santa Fe on NM 14.

Peralta, Don Pedro de

(per-ALL- tuh)

Don Pedro de Peralta

(circa 1584-1666) The Spanish governor of New Mexico who founded Santa Fe. An equestrian statue of Peralta stands in the federal oval between the Joseph M. Montoya Federal Building (which houses Santa Fe's main post office) and Grant Avenue. Paseo de Peralta is named for the city's founder.

peregrino/a (pair-eh-GREE-no/nuh)

"Pilgrim." In Northern New Mexico, the term usually refers to a person making the Easter pilgrimage to the Santuario de Chimayó.

Pet Parade

Saturday morning feature of Fiesta weekend, also known as the *Desfile de los Niños,* "Parade of the Children." The Pet Parade is open to children and their pets, real or stuffed, and adults are allowed to participate only if accompanied by a child. Motorized vehicles are banned, as are religious, political, and commercial messages.

Peregrinos

Peters, Gerald

(1947-) Santa Fe's most prominent entrepreneur. A native of Denver, Peters came to Santa Fe in the 1960s as a student at St. John's College and stayed to amass a fortune in art, real estate, and restaurants. He owns art galleries in Santa Fe and New York, downtown Santa Fe real estate that includes Sena Plaza and Plaza Mercado, and numerous restaurants, including La Casa Sena, the Blue Corn Cafe, and the Rio Chama Steakhouse. Peters is a controversial figure, admired by some for his ambition and work ethic and criticized by others for his aggressive business tactics.

petroglyph (PEH-tro-gliff)

A rock engraving. Over 20,000 images of people, animals, and symbols are carved into the rock of the Petroglyph National Monument on Albuquerque's west side. The vast majority were created by Indians, but there are also many Spanish contributions. The much-marketed Kokopelli character is derived from an Indian petroglyph.

Philmont Scout Ranch

The Boy Scouts' expansive Northern New Mexico retreat. The Scouts acquired the 215-square-mile ranch in 1938 as a gift from Oklahoma oil magnate Waite Phillips. Philmont Scout Ranch is 161 miles from Santa Fe, five miles south of the town of Cimarron.

picante (pee-CAHN-tay)

"Spicy." *Picante* should not be confused with *caliente*, "hot."

Pick, Sam

(1936-) Santa Fe's mayor from 1976 to 1978 and, again, from 1988 to 1994. Pick happily presided over the city's explosive growth in tourism. The gregarious mayor toured the country to promote Santa Fe and was unabashedly pro-development. This pleased some Santa Feans and appalled others, including his successor, Debbie Jaramillo, who won the mayoral office with her campaign against uncontrolled growth.

Sam Pick

Sam Pick's daughter, Cheryl Pick Sommer, owns Kaune's Neighborhood Market.

pico de gallo (PEE-co day GUY-o)

"Beak of the rooster," a spicy, uncooked salsa whose ingredients include tomatoes, onions, and chiles, all chopped into tiny pieces.

Picuris Pueblo (pick-uh-REESE)

One of the Eight Northern Indian Pueblos. Picuris, whose name means "those who paint," was once one of the largest pueblos. Today, it is one of the smallest. The Tiwa-speaking pueblo is too far from any highway to sustain a casino, but it does own a majority interest in the Hotel Santa Fe.

Picuris Pueblo is 57 miles north of Santa Fe via US 84/285, NM 68, and NM 75.

Pilar (pee-LAR)

Northern New Mexico community associated with rafting and kayaking on the Rio Grande rapids. The origin of the settlement's name is uncertain, but Pilar is a common woman's name in New Mexico. It derives from *Nuestra Señora del Pilar*, "Our Lady of the Pillar," a shrine to the Virgin Mary in Zaragoza, Spain.

Pilar is 53 miles from Santa Fe via NM 68, the low road to Taos.

pinche (PEEN-chay)

"Worthless" or "wretched," or, when applied to a person, "mean," "spiteful," or "miserly." John Pen La Farge concludes in *Turn Left at the Sleeping Dog* that Santa Fe has become pinche since its golden age between the 1930s and the 1950s.

When used as an adjective in front of an epithet, pinche is an insult enhancer, roughly equivalent to the English word *f***ing*.

Pink Adobe

Classic Santa Fe restaurant. Founder Rosalea Murphy started the restaurant in 1944 and opened the adjacent Dragon Room bar in 1978.

Murphy's family ran the establishment for seven years after her death in 2000 and then sold it to a Vermont-based company. The absentee owners made some unpopular changes, and "The Pink" and the Dragon Room quickly lost business. Rosalea's daughter, Priscilla Hoback, and her grandson, Joe Hoback, reclaimed the businesses in 2010.

The Pink Adobe is on Old Santa Fe Trail between Paseo de Peralta and East De Vargas Street.

piñon (peen-YOAN)

New Mexico's state tree. In late fall and winter, people look forward to aromatic piñon smoke wafting through the air, and the small pine's edible nuts are valued by New Mexicans of all species. The terrain of Northern New Mexico is technically known as "piñon-juniper woodlands."

Place Names of New Mexico, The

Robert Julyan's 1996 (revised in 1998) compilation of the names, histories, and locations of the cities, towns, villages, rivers, and mountains of New Mexico. The book is the successor to T.M. Pearce's *New Mexico Place Names*, which was published in 1965. Julyan's book is considered a must-have for those interested in New Mexico history.

Placitas (plah-SEE-tuss)

Upscale bedroom community. A *placita*, "little plaza," is an open space surrounded by a cluster of buildings. Placitas, population 4,977, is in

Sandoval County, seven miles east of Bernalillo, and 52 miles southwest of Santa Fe.

plague

Rare, life-threatening disease caused by the bacterial germ *Yersinia pestis*. The plague is usually transmitted to humans by fleas from infected wood rats, rock squirrels, prairie dogs, and other rodents. Dogs that run loose may become carriers when fleas from a dead or dying rodent jump from the dying host to the dog.

About half of the cases of plague in the United States occur in New Mexico, perhaps because there is such a diversity of wild rodents in the state. The greatest number of cases, 27, occurred in 1983; since then, New Mexico has averaged about six cases per year.

Plame Wilson, Valerie

See WILSON, VALERIE PLAME.

plaza

A central courtyard or square. Spanish Colonial towns and villages were organized around a plaza. The surrounding houses provided protection from Indians, and the plaza itself served as a community meeting place.

Plaza Bakery

Bakery and Häagen-Dazs ice cream store on the southwest corner of the Plaza, next to the Five & Dime General Store. Santa Feans like to point out that, per square foot, this is the most profitable Häagen-Dazs store in the country. It may well be true.

The Plaza Bakery building was the unlikely base of operations for the assassination of Josef Stalin's rival, Leon Trotsky. For decades, the building was occupied by Zook's Drugstore, a pharmacy established in 1913 by Lithuanian immigrant John Zook. In 1940, the store was being managed by his daughter, 33-year-old Katie Zook. KGB agent Josef Gregulevich, himself of Lithuanian descent and a suave ladies' man, established a friendship with Katie that allowed him to come and go from the store as he pleased. Gregulevich stayed with her both before and after he orchestrated Trotsky's murder, which was carried out in Mexico City in August 1940.

Plaza Café

The oldest restaurant on the Santa Fe Plaza. A diner was established in the Batts building on the Plaza's west side in 1905. Current ownership began with Greek immigrant Dionysi "Dan" Razatos, who bought the business in 1947. His sons now manage the family business, which was expanded to include the Plaza Café Southside in 2003.

The original Plaza Café suffered a kitchen fire in September 2010. It first appeared that the damage was slight, but further inspection revealed more problems, and the business remained closed for most of the 2011 tourist season. The restaurant, which was closed at the time, was used as a set for the movie *Odd Thomas*, but its name was changed to Pico Mundo Grill for the film.

Plaza, Santa Fe

The city's historical and cultural center. The grassy square is bounded by shops and restaurants on the south, east, and west. On its north side, Indian artists sell handcrafted jewelry and pottery under the portal of the Palace of the Governors. In the summer, the Plaza Bandstand program provides free musical entertainment Monday through Thursday.

pobrecito (po-bray-SEE-toe)

"Poor thing." The word is a combination of *pobre*, "poor," and the diminutive *ito*. It is often used ironically.

Poeh Center (PO-ay)

Pojoaque Pueblo's cultural museum. The Poeh Center was established in 1988 to showcase and preserve pueblo culture, particularly that of the Eight Northern Indian Pueblos. *Poeh* means "pathway" in Tewa, the language spoken at six of the Eight Northern Indian Pueblos. (Picuris and Taos pueblos speak Tiwa.)

The museum's permanent collection, called *Nah Poeh Meng*, "The

Santa Fe plaza

Continuous Path," uses visual art to relate the Pueblo experience. Audio guides are available in Tewa for Pueblo visitors and in English for Anglo visitors. The English-language guides are censored to protect sensitive aspects of Pueblo culture.

The Poeh Center is in Pojoaque, off US 84/285, 16 miles north of Santa Fe.

Pojoaque (*po-AH-key)

Community at the intersection of US 84/285, the road between Santa Fe and Española, and NM 502, the road between Pojoaque and Los Alamos. Stores, gas stations, Pojoaque Pueblo's Cities of Gold casino, and the Poeh Center line the stretch of US 84/285 that runs through Pojoaque. The community, population 1,907, is named for nearby Pojoaque Pueblo.

A Santa Fe resident once forgot her driver's license but wanted the free admission to state museums that is extended to locals on Sundays. The ticket-taker wrote out POJOAQUE on a piece of paper and asked the woman to pronounce it. She did, and was admitted without charge.

Pojoaque is 16 miles north of Santa Fe.

Pojoaque is a Spanish spelling of a Tewa word, so there are variations in its pronunciation, particularly the last syllable. The people who live in the pueblo for which the village is named as well as most Anglos say po-AH-*key*. Spanish speakers say po-AH-*kay*.

Pojoaque Pueblo (*po-AH-key)

The smallest and most financially ambitious of the Eight Northern Indian Pueblos. Pojoaque was once one of the largest pueblos, but its people left their land and joined other pueblos in the 1680 Pueblo Revolt. They returned in 1712 but dispersed again, 200 years later, after a 1912 smallpox epidemic. The pueblo was reconstituted in 1934 – with only 14 people – but its traditions had been lost. Up until 2001, Pojoaque had to invite dancers from other pueblos to help celebrate its feast day.

The Tewa-speaking pueblo benefits from its location near Santa Fe, Española, and Los Alamos. It has exploited this economic advantage with its Cities of Gold casino and Buffalo Thunder Resort. The pueblo also owns the horse racetrack at The Downs at Santa Fe.

Posuwaegeh, an alternative spelling of Pojoaque, is seen on an overpass above US 84/285. The word means "water gathering place."

*The pueblo's name is pronounced po-AH-*key*, not po-AH-*kay*.

politics

Santa Fe and Northern New Mexico are Democratic strongholds. The conventional wisdom is that the Democratic Party in El Norte consists of two wings: Hispanic Norteños who have been party loyalists since the New Deal, and progressive Anglos who tend to vote the issues rather than the party.

When the two wings cooperate, as they usually do, the Democrats are virtually unbeatable, but there are rare occasions when the factions disagree. In the 1997 election for the Third Congressional District, progressives who considered the party's nominee a political hack voted instead

| | PRESIDENTIAL CANDIDATES | | | | | |
| | WINNER AND PERCENTAGE OF POPULAR VOTE | | | | | |
YEAR	SANTA FE COUNTY	%	NEW MEXICO	%	UNITED STATES	%
1984	Mondale	52.1	Reagan	59.7	Reagan	58.8
1988	Dukakis	62.3	Bush	51.9	Bush	53.4
1992	Clinton	60.2	Clinton	45.9	Clinton	43.0
1996	Clinton	60.1	Clinton	49.2	Clinton	49.2
2000	Gore	64.6	Gore	47.9	Bush	47.9
2004	Kerry	69.4	Bush	49.8	Bush	50.7
2008	Obama	76.9	Obama	56.9	Obama	52.9

for the Green Party candidate. The Democratic vote was split, and the Republican Party candidate won the election. But that was an aberration. As the chart shows, Santa Fe County has consistently voted Democratic over the last seven presidential elections.

One occasionally hears Boulder, Colorado, described as the most liberal place in the Rocky Mountain West, but voting returns in the 2008 presidential election indicate otherwise. Boulder County gave Barack Obama 72 percent of its vote, but Santa Fe County gave him almost 77 percent.

Pond, Ashley, Jr.

(1872-1933) Detroit businessman who founded the Los Alamos Ranch School. Pond came to New Mexico to restore his health after contracting typhoid while serving as a Rough Rider in the Spanish-American War. He established the Los Alamos Ranch School in 1917 and remained associated with it until his death in 1933. Los Alamos's Ashley Pond is named for him. Ashley's daughter, Peggy Pond Church, authored *The House at Otowi Bridge*.

Poor New Mexico, so far from God and so close to Texas.

Quote attributed to Manuel Armijo, New Mexico's last governor in the Mexican Period. In truth, the line was probably stolen from Mexican dictator Porfirio Diaz, who is purported to have said: "Poor Mexico, so far from God, and so near the United States."

Po'pay (PO-pay or po-PAY)

Po'pay

(unknown-circa 1688) Leader of the 1680 Pueblo Revolt. In 1675, the Spanish publicly whipped Po'pay, a medicine man from San Juan Pueblo (now called Ohkay Owingeh), for practicing his native religion. Five years later, after moving to Taos Pueblo, he led the independent pueblos in a revolt that killed over 400 Spanish colonists and forced the rest back to Mexico.

Coordinating the timing of the attack among pueblos separated by distance and language required ingenuity. Po'pay had runners deliver a knotted cord to each pueblo, with instructions to undo one knot each day, and to attack on the day the last knot was undone. Paintings and sculptures of the Indian leader show him holding a knotted cord.

Po'pay is believed to have died before the Spanish returned to New Mexico in the reconquista of 1692 and 1693. In 1997, the New Mexico Legislature selected him as the second of two New Mexicans (Senator Dennis Chavez was the first) to be honored with a statue in the National Statuary Hall in the United States Capitol. Some Hispanics objected on the grounds that Po'pay does not represent a culturally harmonious New Mexico, but his defenders noted that the same could be said of the much-memorialized Don Juan de Oñate.

Po'pay's name was once spelled "Popé," but, because he was so violently anti-Spanish, it was changed to Po'pay to avoid the Spanish spelling.

population

The population within the Santa Fe city limits was 67,947 in the 2010 census. The Santa Fe Metropolitan Statistical Area (MSA), which includes all of Santa Fe County, had a population of 144,170 in 2010.

The Santa Fe MSA's population grew rapidly in the last three decades of the 20th century, but slowed in the first decade of the 21st century. As

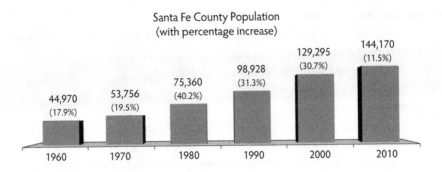

Santa Fe County Population
(with percentage increase)

44,970 (17.9%) — 1960
53,756 (19.5%) — 1970
75,360 (40.2%) — 1980
98,928 (31.3%) — 1990
129,295 (30.7%) — 2000
144,170 (11.5%) — 2010

the chart indicates, the MSA population grew by over 40 percent in the 1970s and by over 30 percent in the 1980s and 1990s, but slowed to 11.5 percent in the 2000s. The reason for the slowdown is unclear, although the increased cost of living in the Santa Fe area is assumed to be a big factor.

portal (pore-TALL)

A long, narrow porch. On a Spanish Pueblo-style building, the portal roof is supported by rough-hewn posts. Santa Fe's best-known portal is on the south face of the Palace of the Governors, where Indian artists sell handcrafted items to tourists.

Portal on the Palace of the Governors

posole (puh-SO-lay)

A thick stew made with dried corn that has been softened with lime or lye, pork, and red chile. Like bizcochitos, blue corn, and calabacitas, posole is a particularly New Mexican dish.

powwow

From the Algonquin *pau wau*, a gathering of Indian musicians, dancers, and other celebrants of Native culture. Most powwows are inter-tribal, which is why much of the singing consists of "vocables," tones and chants that can be sung by people who do not speak the same language.

Albuquerque's Gathering of Nations is billed as the largest powwow in North America.

prairie dog

Subterranean rodent ubiquitous in Santa Fe. Prairie dogs are among the most social of animals. They communicate using a "vocabulary" over 100 identified "words," including different warning sounds for the approach of a domestic dog, a coyote, a human, or a hawk. They can also be a problem. Prairie dogs have unearthed human bones and parts of coffins at Fairview Cemetery, and their many burrows near the runways at Santa Fe Municipal Airport delayed the airport's certification by the FAA. They can also carry plague.

Still, prairie dogs have many admirers, and their removal from construction sites is an ongoing source of contention between developers and animal rights activists. Santa Fe and Boulder, Colorado, are the only places where "humane relocation" of prairie dogs is mandated by law.

Northern New Mexico's Tusas Mountains are named for the creature. (*Tusa* means "prairie dog" in New Mexico Spanish.)

primo/a (PREE-mo/muh)

"Cousin." *Primo hermano* means "first cousin" and *primo segundo* means "second cousin," but most people use *primo* alone to refer to a cousin of any degree of consanguinity.

prison riot

Horrific riot at the New Mexico state penitentiary. In February 1980, rampaging inmates tortured guards and murdered and mutilated 33 suspected snitches in what has been called the most savage prison riot in United States history. *The Devil's Butcher Shop*, a 1983 book by Roger Morris, recounts the uprising in grisly detail.

pueblo

"Townsman" or "town." In the 16th and 17th centuries, Spanish conquistadors applied the term to Indians who lived in permanent villages, and to their villages. The word has much the same meaning today.

The Pueblo people are one of three Indian groups, the Apache and the Navajo being the others, living in present-day New Mexico. Descended from the ancient Anasazi and Mogollon, they are the only truly indigenous New Mexicans. They have survived invasions by the Apache and the Navajo, who appeared between 1300 A.D. and 1500 A.D., by the Spanish in 1598, and by the Americans in 1846. Still, in most cases, they continue to live on – if only on a portion of – their original lands.

New Mexico's Pueblo communities speak different languages and follow different religious practices, so "Pueblo" is not a specific tribal designation. It is best to describe a person as being from, or a member of, a specific pueblo.

In reference to a place, a pueblo can be the ruins of an abandoned village, like Pecos Pueblo, or one of the 19 sovereign political entities recognized by the state of New Mexico and the federal government. The eight pueblos north of Santa Fe – Nambé, Ohkay Owingeh, Picuris, Pojoaque, San Ildefonso, Santa Clara, Taos, and Tesuque – have formed a consortium called the Eight Northern Indian Pueblos.

Pueblo Bonito (bo-NEE-toe)

"Beautiful Village," the largest of the ruins structures at Chaco Can-

Charles Lindbergh's 1929 aerial view of Pueblo Bonito

yon. The building contained over 30 kivas and up to 800 rooms. As many as 1,500 Anasazi once lived in Pueblo Bonito.

pueblo etiquette

Guidelines for visitors to New Mexico's pueblos. Outsiders are often welcome at the pueblos, including on feast days and at dance performances, but they should observe certain rules when visiting.

When to go – Call ahead to make sure that the pueblo is accepting visitors. Not all dances and ceremonies are open to the public.

Where to go – Stay in the public area. Do not wander into non-public buildings and do not enter a private home without an invitation.

What to bring – Yourself. Do not bring alcohol, drugs, pets, or firearms into the pueblo.

Photographs – Ask about the pueblo's general policy. If photography is allowed, there may be a fee, and the fee could be higher for a video camera. Always ask permission before taking a picture of an individual or private property.

Dances and ceremonies – Watch quietly, do not applaud, and do not ask for an explanation of the proceedings.

Cell phones – Turn your cell phone off and leave it in your pocket. Ringtones can disrupt the proceedings, and a mere glance at a cell phone could be mistaken for picture-taking.

Invitation to eat in a private home – Never ask to be invited but accept graciously if an invitation is extended. Do not offer a tip, and do not linger too long after eating.

Pueblo Revival

Inexact name for Spanish Pueblo-style architecture, which is a combination of Spanish building techniques and Pueblo Indian forms. "Pueblo Revival" is a misnomer because it ignores the Spanish contribution.

Pueblo Revolt

Seventeenth-century Indian uprising that drove the Spanish out of New Mexico. The pueblos had long resented being heavily taxed and forced to provide labor, but the immediate cause for the revolt was the Spanish effort to eradicate Native religious practices.

The uprising was organized in Taos Pueblo by a San Juan Pueblo (now called Ohkay Owingeh) medicine man named Po'pay. In August 1680, a combined Pueblo Indian force killed over 400 Spanish colonists before allowing the rest to escape to Mexico.

The Indians retained control of New Mexico until Don Diego de Vargas led a Spanish army back to the region in the reconquista of 1692 and 1693. The Spanish were more tolerant of Native religious practices after their return.

The Pueblo Revolt and DeVargas's reconquista are critical events in New Mexico's colonial history. As might be expected, the descendants of the Spanish settlers and the descendants of the Pueblo rebels have differing views on how these events should be commemorated.

"Tewa Tales of Suspense," Santa Clara Pueblo artist Jason Garcia's perspective on the Pueblo Revolt

puerco (PWAIR-co)

"Pork." Also "muddy," as in the *Rio Puerco*, "Muddy River."

Puye Cliffs National Historic Landmark (POO-yay)

Cliff and mesa-top dwellings once inhabited by ancestors of the people of present-day Santa Clara Pueblo. The dwellings were occupied from 1200 A.D. to 1580 A.D., when their approximately 2,000 inhabitants moved 10 miles west to the Rio Grande, probably because of drought. According to Santa Clara legend, the refugees were aided in their move by a friendly black bear that led them from Puye to the pueblo's current location.

The cliffs were closed to the public for several years due to erosion caused by the Cerro Grande fire of 2000, but Santa Clara Pueblo now offers guided tours of the site. The Puye Cliffs Welcome Center is 30 miles from Santa Fe, off NM 30, a few miles north of Black Mesa. The ruins are seven miles west of the welcome center.

- Q -

quarto centenario (KWAR-toe sen-teh-NAR-ee-o)

Alternate spelling for a 400-year anniversary. (See CUARTOCENTENARIO.)

que (kay)

"What," or "which." The word can also mean "how," as in the Spanglish "Que cute!"

"Que no?" is a rhetorical interrogatory sometimes used to end a sentence. It is the Norteño equivalent of the Canadian "Eh?"

quesadilla (kay-suh-DEE-yuh)

A dish named for its main ingredient, *queso,* "cheese." A quesadilla can be made from one tortilla, which is filled with cheese and other ingredients and then folded onto itself, or from two tortillas, one on the bottom and one on the top. Both flour and corn tortillas are used. Quesadillas are often cut into wedges before being served.

Questa (KWEH-stuh)

Northern New Mexico village on the Enchanted Circle, 22 miles north of Taos. The village's population is 1,770. *Questa* means "ridge" or "slope."

quinceañera (kin-see-en-YEH-ra)

Celebration of a Hispanic girl's 15th birthday. (*Quince* means "fifteen.") A quinceañera is usually an elaborate affair, similar to a debutante's coming-out ball or a Sweet 16 party, with fancy dresses, good food, and music.

- R -

racino (ray-SEE-no)

A horse racetrack with slot machines and, sometimes, casino games. In New Mexico, the state lottery, fraternal and veterans organizations, Indian casinos, and racinos are the only entities legally permitted to offer gaming. Of the five racinos in New Mexico, The Downs at Albuquerque is the closest to Santa Fe.

Rael (rye-EL)

Hispanic surname associated with the theory that crypto Jews moved to New Mexico to escape the Spanish Inquisition. Historian Stanley Hordes suggests that the name may have been shortened from "Israel."

Rail Runner Express

Commuter train that runs from Belen to Santa Fe. The Rail Runner is one of two big infrastructure projects initiated during Governor Bill Richardson's administration, Spaceport America being the other.

Rail Runner Express

The commuter train is popular with people who live in Albuquerque or Rio Rancho but work in Santa Fe. The 85-minute ride from downtown Albuquerque to the Santa Fe Railyard is longer than the 60 minutes it takes to drive, but the train is cheaper; allows the commuter to read, sleep, or access the Internet; and offers views of the real New Mexico, including backyard burros, chickens, horses, and hornos. (Photography is prohibited, however, while the train passes through pueblo land.)

The Rail Runner's Santa Fe depot is in the Railyard, in the California Mission-style building next to Tomasita's restaurant.

Railyard, The Santa Fe

Fifty-acre parcel of city-owned property on Santa Fe's near Westside. The Santa Fe Railway owned the property from 1880 to 1995, when Mayor Debbie Jaramillo organized its purchase by the city. SITE Santa Fe, El Museo Cultural, Warehouse 21, the Farmers Market, Tomasita's restaurant, and the train depot for the Rail Runner Express are all on or adjacent to Railyard property. The Railyard includes a 10-acre park and a public plaza.

RainbowVision

Santa Fe's – and the nation's – first full-service retirement community for gays, lesbians, bisexuals, and transgenders. The 146-unit complex, which includes a community center with a gym, spa, bar, and restaurant, opened in June 2006. The development ran into financial difficulties and filed for Chapter 11 bankruptcy protection in 2011. RainbowVision is on Rodeo Road, just east of St. Francis Drive.

raja (RAH-ha)

Split juniper branches or split cedar branches (also called *cedros*) that are layered above the vigas in Spanish Pueblo-style ceiling construction. Latillas, which are not split, are more common than rajas.

Rancho de Chimayó

Historic restaurant in the village of Chimayó, a favorite with tourists and travel writers. Rancho de Chimayó was established in 1965 in the ancestral home of Arturo and Florence Jaramillo and is still owned and operated by Florence. It serves traditional New Mexican food but is particularly known for its Chimayó cocktail, made with tequila and apple cider, and for its carne adovada. The Rancho operation includes the restaurant, gift shops, and rooms for rent in the adjacent hacienda. Rancho de

Ristras at Rancho de Chimayó

Chimayó is on County Road 98 (Juan Medina Road), 28 miles north of Santa Fe.

Rancho Viejo (RAN-cho vee-AY-ho)

"Old Ranch," Santa Fe County's most ambitious housing development. Rancho Viejo's original developers bought up ranch land south of the city in the 1980s. They donated the campuses of Santa Fe Community College and the Institute for American Indian Arts and made application for the necessary permits. Homebuilding began in the late 1990s when Suncor, a large Arizona company, obtained rights to 2,500 acres of the land with an option for an additional 10,000 acres. The sprawling development currently has about 1,100 occupied homes.

Rancho Viejo lost momentum in the recession. Suncor's longtime New Mexico representative, Ike Pino (brother of former Santa Fe Mayor Debbie Jaramillo), quit the project and took a job with the city, and Suncor sold the development back to its original owners in 2010. Rancho Viejo is south of I-25, about 12 miles from the Santa Fe Plaza.

Ranchos de Taos (RAHN-chos day TA-os)

Northern New Mexico village known for its San Francisco de Asis Church, a wide-hipped adobe building that was a favorite subject of artist Georgia O'Keeffe and photographer Ansel Adams. Ranchos de Taos is also the burial site of actor-director Dennis Hopper.

San Francisco de Asis Church in Ranchos de Taos

According to *The Place Names of New Mexico*, *ranchos de* means something close to the English word "suburb." Ranchos de Taos was so named because Indians from Taos Pueblo were farming there when the Spanish arrived in 1716.

The village, population 2,518, is five miles south of the town of Taos, at the intersection of NM 518 (the High Road to Taos) and NM 68 (the low road to Taos).

Randall Davey Audubon Center

Historic house and 135 acres at the upper end of Upper Canyon Road. Randall Davey, an artist of some renown, bought the house in 1920 and lived in it until his death in 1964. The National Audubon Society acquired the property in 1983 and now uses it as an environmental education center and wildlife refuge. The landscaped grounds are available for weddings and other functions.

Raton (ra-TONE)

City whose name means "mouse" or "squirrel." Raton, population 6,885, came into being in 1880 when the Santa Fe Railway was run through Raton Pass, eight miles north of the city. In 1986, a resident suggested changing the name from Raton to something more appealing, but the idea was rejected by voters. Raton is off I-25, 165 miles northeast of Santa Fe.

rattlesnake

Northern New Mexico's only venomous snake. Rattlesnakes are rarely seen within Santa Fe city limits, but they are common in the surrounding environs. Prairie rattlers are the most numerous, but diamondbacks are found in drier areas.

About 100 people are bitten by rattlesnakes in New Mexico each year, though deaths are extremely rare. Bite victims are advised not to waste time trying to suck out the venom but to get to a hospital or other source of antivenin as soon as possible. Volunteers affiliated with The Wildlife Center will relocate rattlesnakes upon request.

raven

The *Corvus Corax*, Santa Fe's unofficial greeter. Ravens are found in many parts of the United States, but they appeal to people more in Northern New Mexico. Gallery owner Linda Durham had moved from New York and was living in Cerrillos in the 1960s when she began to question her purpose in New Mexico. She told *The New Mexican*, "I stood on the edge of a big cliff and asked for God to give me a sign. 'I don't know why I'm here. Is there a reason?' Just then, two big ravens flew over my shoulder and hung in the updraft, looking at me. For the rest of my life, whenever I see ravens, I am respectful."

"Raven Head"
by Beth Surdut

Ravens are an increasingly popular art theme. Artist Beth Surdut moved to Santa Fe from Florida specifically to create a project called "Listening to Raven." She told *The New Mexican*, "When I started drawing them, a raven came to see me every single day. He would come and he would stand on the turquoise blue railing that went up to the porch. If he couldn't find me on the front porch then he would go to the corrugated tin roof in the back and make noise and dance on it until I came out."

reconquista (reh-con-KEY-stuh)

The "reconquest" of New Mexico by the Spanish after the Pueblo Revolt of 1680. In 1692, newly appointed governor Don Diego de Vargas led an expedition from El Paso del Norte to reclaim New Mexico from the rebellious Pueblo Indians who had expelled the Spanish 12 years earlier. After a long trek up the Camino Real, DeVargas's men marched into Santa Fe, surrounded the Palace of the Governors, and convinced its occupiers to surrender. This peaceful entry into Santa Fe in 1692 is the entrada, "procession," celebrated in the annual Fiesta de Santa Fe.

DeVargas marched back to El Paso del Norte with plans to return to Santa Fe permanently the following year. When he returned in 1693, however, he found that the Indians had reconsidered their surrender. This time, the Spanish reclaimed Santa Fe by force and spent the next few years subjugating the defiant pueblos. It was during this period that the statue of the Virgin Mary that accompanied DeVargas from El Paso del Norte became known as La Conquistadora.

Red or green?

New Mexico's official state question. Waiters ask "Red or green?" to determine whether diners prefer red or green chile with their meal. Those who want both answer "Christmas," which is the official state answer.

Red River

Northern New Mexico tourist destination. Once a mining town, Red River now caters to visitors interested in skiing, off-roading, jeep tours, and other outdoor recreational pursuits. It is particularly popular with tourists from Texas and Oklahoma.

Like Angel Fire and Eagle Nest, Red River is sometimes called an "Anglo village," one established in the 19th or 20th century, as opposed to a much older, historically Hispanic village like Chimayó or Truchas. Red River is on the Enchanted Circle, 34 miles north of Taos via NM 522 and NM 38.

Red Sky at Morning

1968 coming-of-age novel by the late Santa Fe author Richard Bradford. The book recounts the trials of Josh Arnold, an Anglo transplant to the fictional New Mexico village of Corazon Sagrado during World War II. A movie version of the book starring Richard Thomas was released in 1971.

refritos (reh-FREE-toes)

Short for *frijoles refritos*, "refried beans." The beans, usually pinto beans, are served as an ingredient in bean burritos and as a separate side dish. Refritos are a staple of Mexican and New Mexican cuisine.

repisa (reh-PEE-suh)
"Shelf" or "mantelpiece."

Reporter, Santa Fe
See *SANTA FE REPORTER.*

reredos (reh-RAY-dose)
Painted or carved screens displayed behind an altar. Like retablos and bultos, reredos are considered a Spanish colonial art form.

Cristo Rey Church was designed to showcase the stone reredos that once graced *La Castrense*, a Spanish military chapel that stood on the Santa Fe Plaza until it was demolished in 1859. The reredos were stored at St. Francis Cathedral before their installation in Cristo Rey in 1940.

retablo (reh-TAH-blow)
A two-dimensional santo, or representation of a saint. Retablos are usually painted on wooden panels.

ribbon shirt
Loose-fitting shirt decorated with ribbons. The shirts were originally made by Plains Indians from cloth acquired in trade. The style was patterned after the wide-sleeved shirts worn by early white settlers, with ribbons added for decoration. In Northern New Mexico, ribbon shirts are worn by Anglos, Hispanics, and Indians on special occasions like feast days and fiestas.

Bill Richardson

Richardson, Bill
(1947-) New Mexico's governor from 2003 to 2011. William Blaine Richardson was born in California to an American father and Mexican mother and spent his

childhood in Mexico City, where his father was a Citibank executive. After prep school in Massachusetts, he attended Tufts University, where he was a star pitcher on the baseball team. (For years, he claimed to have been drafted by the major leagues, but this was disproved by the *Albuquerque Journal* in 2005.)

Richardson began his political career as a congressional staffer in Washington. Believing that he would do well in a heavily Hispanic state, he moved to New Mexico to run for Congress in 1978. Defeated in his first bid for office, he was eventually elected to represent the state's newly created and heavily Democratic Third Congressional District, which includes Northern New Mexico. Richardson held the seat until 1997, when President Clinton appointed him ambassador to the United Nations. In 1998, he was appointed secretary of energy and served in that capacity until the end of the Clinton administration.

The ex-congressman was elected governor of New Mexico in 2002 and reelected in 2006. The Richardson administration will be remembered for the Rail Runner Express, Spaceport America, attracting movie-makers to the state through generous subsidies, and, in the end, allegations of cronyism and financial impropriety.

Governor Richardson campaigned for the Democratic nomination for president in the 2008 election but gave up after poor showings in the early caucuses and primaries. He ultimately endorsed Barack Obama over Hillary Clinton, an act that earned him the enmity of Bill Clinton and an appointment as secretary of commerce in the new Obama administration. He was asked to withdraw before the confirmation hearings, however, because of an ongoing investigation into pay-to-play practices in New Mexico.

Richardson was named chairman of Global Positioning Strategies, a Washington, D.C.-based consulting firm, after leaving the Governor's Mansion in 2011. He maintains an office and a residence in Santa Fe.

rico/a (REE-co, REE-cuh)
"Rich," usually a reference to a rich man or woman.

Rinconada (rin-cone-AH-dah)
Northern New Mexico community at the junction of three creeks.

Rincon means "corner" but can also mean "crossroads," and the village is probably named for its location at the creek junction. Rinconada is 48 miles north of Santa Fe on NM 68 (the low road to Taos), near the county line between Rio Arriba and Taos counties.

rio (REE-o)

"River." In New Mexico, waterways like the Rio Grande that were named by the Spanish are always called rios. Those that run through the mostly English-speaking parts of the state, like the Pecos River, are usually called rivers.

Rio Abajo (uh-BAH-ho)

"Lower river," one of two distinct regions of New Mexico in the Spanish Colonial Period. New Mexico's early Spanish settlements were concentrated along the Rio Grande and, because Apache raiders controlled southern New Mexico, most of them were north of Belen.

In the 18th and 19th centuries, this colonized part of New Mexico was divided into the Rio Abajo, or "Lower River," region and the Rio Arriba, or "Upper River," region. The Rio Abajo stretched north from Belen to La Bajada Hill. Until the 20th century, this relatively flat land was dominated by a few wealthy landowners, just as it is now dominated by the ever-expanding city of Albuquerque.

Unlike Rio Arriba, which has been preserved in a county name, Rio Abajo is not often heard in contemporary New Mexico.

Rio Arriba (uh-REE-buh)

"Upper river," that part of Spanish New Mexico now known as Northern New Mexico. The Rio Arriba region is more mountainous than the Rio Abajo, which accounts for its history of comparatively smaller land holdings and more isolated villages.

Rio Arriba County

"Upper River" County, the heart of Northern New Mexico. Old traditions are strong here, which is why tourists flock to the churches, restaurants, and shops in picturesque villages like Chimayó and Truchas.

Like the rest of Northern New Mexico, Rio Arriba County has experienced great social tension as native Hispanics struggle to reach a balance between their traditional lifestyle and the unrelenting pressure of mainstream America. In 1967, the Alianza, a group of Nuevomexicanos whose members believed that their ancestors had been cheated out of their land by unscrupulous Anglos, raided the Rio Arriba County Courthouse in Tierra Amarilla.

Today, the tension is reflected in the disheartening rate of drug abuse. From 2001 to 2005, Rio Arriba County led the nation in drug overdoses with 42.5 deaths per 100,000 residents. (The national rate for the same period was 7.3 per 100,000.) The problem does not seem to be abating: from 2006 to 2008, the county rate was 52.2 deaths per 100,000, and in 2010, state health officials expressed concern that overdoses among people under 21 were on the rise.

Rio Arriba County is due north of Santa Fe County.

Rio Chama (CHA-muh)

One of Northern New Mexico's principal rivers, a major tributary of the Rio Grande. The Rio Chama heads just over the Colorado border and flows south into New Mexico, passing through or near the villages of Chama, Tierra Amarilla, and Abiquiu before its confluence with the Rio Grande just north of Española. The river is popular with fishermen, rafters, and kayakers. It is also the conduit for water delivered to New Mexico via the San Juan-Chama Diversion Project.

Unlike the Rio Grande, which has only a Spanish name, and the Pecos River, which is usually called by its English name, the Chama is known as both the Rio Chama and the Chama River.

Gerald Peters's Rio Chama bar and restaurant is next door to the Roundhouse on Old Santa Fe Trail. Politicians and lobbyists crowd the place during legislative sessions.

Rio en Medio (MAY-dee-o)

Northern New Mexico community named for the "middle river" that flows through it before emptying into the Santa Cruz reservoir. Rio en Medio is northeast of Tesuque, at the end of NM 592.

Rio Grande (*GRAND, GRAHN-day)

New Mexico's defining "Big River." The Rio Grande heads in the Rocky Mountains of southwest Colorado on the eastern slope of the Continental Divide. It enters New Mexico 40-odd miles northwest of Taos and flows down the middle of the state for about 470 miles to El Paso. From there, the river delineates the 1,248-mile border between Texas and Mexico before finally emptying into the Gulf of Mexico.

Because access to water is crucial, the Rio Grande corridor is, and has always been, the most heavily populated part of New Mexico.

*The pronunciation of *grande* in the river's name varies. Some Anglos say GRAND. Others, including all Spanish speakers and most local newscasters, say GRAHN-day. Either is acceptable in the name of the river.

Rio Grande cutthroat trout

New Mexico's state fish. The cutthroat trout once thrived throughout the Rio Grande basin, but, because of shallow and polluted water, it is now found in only 10 percent of its historic range. The fish have been stocked in the Santa Fe Municipal Watershed's reservoirs in an attempt to increase their population.

"Santa Fe Current"
by Collette Hosmer

Twenty-seven cutthroat trout sculpted from granite appear to leap from a bed of gravel in a permanent art installation at the Santa Fe Community Convention Center.

Rio Grande Gorge

Deep river canyon that runs from northwest to southeast of Taos. The gorge is part of a longer rift valley that was created by tectonic shifts.

This means that, although the Rio Grande runs through the gorge, the river did not create it – the gorge was there first, and the water simply followed the riverbed of least resistance. The canyon reaches its greatest depth, about 800 feet, just south of Taos. White-water rafters and kayakers navigate the river through the 17-mile stretch of the gorge called the Taos Box.

Rio Grande Gorge Bridge

Cantilever truss bridge that spans the Rio Grande Gorge. At 650 feet above the river, the bridge offers spectators a dramatic view of the gorge. It has been the scene of numerous suicides, a few accidental deaths, and the murder of an Española man who was thrown off of it by drug-addled car thieves. The Rio Grande Gorge Bridge was featured in the movies *Natural Born Killers* (1994) and *Terminator Salvation* (2009). It is 11 miles west of Taos, on US 64.

Rio Grande Gorge Bridge

Rio Grande Sun

Weekly subscription newspaper based in Española. Established in 1956 by publishers Robert and Ruth Trapp, the Wednesday paper primarily covers Española and Northern New Mexico but often scoops the big-city papers with its investigative pieces on statewide issues. The *Sun* does not make political endorsements.

Rio Rancho (REE-o RAN-cho)

New Mexico's third-largest (behind Albuquerque and Las Cruces) and fastest-growing city. Rio Rancho's population, currently 87,521, grew by 69 percent between 2000 and 2010, surpassing Santa Fe's population sometime in 2007.

Rio Rancho got its start in the 1960s and 1970s as Rio Rancho Estates, an aggressively marketed retirement community. (Art imitates life in David Mamet's 1984 play *Glengarry Glen Ross*. The references in the play to a development called Rio Rancho are believed to be based on the actual Rio Rancho Estates.)

The city boomed in the 1980s and 1990s, in part because of the growth of resident Intel Corporation, but mostly because its housing prices compared so favorably with those of Albuquerque and Santa Fe. The city still benefits from the disparity. A Rio Rancho spokesman commented that residents feel more secure because of the presence of so many police cars driven home by officers who work in other jurisdictions but live in Rio Rancho.

The city is just west of I-25, nine miles north of Albuquerque and 50 miles southwest of Santa Fe.

ristra (REE-struh)

String of red chiles. The chiles are strung together for drying and storage, and for decoration. (Ristras sold for decoration have been treated with chemicals to preserve their color and gloss. They are not edible.)

Roadrunner

roadrunner

New Mexico's state bird. The long-legged cuckoo is the mascot for the New Mexico School for the Deaf and the logo for the Rail Runner Express. Roadrunners are occasionally seen in Northern New Mexico but are more common in the southern part of the state, where it is both hotter and drier.

Rociada (ro-see-AH-duh)

Northern New Mexico valley community whose name means "sprinkled with dew." Rociada is 95 miles northeast of Santa Fe via I-25 north, NM 518 north, and NM 94 north.

rodeo (*RO-dee-o)

An exhibition of cowboy skills. The word derives from *rodear*, "to surround" or "to encircle," and was first used to describe a cattle roundup.

*In Santa Fe, when speaking of the Rodeo Grounds or Rodeo Road, the Anglo RO-dee-o is the correct pronunciation. The Spanish ro-DAY-o is appropriate only in a Spanish phrase like *Rodeo de Santa Fe*.

Rodeo
de
Santa Fe

Rodeo de Santa Fe (ro-DAY-o)

Santa Fe's annual cowboy competition. The rodeo was inaugurated in 1949 and is one of the oldest on the Professional Rodeo Cowboys Association circuit. Festivities begin in late June with a parade featuring 70-odd cowboys and cowgirls riding behind the event's mascot, *El Toro Diablo*, "The Devil Bull," which was designed by Zozobra creator Will Shuster. The rodeo is held at the Rodeo Grounds on Rodeo Road.

Rogers, Millicent

(1902-1953) Madcap Standard Oil heiress who settled – and settled down – in Taos. Rogers lived a glamorous and tumultuous life, including three failed marriages, in New York and Europe in the 1920s and 1930s.

Her life changed when she moved to Taos in 1947. Always interested in fashion and art, Rogers adapted Indian clothing to her own style and started collecting pottery from Taos Pueblo, as well as Spanish Colonial art and paintings from her Anglo friends in the Taos art colony. At her death at age 50, the woman who wore furs and diamonds for most of her life was buried in Taos in a simple Indian blouse and skirt.

In 1956, one of her three sons established the Millicent Rogers Museum to showcase her collection of art, textiles, and jewelry. The museum is four miles north of the Taos plaza.

Rosario Cemetery (ro-SAH-ree-o)

Santa Fe cemetery across from DeVargas Mall, adjacent to the much larger Santa Fe National Cemetery. Among Rosario's 7,500-plus graves are those of Fray Angélico Chávez and two Japanese men who died in the Santa Fe internment camp.

During holidays, Rosario Cemetery can be a festive place, particularly in contrast to the staid National Cemetery. At Christmas, Rosario's graves are bordered by farolitos and its trees are decorated with ornaments.

Rosario Chapel

Historic chapel on the grounds of Rosario Cemetery. Rosario Chapel is situated on the approximate site of Don Diego de Vargas's encampment during his 1693 reconquista of New Mexico. The chapel was built in 1807 and expanded in 1914.

According to legend, DeVargas was so grateful for his victory over the rebellious pueblos that he vowed that each year the statue of the Virgin Mary known as La Conquistadora would be returned to the spot of his encampment for a novena of masses. Every year, in June or July, depending on the religious calendar, La Conquistadora is taken from her shrine in St. Francis Cathedral and carried in a procession to Rosario Chapel for the novena.

Roswell (ROZ-well)

New Mexico's fifth most populous city, behind Albuquerque, Las Cruces, Rio Rancho, and Santa Fe. Roswell, population 48,366, is famous for a supposed UFO incident that is said to have occurred there in 1947. The city is home to the New Mexico Military Institute and is the birthplace of artist Peter Hurd, singer John Denver, and actress Demi Moore. Roswell is 192 miles southeast of Santa Fe.

Rothenberg, Susan

(1945-) Internationally known contemporary artist and Santa Fe-area resident. Rothenberg lives on a 750-acre ranch near the village of Galisteo with her even more famous husband, conceptual artist Bruce Nauman.

Rothenberg's paintings were shown at the Georgia O'Keeffe Museum in 2010. Although she says that O'Keeffe's works do not speak to her, Rothenberg's show brought up the inevitable comparisons to New Mexico's best-known painter. Art critic David Belcher wrote in *The New York Times*, "If O'Keeffe's version of this state is a staid and otherworldly landscape of honey-colored plateaus, mountains and desert plains, Ms. Rothenberg's is about a delirious, often physically indeterminate setting for sometimes ghastly scenes, what she calls the 'melodrama of nature'."

Rough Riders

Spanish-American War cavalry troop that included 400 volunteers from New Mexico, more men than from any other state. The unit was organized by future president Teddy Roosevelt, who thought that cowboys would make good soldiers. The men proved him right in their famous charge up Cuba's San Juan Hill.

Teddy Roosevelt in Las Vegas at the first Rough Riders reunion in 1899

For many years, the Rough Riders held reunions in Las Vegas, New Mexico, where there is a museum dedicated to them.

Roundhouse

Nickname for the New Mexico state capitol. The round building was originally designed to represent a kiva but came to resemble the Zia sun symbol when projections were added at the cardinal points.

The House and Senate chambers are on the first (basement) floor, the building's entrances and open rotunda are on the second (ground) floor, committee rooms are on the third floor, and the offices of the governor and the lieutenant governor are on the fourth floor.

The Capitol Art Collection includes almost 600 works by Anglo, Hispanic, and Indian artists from around New Mexico. The capitol and the art collection are open for self-guided tours.

The Roundhouse is on the corner of Paseo de Peralta and Old Santa Fe Trail.

The Roundhouse

Route 66

Pre-interstate highway that passed through New Mexico on its route from Chicago to Los Angeles. From 1926 to 1938, Route 66 entered Santa Fe from the east and followed a series of tortuous switchbacks down La Bajada Hill. In 1938, the highway was straightened so that it followed approximately the same course that I-40 follows today, and it no longer passed through Santa Fe. In 2001, the Museum of Indian Arts and Culture celebrated the 75th anniversary of Route 66 with an exhibit of memorabilia called "Get Your Kitsch on Route 66."

Ruidoso (*ree-uh-DOE-so, rue-ih-DOE-so)

Resort town in south-central New Mexico. The town is named for the *Rio Ruidoso*, "Noisy River," that runs through it. The mountain community, population 8,029, is popular with Texans and Oklahomans – and New Mexicans – who live in flatter, drier places.

Ruidoso is 194 miles south of Santa Fe via US 285 south and US 54 west.

*Anglos say ree-uh-DOE-so; Spanish speakers say rue-ih-DOE-so.

- S -

Sagel, Jim

(1947-1998) Literary interpreter of Northern New Mexico's Hispanic culture. An Anglo, Sagel was born and raised in Colorado. He moved to Española in 1970 and married a local girl named Teresa Archuleta. Fascinated by the culture he had married into, he quickly became proficient in Spanish and began writing fiction, nonfiction, and poetry in English, Spanish, and the version of Spanglish spoken in Northern New Mexico.

In 1981, Sagel won the *Premio Casa de las Americas* award (considered by some to be the Latin American equivalent of the Pulitzer Prize) for *Tunomás Honey*, a Spanish-language collection of short stories. The award created some controversy in Chicano literary circles when it was disclosed that the author was an Anglo.

Sagel succumbed to chronic depression and hanged himself in 1998.

saguaro cactus (suh-GWAH-ro)

Cactus *not* found in New Mexico. While New Mexico is home to many varieties of cacti, the saguaro, which is native to Arizona, is not one of them. Ads promoting New Mexico occasionally feature sombreros and saguaros, neither of which is found in the state.

sala (SAH-luh)

"Room," usually the living room. Sala can also mean "hall."

salsa (SALL-suh)

"Sauce" – hot sauce, a type of music, or a dance. Salsa is an often-fiery mixture of chiles, tomatoes, onions, and other ingredients. The condiment outsold ketchup in the United States for the first time in 1992.

Afro-Caribbean salsa music and dance are fast and compellingly rhythmic. Though not native to New Mexico, the music is popular in Santa Fe.

salt cedar

See TAMARISK.

Saltillo tile (sall-TEE-yo)

Naturally colored, reddish-brown floor tiles that originated in Saltillo, Mexico. The tiles are sometimes set in the floor unglazed and then sealed.

San Felipe Pueblo (fuh-LEE-pay)

Pueblo about halfway between Albuquerque and Santa Fe. San Felipe Pueblo's Hollywood Casino, Hollywood Hills Speedway, gas station, convenience store, and diner are just off I-25.

According to pueblo oral tradition, the community was named San Felipe by the Spanish in 1591. The Keresan-speaking pueblo may have been named for Saint Philip, one of the 12 disciples, or for one of the five Spanish kings named Philip. San Felipe is 30 miles southwest of Santa Fe.

San Francisco Street

Downtown Santa Fe's busiest shopping street. The third-of-a-mile stretch of San Francisco Street between the Eldorado Hotel on the west and St. Francis Cathedral on the east passes by the Lensic Theater, Burro Alley, the Five & Dime store, the Plaza, La Fonda, and numerous galleries, boutique shops, and restaurants.

Most of the missionaries who came to New Spain were Franciscans, members of the Catholic order founded by Saint Francis of Assisi. Many places in New Mexico are named for San Francisco.

San Ildefonso Pueblo (ill-duh-FAHN-so)

One of the Eight Northern Indian Pueblos. Don Juan de Oñate named the pueblo in honor of Saint Ildephonse, the 7th-century Archbishop of Toledo. The Tewa-speaking pueblo is known for the black-on-black pottery perfected by Maria Martinez and for Black Mesa, where its people took refuge during DeVargas's reconquest of New Mexico.

San Ildefonso Pueblo is off NM 502, 23 miles north of Santa Fe.

San Juan-Chama Diversion Project

Massive civil engineering project that diverts water from the Colorado River Basin to the Rio Grande Basin. Water is channeled from tributaries of the San Juan River on the western slope of the Continental Divide through a 12.8-mile tunnel into Willow Creek and the Rio Chama on the eastern slope of the Divide. The Chama merges with the Rio Grande just north of the city of Española, and the Rio Grande delivers the diverted water farther downstream.

Most of the San Juan-Chama water is consumed by the city of Albuquerque and by the Middle Rio Grande Conservancy District, a giant irrigation project that supplies water to farms between Cochiti and Socorro.

San Juan Pueblo

See OHKAY OWINGEH.

San Miguel County (mee-GHEL)

The county immediately east of Santa Fe County. Rural San Miguel County encompasses the Pecos National Historical Monument, near Pecos; United World College, near Las Vegas; Don Imus's ranch for sick kids, near Ribera; and Trementina Base, the Scientologists' secret archive, near the village of Trementina. Las Vegas is the seat of San Miguel County.

Many places in New Mexico are named San Miguel for Saint Michael the Archangel.

San Miguel Mission

The oldest church still in use in the United States. San Miguel Mission, also called San Miguel Cha-

San Miguel Mission

pel, was built between 1610 and 1628 by Mexican Indians who came to New Mexico as servants of the Spanish. The structure was destroyed in 1640, rebuilt, and destroyed again in the Pueblo Revolt of 1680. Its current incarnation dates from about 1710.

San Miguel Mission, which is open to the public, is on Old Santa Fe Trail at its intersection with East DeVargas Street.

San Ysidro (ee-SEE-dro)

The patron saint of farmers, named for Saint Isidore, who lived in Madrid in the 11th century. More than one community in New Mexico is named San Ysidro. The one closest to Santa Fe is about 70 miles away, at the intersection of US 550 and NM 4.

The name is sometimes spelled "Isidro." San Isidro Plazas I and II are shopping centers on Santa Fe's Southside, at the intersection of Cerrillos Road and Zafarano Drive.

Sanbusco (san-BOO-sco)

Enclosed mini-mall one block off Guadalupe Street, near the western end of Montezuma Avenue. Sanbusco's name is an acronym for the old Santa Fe Builders Supply Company, whose premises it now occupies.

Sanchez, John

(1963-) New Mexico's Republican lieutenant governor. Sanchez was elected in 2010 with Governor Susana Martinez. A native of Albuquerque, he started a successful roofing company after graduating from high school. He served in the New Mexico Legislature for two years before winning the Republican nomination for governor in 2002. He lost that race to Democrat Bill Richardson.

John Sanchez

Sanchez made a run for the Republican nomination for the U.S. Senate seat being vacated by Jeff Bingaman, but withdrew from the race in early 2012.

lountains (san-DEE-uh)

Albuquerque's mountain range. The Sandias run north-south for 28 miles just east of Albuquerque. The Sandia Peak Tramway transports passengers to and from the 10,378-foot summit of Sandia Peak.

Sandia means "watermelon." The name may stem from the mountains' reddish glow or, perhaps, from Sandia Pueblo, where the Spanish mistook the Indians' squash for watermelons.

Sandia National Laboratories

Research facility adjacent to Kirtland Air Force Base in Albuquerque. Like Los Alamos National Laboratory, Sandia works on nuclear weapons and other advanced defense systems for the United States Department of Energy. The facility's thousands of employees (it is one of New Mexico's largest employers) also work on arms control verification, pulsed-power research, and semiconductor technology.

Sandia Peak Tramway

Albuquerque cable-car system that carries passengers 4,000 feet up the western face of the Sandia Mountains. Some people take the tram up to Sandia Peak, go for a hike along the ridge or have a meal at the High Finance Restaurant, and then ride back down. In the winter, skiers can take the cable car up the western slope and ski down through Sandia Ski Area on the eastern slope. (Chairlifts run up the eastern slope, so it is easy to return to the tram for the ride back down the western face.)

Sandia Peak Tramway

The Sandia Peak Tramway was conceived and built by Ben Abruzzo. It opened in 1966 and is still owned and operated by the Abruzzo family.

At 2.7 miles in length, the Sandia Tramway was for decades the world's longest tramway, but it has since been eclipsed by Armenia's 3.5-mile-long Tatev Tramway.

Sandia Pueblo

Tiwa-speaking pueblo in Sandoval County. Sandia's casino is the most profitable in New Mexico, largely because of its proximity to the city of Albuquerque. *Sandia* means "watermelon."

Sandia Pueblo is off I-25, 46 miles south of Santa Fe.

Sangre de Cristo Mountains (SAHN-gray day CREE-stow)

Northern New Mexico's signature mountains, the southernmost extension of the Rockies. The Sangres run east of the Rio Grande, as far south as Santa Fe. New Mexico's highest peaks are all in the Sangres, and most of the mountains are protected from development by their location within the Pecos Wilderness.

The name *Sangre de Cristo*, "Blood of Christ," is of uncertain derivation. The popular story is that a priest dying from wounds received in the 1680 Pueblo Revolt asked for a sign from God. He received his answer and exclaimed, "Sangre de Cristo!" when he looked to the east and saw the mountains glowing red in the evening sun. *The Place Names of New Mexico* suggests that this story is apocryphal, however, as the name dates from the early 19th century, more than 200 years after the Pueblo Revolt. It is more likely that the mountains were named by *Los Hermanos Penitentes*, "The Brotherhood of Penitents," who were very active in that period.

Santa Ana Pueblo (*ANN-uh, AH-nuh)

Large pueblo named for Saint Anne, mother of the Virgin Mary. The Keresan-speaking pueblo is about 50 miles from Santa Fe, west of I-25 near the town of Bernalillo. Santa Ana Pueblo operates a casino on US 550 and a gravel operation that can be seen from I-25.

*Anglos often say ANN-uh, while Hispanics say AH-nuh.

Santa Clara Pueblo

One of the Eight Northern Indian Pueblos. Santa Clara is known for the Puyé Cliff Dwellings, for Santa Clara Canyon, and for red and black pottery. The Tewa-speaking pueblo is named for Saint Clare of Assisi, a

:r of Saint Francis. The pueblo owns the 124-room Santa Claran Hotel, the Santa Claran Casino, and a bowling alley, all in Española. It also owns the Black Mesa Golf Club, which is off US 84/285 just south of Española.

Santa Clara Pueblo is 25 miles north of Santa Fe on NM 30.

Santa Cruz (CRUISE)

"Holy Cross," a northern New Mexico community two miles east of Española. Santa Cruz was named by Don Diego de Vargas in 1695. He called it *La Villa Nueva de la Santa Cruz de la Cañada,* "The New Town of the Holy Cross of the Canyon."

Santa Fe (*SAN-tuh FAY)

A city shaped by isolation. Santa Fe was historically one of the most remote European outposts in the New World. Travel to the city required a long and dangerous trek up the Camino Real from Mexico or down the Santa Fe Trail from the United States, so only people who were uncomfortable elsewhere bothered to make the trip. These people included crypto Jews hoping to evade the Inquisition and Anglos with limited options in the United States.

The Atchison, Topeka, and Santa Fe Railway came through New Mexico in 1880, but bypassed its namesake city. Had it not done so, Santa Fe would have grown rapidly, like Albuquerque, and its character would have changed. Instead, it remained off the beaten track. Its isolation appealed to Anglo artists and intellectuals seeking an alternative to mainstream America.

In other places, buildings were modernized and minorities were encouraged to assimilate into the American melting pot. In Santa Fe, Anglo immigrants worked to protect not just the city's architectural heritage, but its cultural heritage as well. Contemporary Santa Fe is a product of this history.

*There are several ways to pronounce the city's name. Local Anglos say SAN-tuh FAY. Gringos, particularly those from Texas and the Southern states, tend to ignore the *t* and underemphasize *Fe*, saying something like SAN-uh fay. When used in a Spanish phrase like El Museo Cultural de Santa Fe, the city's name is pronounced SAHN-tah FAY.

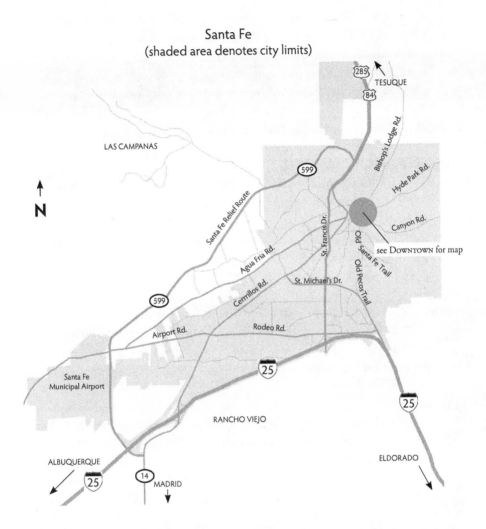

Santa Fe
(shaded area denotes city limits)

Santa Fe Animal Shelter and Humane Society

Animal shelter that has benefited from the largesse of Santa Fe's wealthiest residents. Newspaper heiress Amelia White established the shelter in 1939. In 1994, it received $1 million from the estate of homebuilder Betty Stewart. It has since been the recipient of other large grants, including from Robin Sommers, founder of the Santa Fe Natural Tobacco Company. One of the shelter's buildings is named for Sommers.

The animal shelter was housed in a modest building on Cerrillos Road until 2005, when it moved into its current space on Caja del Rio Road, off NM 599. The state-of-the-art facility includes two buildings and a 100-acre campus. The nonprofit serves more than 10,000 lost, stray, abandoned, or injured animals each year.

Santa Fe Art Institute (SFAI)

Nonprofit organization dedicated to the arts. The SFAI was founded in 1985 as a place for emerging artists to study with visiting artists. In 1999, it moved into a 17,000-square-foot building complex on the grounds of the College of Santa Fe (now the Santa Fe University of Art and Design) that was funded by a gift from Anne and John Marion. The SFAI hosts public lectures, workshops, and exhibitions.

Santa Fe: Autobiography of a Southwestern Town

Oliver La Farge's patchwork history of Santa Fe. The author used news articles printed in *The New Mexican* between 1849 and 1959 to describe the city's evolution over that period.

Santa Fe Baldy

The highest mountain in Santa Fe County. The peak appears bald when viewed from Santa Fe because the only part of the mountain visible from the city is above the tree line.

The strenuous, round-trip hike from the parking lot of Ski Santa Fe, at 10,250 feet, to the top of Baldy, at 12,622 feet, takes about eight hours.

Santa Fe Century

One-hundred-mile bicycle ride. The annual event, which began in 1985, recently attracted over 2,600 riders, over half of them from out of state. The race is held in May. Cyclists take off from Santa Fe, bike south down NM 14 (the Turquoise Trail) before returning to Santa Fe on NM 41 and NM 85. There are 25-, 50-, and 75-mile alternative routes for those who choose not to ride the entire 100 miles.

Santa Fe Community College (SFCC)

Ever-expanding educational institution. Santa Fe Community College had its modest beginning in 1983 in temporary space at the School for the Deaf. By 1988, it was holding classes on its own 366-acre campus, on land donated by the developers of Rancho Viejo.

The school now includes a Fitness Education Center, an Early Childhood Development Center, a Fine Arts Center, and an Instructional Technology Center. About 7,000 students seeking two-year degrees enroll in for-credit classes each semester, with many more attending non-credit classes as continuing education students. University professors from around the country retire to the Santa Fe area, and some of them teach a class or two at the community college, so the quality of teaching at the school is high.

SFCC will soon be opening a Higher Education Center, where students can pursue baccalaureate degrees from the University of New Mexico and other four-year institutions. The Higher Education Center will be on 15 acres near the Santa Fe University of Art and Design.

Santa Fe Community College's main campus is off Richards Avenue, south of I-25.

Santa Fe Community Convention Center

Santa Fe's new convention and meeting space. The 72,000-square-foot facility is downtown on the site of the old Santa Fe High School's Sweeney Gymnasium, which was converted into a convention center when the school moved. The Sweeney Center, as it was called, served as the city's primary meeting space until 2008, when it was demolished and replaced by the current, much-larger building.

It was discovered during its construction that the new convention center sits atop a pre-Columbian pueblo. Excavation for the underground parking garage uncovered human remains, at least one kiva, and numerous tools and potshards. The finds were reburied on site after negotiations with Tesuque Pueblo, the Indian community nearest to Santa Fe.

The Santa Fe Community Convention Center is on the corner of Grant Avenue and Marcy Street.

Santa Fe County

The third most populous, after Bernalillo and Doña Ana, of New Mexico's 33 counties. The city of Santa Fe and the communities surrounding it make up more than half of the county's population of 144,170. Santa Fe County constitutes the Santa Fe metropolitan statistical area (MSA).

The county is governed by a five-member board of county commissioners. Santa Fe city residents pay property taxes to the county and vote in both city and county elections.

Santa Fe Downs

See DOWNS AT SANTA FE.

Santa Fe film festivals

The original Santa Fe Film Festival was founded in 2000 by *New Mexico Magazine* associate editor Jon Bowman. Most of Santa Fe's professional actors, including Alan Arkin, Val Kilmer, Ali MacGraw, Shirley MacLaine, and Wes Studi, have participated in the festival in some capacity. The Santa Fe Independent Film Festival was established in 2009 by David Moore and Jacques Paisner. Both festivals take place in October.

Santa Fe High School

The oldest and largest of Santa Fe's two public high schools. By most measures, Santa Fe High performs better academically than Capital High School, which serves the poorer side of town.

Santa Fe High, founded in 1899, was located downtown until 1964, when it was relocated to its current location on the corner of Yucca Street and Siringo Road. The old, downtown school buildings now serve as offices for the City of Santa Fe.

The student population of approximately 1,700 roots for the Demons and the Demonettes. Some Catholic parents have lobbied, unsuccessfully, to have the school mascot changed to something less demonic.

Santa Fe Indian School

Secondary school (grades 7 through 12) for New Mexico Indians. The school serves approximately 700 students, about 500 of whom live on campus. Most of its students are from New Mexico – from one of the state's 19 pueblos, the Mescalero or Jicarilla Apache tribes, or the Navajo Nation – although several other tribes are represented by kids whose parents have moved to the area from other states.

The Santa Fe Indian School was established in 1890 and was run by the federal government until 1977, when the 19 pueblos took over its administration. The campus is now considered Indian country, which means that its governing body, the All Indian Pueblo Council, has limited sovereignty on school grounds, just as the individual tribes and pueblos have limited sovereignty on their own land.

In 2008, the school's governing board decided to demolish many of the older buildings on campus, some dating back to 1895, without consulting any other authority. Local preservationists deemed the action arbitrary if not illegal. The Paolo Soleri amphitheater, which is on school property, was also slated for demolition but was spared when school alumni and others protested.

The Santa Fe Indian School's 115 acres front Cerrillos Road, just south of Baca Street. The Indian Health Service Hospital is on federal land adjacent to the school.

Santa Fe Institute (SFI)

Multidisciplinary think tank devoted to the study of "complex adaptive systems." The Santa Fe Institute was founded in December 1983 by George Cowan, former director of research at Los Alamos National Laboratory; Murray Gell-Mann, Nobel Prize-winning physicist; and other scientists, most of them from LANL. Among other things, SFI studies the ways in which individual plants and businesses organize themselves into ecosystems and economies. The Institute's research center is on Hyde Park Road.

Permanent staff numbers in the twenties, but each year the facility hosts up to 150 visiting scientists and other scholars. SFI's eclectic, interdisciplinary approach is exemplified by the presence of novelist Cormac McCarthy, who maintains an office on campus, and Valerie Plame Wilson, who serves part time as director of community relations. In an interview with *Santa Fean* magazine, Plame Wilson said, "I really do believe that the work they are doing at the Santa Fe Institute will save the world. They are asking the big questions – of poverty, of climate change, of cancer ....”

SFI periodically sponsors free community lectures. They are usually held at the James A. Little Theater, on the School for the Deaf campus.

Santa Fe Municipal Airport

Santa Fe's limited-service airport. American Eagle currently provides regular flights to Los Angeles and Dallas, but for most of its history, the airport offered intermittent and infrequent commuter flights. (Santa Fe is popularly believed to be the state capital that is least accessible by air, but Concord, New Hampshire, which has *no* commercial flights, holds that title.) Santa Feans periodically discuss whether the airport should be upgraded, but most seem to agree with former Mayor Debbie Jaramillo, who said, “Santa Fe has a perfectly good airport. We keep it in Albuquerque.”

The Santa Fe Municipal Airport terminal building was designed by John Gaw Meem. The airport is in the far southwest corner of the city, at the western end of Airport Road.

Santa Fe Municipal Watershed

The Santa Fe River basin in the Sangre de Cristo Mountains. The watershed encompasses 17,260 acres on both sides of the river, from just east of the Ski Santa Fe slopes down to the city's water treatment plant on Upper Canyon Road. For most of Santa Fe's early history, the Santa Fe River canyon was used as a route to the mountains for high-country grazing, firewood collection, and recreation. In 1932, the watershed was closed to the public to allow the forest to regenerate and to stop pollution caused by grazing. It has been closed ever since.

The Santa Fe River was dammed to create the Nichols Reservoir in 1928. The McClure Reservoir followed in 1942. The watershed typically supplies about 40 percent of the city's water, with the remainder coming from the Rio Grande, either from wells or from the Buckman Direct Diversion Project.

Santa Fe National Cemetery

The burial site of more than 45,000 military veterans and their spouses. The 78.6-acre cemetery was established in 1875. It is the final resting place of Charles Bent, New Mexico's first governor in the Territorial Period, three African-American Buffalo Soldiers, artist Will Shuster, authors Oliver La Farge and Tony Hillerman, Santa Fe Opera founder John Crosby, numerous Medal of Honor winners, and other veterans from every conflict since the Civil War.

The cemetery's saddest story may be that of Private Dennis O'Leary, who died in 1901 while serving at Fort Wingate, a frontier outpost 12 miles east of Gallup. O'Leary was a sickly and lonely soldier who disappeared from the fort for several weeks and then returned with no explanation for his absence. Sentenced to the guardhouse for being absent without leave, he served his time without complaint. Soon after his release, however, on April 1, 1901, O'Leary shot himself. A suicide note explained that he had left a "Memento" of his death in the nearby hills and asked the army to retrieve it.

Dennis O'Leary's grave marker at Santa Fe National Cemetery

Troopers in a buckboard wagon followed O'Leary's directions to the place he described and found there an almost life-sized sandstone carving of a soldier. The sculpted figure leans back against a tree, on whose trunk is inscribed: "DENNIS O'LEARY, Pvt, Co I, 23rd INFTY, died April 1, 1901 Age 23 yrs & 9 mo." The soldiers realized then that O'Leary had carved his own tombstone, including the anticipated date of his death, while hiding in the mountains. They hauled the carving back to the fort and placed it on his grave. In 1910, Fort Wingate's graves were moved to Santa Fe National Cemetery, where the unusual marker can be seen today.

Santa Fe National Cemetery is on North Guadalupe Street, just north of the civilian Rosario Cemetery.

Santa Fe National Forest

One of two national forests in Northern New Mexico, the other being the Carson National Forest. The 1.6-million-acre Santa Fe National Forest covers the southern extension of the Sangre de Cristo Mountains and much of the Jemez Mountains. Most of the Pecos Wilderness is in the Santa Fe National Forest.

Santa Fe Natural Tobacco Company

One of Santa Fe's most successful business start-ups. Founded in 1982 by Robin Sommers, the company was acquired in 2002 by R.J. Reynolds for $340 million. The company's American Spirit cigarettes are not manufactured in Santa Fe, though over 100 people are employed at the company's office near the intersection of Cerrillos Road and I-25.

Santa Fe New Mexican, The

See NEW MEXICAN, THE SANTA FE.

Santa Fe Opera

World-class seasonal opera. Founded by John Crosby in 1957, Santa Fe's open-air opera underwent a $14-million renovation in 1997. As part of the renovation, all 2,128 seats were sheltered from the rain, and a scrolling libretto was installed on each seatback.

Santa Fe Opera

Opera season runs from early July to late August, with five productions playing in rotation. The Santa Fe Opera is on US 84/285, seven miles north of the Plaza.

Santa Fe Place

The newer and larger of Santa Fe's two enclosed shopping malls. Santa Fe Place, which was called Villa Linda Mall when it opened in 1985, was renamed in 2005 after a change of ownership. The 573,000-square-foot center houses three major department stores and the usual assortment of smaller retail outlets.

Because it is on Santa Fe's Southside, which has a younger demographic, the mall attracts more teenagers than DeVargas Center, which is close to downtown.

Santa Fe Place is on the southeast corner of Rodeo Road and Cerrillos Road.

Santa Fe Playhouse

The oldest continuously operating theater west of the Mississippi. Established as the Santa Fe Little Theater by writer Mary Austin in 1922, the community playhouse stages locally produced entertainments year-round but is best known for the Fiesta Melodrama, which runs from late August through Fiesta weekend. Twenty-five percent of the theater's productions are "pay-what-you-wish."

Santa Fe Playhouse is on East DeVargas Street, in the old Barrio de Analco neighborhood.

Santa Fe Prep

Santa Fe's most expensive private high school. Founded in 1961, the Eastside school has an enrollment of about 340 students on a 13-acre campus on Camino Cruz Blanca. Annual tuition and fees approach $20,000, which is almost three times that of St. Michael's, the city's other private high school. Santa Fe Prep's sports teams are called the Blue Griffins.

Notable Prep graduates include designer Tom Ford, actress Anna Gunn (who plays Skyler White on the TV series *Breaking Bad*), and supermodel Arizona Muse.

Santa Fe Pride

Santa Fe's annual gay pride celebration. The mid-June festival began in 2001 as a one-day affair but has since evolved into a 10-day arts and culture marathon. The main event is the Saturday Gay Pride Parade, which starts at the Roundhouse and meanders down Paseo de Peralta to the Railyard. The festival is sponsored by Santa Fe's Human Rights Alliance.

Santa Fe has historically been welcoming to gays and lesbians, and this has not changed. According to a study by the Human Rights Campaign, Santa Fe is second only to San Francisco in the percentage of same-sex households.

Santa Fe Public Library

The city's three-branch library system. The Main Library opened downtown in 1908 in what is now the Fray Angélico Chávez History Library. It is currently housed in a Territorial-style building, designed by John Gaw Meem, that once contained Santa Fe's municipal offices. The Main Library is on the corner of Washington Avenue and Marcy Street.

The Oliver La Farge Branch opened in 1978 in the Llano Neighborhood Center, on Llano Street near its intersection with Siringo Road. The Southside Library opened in 2007 at the intersection of Jaguar Drive and Country Club Road.

Santa Fe Railway

The railroad that bypassed its namesake. The Atchison, Topeka, and Santa Fe Railway (usually referred to as "the Santa Fe Railway" or simply "the Santa Fe") reached Raton Pass in 1878 and Las Vegas, New Mexico, in 1879. Then, contrary to the expectations of Santa Fe's citizens, the railway was run south of town, through less challenging terrain, and then on to Albuquerque. Santa Fe's disappointed citizens, led by Archbishop Lamy, approved a bond issue to build an 18-mile spur from Santa Fe to the main line. That spur still runs from Santa Fe to the town of Lamy.

The Santa Fe Railway had a mighty effect on its namesake's development, mostly because it made the city easily accessible to tourists for the first time. The company also saved La Fonda, Santa Fe's oldest hotel. When La Fonda went broke in 1925, the railroad bought the property and leased it to the Fred Harvey Company, which ran it as a Harvey House hotel from 1926 to 1968.

The Santa Fe Railway merged with Burlington Northern in 1995 and is now part of the Burlington Northern Santa Fe Railway. The Santa Fe Southern Railway and the Rail Runner Express still use the spur line.

Santa Fe Reporter

Santa Fe's free, alternative newspaper. The weekly *Reporter* covers the arts and culture scene as well as local news stories that it believes have been overlooked or underplayed by *The New Mexican*. It is known for its annual Best of Santa Fe awards and for the *Annual Manual*, a locals' guide to living in Santa Fe. The paper is distributed to its ubiquitous red boxes on Wednesday mornings.

Richard McCord founded the *Santa Fe Reporter* in 1974. In 1988, he sold it to Rockefeller heiress Hope Aldrich, who in turn sold it to the *Willamette Week*, a Portland, Oregon, alternative paper, in 1997.

The *Reporter* endorsed Ralph Nader for president in 2000, John Kerry in 2004, and Barack Obama in 2008.

Santa Fe Review, The

The online "Journal of Commentary and Reportage" intermittently maintained by science writer and Santa Fe resident George Johnson. The blog addresses complex local issues like regional water policy, the real or imagined dangers of electromagnetic waves, and Santa Fe's escarpment ordinance.

Johnson does not hesitate to skewer people that he feels have offended Santa Fe sensibilities. He has criticized portfolio manager Andrew Davis for his 23,000-square-foot ridge-top mansion, physicist Bill Bruno for his opposition to expanding Wi-Fi access, and the administrators of the Santa Fe Indian School for the destruction of historic buildings on the school campus. *The Santa Fe Review*'s web address is santafereview.com.

Santa Fe Ring

Shadowy group of lawyers, politicians, businessmen, and ranchers who controlled much of New Mexico during the late Territorial Period. Some members of the Ring acquired vast tracts of land from heirs to Spanish and Mexican land grants. Thomas B. Catron, who is often identified as the leader of the Ring, became one of the largest landowners in the country.

Not everyone agrees that the Santa Fe Ring was as powerful or nefarious as it is usually portrayed. Thomas B. Catron III, a Santa Fe lawyer and grandson of the group's purported leader, said, "... the idea that [the Ring] was an early type of Mafia is overblown."

Santa Fe River

Santa Fe's intermittent waterway. The river heads in the Sangre de Cristo Mountains northeast of town and runs for about 46 miles to its confluence with the Rio Grande just south of Cochiti Lake.

In 2007, the Santa Fe River was designated "America's Most Endangered River" by the national advocacy group American Rivers. The problem is a lack of water: runoff from the Santa Fe Municipal Watershed is held in reservoirs east of the city, so the 13-mile stretch of the river that runs through the city is dry unless the reservoirs are full enough to warrant releases. In recent years, the city has made an effort to release more water into the river in the summer.

Santa Fe shuffle

The shuffle between two or three part-time jobs. Santa Fe is a notoriously difficult place for newcomers to find desirable full-time employment.

Santa Fe ski area

See SKI SANTA FE.

Santa Fe Southern Railway (SFSR)

The train that runs along the 18-mile rail spur from Santa Fe to Lamy. The SFSR, which has been in operation since 1992, hauls some freight but is mostly known for its round-trip tourist runs. The scenic ride takes about four hours, including a two-hour stopover in Lamy.

In 2010, the Santa Fe Southern Railway was acquired by STI-GLOB-AL, Ltd., an Australian company that uses the train as a test platform for rail-safety technology.

Santa Fe style

Generic term for the architecture, interior decoration, clothing, cuisine, and jewelry associated with Santa Fe.

The architectural style, sometimes called "adobe architecture," is distinguished by flat roofs and brown or tan stucco finishes. Spanish Pueblo and Territorial are the two types of Santa Fe-style architecture.

Santa Fe-style interior decor includes Spanish Colonial artworks like retablos, bultos, and straw appliqué crosses as well as Indian pots, blankets, and kachinas.

Santa Fe-style clothing includes broomstick skirts and wide concha belts for women, and bolo ties, cowboy boots, and turquoise jewelry for both men and women.

Although there are restaurants called "The Santa Fe Grill," or "The Santa Fe Café" across the country, there is no such thing as Santa Fe-style cuisine. Most Santa Fe restaurants serve New Mexican food, which is much like Mexican cooking except that it makes greater use of spicy chiles and includes regional favorites like bizcochitos, blue corn, posole, and sopaipillas. (See NEW MEXICAN FOOD.)

Santa Fe Style

1986 coffee-table book by Christine Mather and Sharon Woods. The book's focus on interior design and architectural detail capitalized on the national interest in all things Santa Fe.

Santa Fe Trail

Wagon route from Independence, Missouri, to Santa Fe that served as New Mexico's primary trade route from 1821 to 1880. Traffic along the 780-mile trail (a trail is by definition a road that develops through repeated use) began in 1821, when newly independent Mexico first allowed trade with the United States. The Santa Fe Trail quickly eclipsed the Camino Real as Northern New Mexico's main highway for goods and supplies. It became even more important after 1846, when New Mexico was annexed by the United States in the Mexican-American War.

The Trail's longer Mountain Branch ran through Raton Pass. The Cimarron Cutoff, which was shorter but more hazardous due to infrequent water sources and Indian attacks, entered New Mexico north of Clayton and rejoined the Mountain Branch at the town of Watrous, near Fort Union. From there, the Trail followed essentially the same route that I-25 follows today before terminating in Santa Fe. Ruts from wagon wheels are still visible in many places in northeast New Mexico.

Of the two branches of the Santa Fe Trail, the Cimarron Cutoff is the one that did *not* go near the town of Cimarron. The confusion arises be-

Santa Fe Trail

cause the Cutoff and the town are each named for a different Cimarron River: the town is named for a river that begins in the Sangre de Cristos and drains into the Canadian River without leaving New Mexico, while the Cutoff is named for a much longer river that heads in New Mexico but meanders through Colorado, Oklahoma, and Kansas before returning to Oklahoma and draining into the Arkansas River. In New Mexico, this longer river is called the Dry Cimarron.

The Santa Fe Trail's importance waned quickly with the arrival of the Santa Fe Railway in 1880.

Santa Fe Trend

Magazine published three times a year, in fall, spring, and summer. *Trend* focuses on art, architecture, and fashion. It was started in 2000 by publisher Cynthia Canyon.

Santa Fe University of Art and Design

The school once known as the College of Santa Fe. The Santa Fe University of Art and Design is one of the city's two expensive private colleges, the other being St. John's College.

In 1859, Bishop Jean Baptiste Lamy brought four Christian Brothers from France to Santa Fe to start a school for boys. St. Michael's College, as the school came to be known, was housed in what is now the Lamy Building, a state office building across from the Roundhouse on Old Santa Fe Trail. (Some Santa Fe old-timers still refer to Old Santa Fe Trail as College Street.) Future hotelier Conrad Hilton, a native of San Antonio, New Mexico, briefly attended St. Michaels College.

The school moved to its current location, the former site of Bruns Army Hospital, in 1946. In 1966, St. Michaels changed its name to the College of Santa Fe and began accepting women. The Greer Garson Theater and Fogelson Library are named for film star Greer Garson and her husband, Buddy Fogelson, who were major benefactors through the 1960s, 1970s, and 1980s.

The college was nearly closed in a severe financial crisis in 2008 and 2009. It narrowly escaped that fate when the City of Santa Fe bought the 100-acre campus and leased most of it to Laureate Education, the for-profit parent company of Sylvan Learning Centers. Laureate renamed the school the Santa Fe University of Art and Design.

The school focuses on filmmaking, performing, writing, and the visual arts. Santa Fe film buffs appreciate the college's movie theater, called The Screen, both for the films it runs and for the state-of-the-art theater.

The entrance to the Santa Fe University of Art and Design is on St. Michael's Drive, just east of its intersection with Cerrillos Road.

Santa Fean (SAN-tuh FAY-un)

A person who lives in Santa Fe.

Santa Fean magazine

Glossy, bi-monthly magazine devoted to the art of living in Santa Fe. The *Santa Fean* was started in 1972 by partners Marian Love and Betty Bauer. It is currently owned by Bruce Adams, who worked for the founders in the 1980s and 1990s. The periodical covers art, architecture, and design, and frequently does profiles of local celebrities like Val Kilmer, Ali MacGraw, Wes Studi, and Valerie Plame Wilson.

The *Santa Fean* attracts upper-income readers. In 2001, the magazine reported that the average household income of its subscribers was over $270,000.

Santa Rosa

The "Scuba Capital of the Southwest." Santa Rosa, population 2,848, is known for the Blue Hole, an artesian well big enough to be used by scuba divers. The city is named for Santa Rosa de Lima (1586-1617), the first Catholic saint of the Americas.

Santa Rosa is on I-40, 121 miles southeast of Santa Fe.

Santacafé

Fine dining restaurant housed in a historic property. Santacafé, which opened in 1983, is in a house once owned by Padre Jose Manuel Gallegos, a Catholic priest who was defrocked by Bishop Jean Baptiste Lamy in 1852 and who later became a politician. Santacafé owners Bobby Morean and Judith Ebbinghaus explain that the covered well in the bar area was dug inside the house because Gallegos feared that his political enemies might poison his outdoor well. The establishment serves American cuisine with a Southwestern flair. Santacafé is on Washington Avenue, between Marcy Street and Paseo de Peralta.

Santafesino (sahn-tuh-fay-SEE-no)

One who lives in Santa Fe. *Santa Fean* is the more common term.

santero/a (sahn-TAIR-o/uh)

An artist who paints or carves santos, depictions of saints.

santo (SAHN-toe)

A painted or carved depiction of a saint. Two-dimensional paintings are called retablos, and three-dimensional wooden carvings are called bultos. Santos are a Spanish Colonial art form.

Santo Domingo Pueblo

See Kewa Pueblo.

Santo Niño de Atocha (NEEN-yo day ah-TOE-cha)

Santo Niño de Atocha

"The Holy Child of Atocha," an image of the Christ child popular in Mexico and the American Southwest. The legend of Santo Niño de Atocha originated during the Moorish occupation of Spain, when Christians in the village of Atocha were imprisoned and denied food unless it was delivered by children. Childless couples who would have otherwise starved were brought food by an unknown boy, whom they assumed to be an incarnation of the Christ child. The mysterious child later appeared in Mexico, where he guided miners out of a cave-in. Santo Niño de Atocha is usually depicted holding a basket and a staff and wearing the attire of a religious pilgrim, including a cape and feathered hat.

santuario (sahn-too-AH-ree-o)
"Sanctuary."

Santuario de Chimayó
(sahn-too-AH-ree-o deh chee-my-O)

The historic adobe church in the village of Chimayó, one of Northern New Mexico's premier tourist attractions. Built in 1813, the old church is a masterpiece of Spanish Colonial folk art, and many people visit it for that reason alone. Others come to the "Lourdes of America" for spiritual or health reasons: its holy dirt is thought to have curative powers.

Santuario de Chimayó

During the Holy Week before Easter, thousands of peregrinos make a pilgrimage to the Santuario.

Santuario de Guadalupe (sahn-too-AH-ree-o deh gwah-duh-LOO-pay)
The oldest church in the United States dedicated to Our Lady of Guadalupe. Constructed in the late 18th century, the Santa Fe church has experienced a recent renaissance. The building fell into disrepair after 1961, when a new, larger church was built next door. Unable to afford the upkeep on the old building, the parish deconsecrated it and leased it to the secular Historic Guadalupe Foundation, which rented it out for art exhibits and musical performances. Catholics who were offended when alcohol was served at art openings were outraged when the facility was rented to a Wiccan group, and the Santa Fe Archdiocese was happy to reclaim the church when the foundation's lease expired in 2006.

The Santuario de Guadalupe has thrived since then, primarily because it now attracts large numbers of Spanish-speaking immigrants. Church members serve free lunches three times a week to the mostly undocumented day laborers who wait for work on a corner across from the church. A statue of Our Lady of Guadalupe was erected in the churchyard in 2008.

The old church is on the corner of Guadalupe and Agua Fria streets in downtown Santa Fe.

School for Advanced Research (SAR)

The nation's first research institution dedicated to the study of the archaeology and ethnology of the American Southwest. The School of American Archaeology, as it was initially known, was founded in 1907 with Edgar Lee Hewett as its first director. In 1917, the name of the institution was changed to the School for American Research. The name was changed again, in 2007, when it became the School for Advanced Research, a name that reflects the institution's increasingly global perspective. The SAR is housed in *El Delirio*, "The Madness," a Garcia Street house once owned by philanthropist Amelia White.

School for the Deaf, New Mexico (NMSD)

New Mexico's oldest state educational institution, established in 1887. NMSD's student body consists of about 120 K-12 students, and the roadrunner is the school mascot. The school's 30-acre campus is on the southwest corner of Cerrillos Road and St. Francis Drive, on some of Santa Fe's most valuable real estate. The James A. Little Theater is on the grounds of NMSD.

Scottish Rite Temple

An important link in Santa Fe's architectural evolution. In the late 19th century, the city's two big public-building projects were St. Francis Cathedral and the Federal Courthouse. The Romanesque cathedral and the Greek Revival courthouse reflected the architectural fashion of the times, but neither had any connection to Santa Fe's history. By 1910, however, when the Masonic Temple was being contemplated, Santa Fe's city fathers – many of whom were Masons – recognized that the city's architecture was a big tourist draw. With that in mind, they rejected the temple's original neoclassical design in favor of a California Mission style with distinct Moorish elements, a motif that they thought would better reflect the city's Spanish heritage.

Scottish Rite Temple

The irony is that by the time the building was dedicated in 1912, what is now known as Santa Fe-style architecture had become better defined, and the salmon-pink Temple was criticized for being out of synch with the rest of the city. To the relief of those who appreciate architectural diversity, the Masons refused to alter the historic building.

The Scottish Rite Temple is in downtown Santa Fe on the corner of Paseo de Peralta and Washington Avenue.

seco/a (SEH-co/uh)

"Dry." Arroyo Seco is a place name in both Santa Fe County and Taos County. Carne seca is dried meat.

Sena Plaza (SEH-nuh)

Enclosed courtyard off Palace Avenue in downtown Santa Fe. In the 19th century, the property was owned by Don Jose and Doña Isabel Sena, who added on to their original small house to make room for their many children. (One of their sons, also named Jose Sena, served as mayor of Santa Fe from 1908 to 1910.) The additions gradually created a hacienda surrounding an open courtyard.

Mayor Jose D. Sena

Second stories were added to the houses in a major renovation of the property in 1927, and additional improvements were made after developer Gerald Peters bought the plaza in the early 1980s. In 1983, Peters opened La Casa Sena, "The Sena House," the restaurant that still serves as the plaza's anchor business. Sena Plaza is on Palace Avenue, one block east of the Plaza.

Servants of the Paraclete

The Catholic religious order that tried to rehabilitate pedophiles. The Servants of the Paraclete operates a treatment center for troubled priests in Jemez Springs, and some of the men referred to the center after its founding in 1947 were sent there because they had had sexual relations with children. The order's founder, Father Gerald Fitzgerald, recognized early on that pedophiles were poor candidates for rehabilitation and recommended to the church hierarchy that they be defrocked. After his death in 1969, however, the center allowed "rehabilitated" pedophiles to return to priestly duties in parishes around New Mexico and elsewhere. Most re-offended.

Father Fitzgerald's many letters to his superiors, which were unsealed in 2007, refute claims by church leaders that they were unaware of the magnitude of the problem.

Seton Village

Historic residential area south of Santa Fe. The village is named for artist, author, and naturalist Ernest Thompson Seton (1860-1946), who co-founded the Boy Scouts of America and is credited with introducing American Indian lore to the Scouts.

Seton built a 32-room "castle" of stone and rough-hewn timbers and lived in it from 1933 until his death in 1946. In 2003, Seton's daughter sold the property to a private school called the Academy for the Love of Learning. The school was in the process of renovating Seton Castle when it was destroyed by a fire.

Seton Village is seven and a half miles south of the Plaza via Old Las Vegas Highway and Arroyo Hondo Road. It is a mile and a half east of I-25.

Shed, The

Classic Santa Fe restaurant. Thornton and Polly Carswell opened The Shed in 1953, and their grandson Joshua is the current chef. The family also owns La Choza, which opened on Alarid Street in 1983. While both restaurants serve New Mexican food, The Shed is more expensive because of its ambience and downtown location. The restaurant is in a rambling hacienda that dates back to 1692, and its small rooms, low doorways, and brightly colored walls add an old-world flavor to the dining experience. The Shed is on Palace Avenue, just east of the Plaza.

Sheehan, Michael

(1939-) Leader of the Catholic Archdiocese of Santa Fe. Sheehan was born in Kansas and ordained in 1964. Formerly First Bishop of Lubbock, Texas, Archbishop Sheehan was assigned to Santa Fe in 1993 after a series of sex scandals forced the resignation of his predecessor, the late Archbishop Robert Sanchez.

shepherd's bed

A raised sleeping platform. The bed was placed directly above or ad-

Shepherd's bed in an old adobe home, 1912

jacent to a kiva fireplace to take advantage of the rising heat. Shepherd's beds are occasionally seen in modern Santa Fe-style homes.

Shidoni Foundry (shih-DOE-nee)

Art foundry, gallery, and sculpture garden on eight acres in Tesuque. Founded in 1971 as a two-man operation, Shidoni (the word is a Navajo greeting to a friend) now employs 40 people. The foundry has done work for Allan Houser and Glenna Goodacre, among many other local sculptors.

Shidoni is on Bishop's Lodge Road, five miles north of Santa Fe.

Will Shuster

Shuster, Will

(1893-1969) Painter, creator of Zozobra, and the best-known of Los Cinco Pintores. Born in Philadelphia, William Howard Shuster moved to Santa Fe in 1920 to combat tuberculosis, which he contracted after a gas attack in World War I.

In 1921, he joined four other artists to form Los Cinco Pintores, "The Five Painters," who exhibited their work together and lived near each other on Camino del Monte Sol. In 1924 (some sources say 1925 or

1926), Shuster and Gustave Baumann created Zozobra, the giant marionette that is burned each year during Fiesta. Will Shuster is buried in Santa Fe National Cemetery.

Sides, Hampton

(1962-) Popular historian and Santa Fe resident. Sides is a native of Memphis, Tennessee, and a graduate of Yale. He moved to the area in 1994 when he was working as an editor at *Outside* magazine and the publication relocated from Chicago to Santa Fe.

Hampton Sides

Since moving to New Mexico, Sides has published three best-selling histories: *Ghost Soldiers* (2001), *Blood and Thunder: An Epic of the American West* (2006), and *Hellhound on His Trail* (2010). All three were written in a Santa Fe coffee shop. He appeared on *The Colbert Report* in May 2010 to discuss *Hellhound*, the story of Martin Luther King assassin James Earl Ray.

Sides has three sons who are, or have been, standout soccer players for Santa Fe Prep, and he is a regular at their games. The author has established a trust through the Santa Fe Community Foundation to preserve the memory of World War II veterans of the Pacific Theater.

Sikh (SEEK)

A follower of the major religion of Punjab, India; in Northern New Mexico, a member of the offshoot of that religion that was brought to the United States in 1969 by the late spiritual leader Yogi Bhajan.

The hundreds of Sikhs who are associated with the Española *gurdwara*, "temple," are almost exclusively Anglo converts. When they become Sikhs, they change their surname to Khalsa, hide their unshorn hair under turbans, wear white clothing, and practice kundalini yoga. The 3HO (happy, healthy, holy) organization claims thousands of American followers, and its members control numerous businesses, including Akal Security and Golden Temple, which makes Peace Cereal and Yogi Tea.

The Sikhs are well integrated into Northern New Mexico. New Mexico governors have spoken at their annual Peace Prayer Day, and Sikhs have offered the invocation at the opening of the New Mexico Legislature. Flags across the state were flown at half-mast after Yogi Bhajan's death in 2004.

Silver City

Old mining town in southwest New Mexico. The Silver City town site was a regular camping ground for nomadic Apaches before it was settled by Anglos in the late 19th century. Senator Jeff Bingaman is from Silver City. The town, population 10,315, is the seat of Grant County.

Silver City is 298 miles southwest of Santa Fe via I-25 south and NM 152 west.

silvery minnow

Iconic endangered species. When the Rio Grande began to dry up in the summer of 2000, the courts mandated a release of water from Abiquiu Reservoir specifically to ensure the two-inch minnow's survival. The release worked to save the fish but heightened tensions between environmentalists and farmers and communities along the river, who saw the minnow as a threat to their own water rights.

Simmons, Marc

(1937-) New Mexico's best-known living historian. His 2005 biography by Phyllis S. Morgan is titled *Marc Simmons of New Mexico: Maverick Historian.* The subtitle is particularly apt – Simmons worked as a cowboy while earning a Ph.D. in history from the University of New Mexico and has for decades lived off the grid in a house he built with his own hands near the village of Cerrillos.

The prolific Simmons has written more than 40 books, 1,400 newspaper and magazine articles, and 50 scholarly articles. He writes a weekly column called "Trail Dust" for *The New Mexican.*

sipapu (SEE-pah-poo)

In Pueblo creation myth, the hole through which the first people emerged from the underworld. Ceremonial kivas have a hole in the floor representing a sipapu.

The Sipapu Ski Resort is a small ski area in the Sangre de Cristo Mountains, 62 miles north of Santa Fe.

SITE Santa Fe (SITE is not an acronym)

Santa Fe's premier contemporary art venue. The 18,000-square-foot building was a beer warehouse until 1995, when Anne and John Marion funded its transformation into an art space. SITE has no permanent collection but exhibits conceptual and abstract works in its biennial shows. SITE Santa Fe is in the Railyard, on the corner of Paseo de Peralta and Guadalupe Street.

Ski Santa Fe

Santa Fe's winter tourism draw. With a parking lot at 10,350 feet and ski runs beginning at 12,075 feet, the Santa Fe ski area is one of the highest in the country. It boasts 1,725 vertical feet of skiing and seven lifts that can transport 9,350 people per hour. The chairlift also opens in the fall, allowing leaf-peepers to view the color-changing aspens from the summit of Tesuque Peak. Ski Santa Fe is owned by the Abruzzo family of Albuquerque.

The 16-mile drive from the Plaza up Hyde Park Road to the ski area takes about 45 minutes.

Smokey Bear

(1950-1976)   Ursine star of the U.S. Forest Service's campaign to stamp out forest fires. Smokey Bear (not *the* Bear) was a black bear cub that was found cowering in a tree after a 1950 forest fire in south-central New Mexico. He was brought to Santa Fe, where he was treated by Dr. Edwin Smith, founder of Smith Veterinary Hospital. Smokey died in a Washington, D.C., zoo in 1976.

snap

To suddenly realize. In other places, *to snap* means to finally lose it. In New Mexico, it means to finally get it. A Norteño might say, "I thought

I knew her from somewhere, and then I snapped – she's my cousin's girl-friend!"

sobador/a (so-bah-DOOR/DOOR-uh)

A folk chiropractor or massage therapist, one who effects cures by ma-nipulating the skeleton and massaging the skin.

Socorro (suh-CORE-o)

City near the National Wildlife Refuge at Bosque del Apache. Socorro, which means "succor" or "aid," was named by Don Juan de Oñate after friendly Indians fed his party there in 1598. The community was aban-doned after the 1680 Pueblo Revolt and was not resettled until 1815.

Socorro, population 9,051, is home to the New Mexico Institute of Mining and Technology. The city is 136 miles south of Santa Fe, near the intersection of I-25 and US 60.

Somos Un Pueblo Unido (SO-mos oon PWEB-lo oo-NEE-doe)

"We Are a People United," a Santa Fe-based immigrants' rights group. The group was founded in 1995 in response to California's passage of Proposition 187, a proposed law that would have prohibited illegal im-migrants from using the state's social services. (The law was overturned by the courts before it took effect.)

In 1999, Somos initiated a campaign that led to a Santa Fe City Coun-cil resolution that prohibits city employees from asking immigrants about their legal status. In 2002, the group successfully lobbied the New Mexi-co Legislature for a law that allows undocumented immigrants to obtain New Mexico driver's licenses. (Governor Susana Martinez has made the repeal of this law a priority for her administration.) And in 2005, Somos led the effort to pass a bill that allows undocumented students access to state educational institutions at in-state tuition rates.

Somos estimates that there are between 10,000 and 15,000 undocu-mented people living in Santa Fe.

sopaipilla (so-pah-PEE-yuh)

Puffy fried bread served in New Mexico restaurants. Sopaipillas are often split and filled with honey, and they are usually eaten during the meal – not as a dessert – to counter the heat from spicy chiles. Actor Alan Arkin said of the deep-fried sopaipilla, "It'll kill you in a minute, but it's a good death."

South Capitol

Old Santa Fe neighborhood. The South Capitol area is bounded by Paseo de Peralta and Cerrillos Road to the north, Cordova Road to the south, Old Santa Fe Trail to the east, and St. Francis Drive to the west.

The South Capitol Campus is a cluster of state office buildings on the southwest corner of the intersection of St. Francis Drive and Cordova Road. A Rail Runner Express station is centered in the middle of the 30-acre property.

Southside

The fastest-growing part of Santa Fe. Boundaries are debatable, but the Southside has been defined as broadly as the area south of St. Michael's Drive/Osage Avenue and west of St. Francis Drive. Rodeo/Airport Road (it is the same road; the name changes as it crosses Cerrillos Road) is its main thoroughfare.

Compared to Santa Fe's older neighborhoods to the north and east, the Southside has more affordable housing, more big box stores, more people per household, more children, more Hispanic residents (both native Santa Feans and recent immigrants), and, in certain areas, more crime. Over the years, public facilities have been built to accommodate the growing population. These include Villa Linda Mall (now called Santa Fe Place) in 1985, Capital High School in 1988, the Genoveva Chavez Community Center in 2000, and the Southside Library in 2007.

Southwestern Association for Indian Arts (SWAIA)

Nonprofit organization formed in 1922 to support Indian culture. SWAIA (the acronym, which is used more often than the entire name, is pronounced as a single word) is best known for its sponsorship of Santa Fe's annual Indian Market.

Spaceport America

The world's first purpose-built commercial spaceport. Spaceport America is the brainchild of three ambitious parents: New Mexico Governor Bill Richardson, who advocated for the Spaceport as an economic development project for the southern part of the state; British entrepreneur Richard Branson, whose Virgin Galactic company is the Spaceport's anchor tenant and who hopes to take the lead in space tourism; and Burt Rutan, the aircraft designer whose Scaled Composites company developed the mother ship and space plane that will transport wealthy tourists into space. According to Virgin Galactic's promotional material, a fare of $200,000 will allow passengers a few minutes of gravity-defying flight 62 miles above the Earth's surface.

The 27-square-mile Spaceport facility is in southern New Mexico, 30 miles east of Truth or Consequences and 45 miles north of Las Cruces.

Spanish Colonial Arts Society

Nonprofit organization devoted to the preservation and promotion of decorative and functional objects from the Spanish Colonial Period. The Society was founded by writer Mary Austin and artist Frank Applegate in 1925 and began sponsoring Spanish Market in 1926. It is headquartered in the Museum of Spanish Colonial Art.

Spanish Colonial Period

The first 223 years of New Mexico's history, when it was part of Spain's New World colonial empire The Spanish Colonial Period lasted from 1598, when Don Juan de Oñate led his soldiers into New Mexico, until 1821, when Mexico achieved independence from Spain. Northern New Mexico's unique culture was shaped during this long period of isolation.

Spanish Market

Exhibition and sale of Hispanic art. The festive mid-summer event features about 200 booths displaying bultos, retablos, tinwork, straw appliqué, and other traditional art forms. Artist Frank Applegate and writer Mary Austin, founders of the Spanish Colonial Arts Society, organized the first market in 1926 with just 15 artists. It faded out after 1939 but was reinvigorated in 1965. Today, it is the largest exhibition of traditional Spanish art in the country.

Spanish Market has become a biannual event. The summer market is held on and around the Plaza the last weekend in July. The smaller winter market is held in the Santa Fe Community Convention Center on the first weekend in December.

Contemporary Hispanic Market was formed in 1985 by an independent group of artists whose work did not meet the Spanish Colonial Arts Society's definition of "traditional." Contemporary Hispanic Market is held at the same time as the summer Spanish Market.

Spanish Pueblo style

One of two distinct types of Santa Fe-style architecture. Spanish Pueblo style represents the architecture of the Spanish Colonial Period, before kiln-dried bricks and milled window and door frames were widely available. It is characterized by soft edges and curved lines, deep-set windows, vigas extending through exterior walls, and rough-hewn lintels, columns, and corbels. (The other type of Santa Fe-style architecture, called Territorial style, does include red bricks and milled woodwork. Territorial style appears more finished than Spanish Pueblo style.)

The New Mexico Museum of Art is a good example of Spanish Pueblo-style architecture.

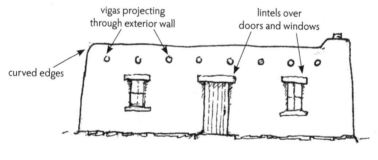

Spanish Pueblo style

Spitz Clock

Oversized pocket watch that stands on the northwest corner of the Santa Fe Plaza near the New Mexico Museum of Art. The 1880s-era monument clock serves as a meeting place and reference point for tourists exploring the Plaza.

Spitz clock

The original clock stood in front of the Spitz brothers' jewelry store on San Francisco Street, on the south side of the Plaza. It had to be replaced in 1915 after a truck – one of the first in Santa Fe – collided with it and damaged it beyond repair. The replacement clock stood until 1967, when construction of a portal over the San Francisco Street sidewalk required its removal. Bernard Spitz donated the clock to the city, and it was ensconced in its present location in 1974.

The Spitz clock played a small role in Santa Fe's spy history. In 1945, physicist Klaus Fuchs and KGB courier Harry Gold synchronized their watches to the clock before meeting at the Castillo Street Bridge. Fuchs turned over America's atomic secrets at that meeting.

split estate

Property-right system in which the surface rights to land and the sub-surface mineral rights to the same land are separately owned. In 2007, landowners in the Galisteo Basin south of Santa Fe were shocked when an oil company announced plans to build roads and drill wells on their land. The state and Santa Fe County managed to delay the drilling, but the issue died only when the price of oil dropped and the company canceled its plans. People buying land in New Mexico are advised to inquire about subsurface mineral rights.

Springer

Northern New Mexico town on I-25 between Wagon Mound and Raton. Once part of the Maxwell Land Grant, Springer is near the point at which the Cimarron Cutoff rejoins the main branch of the Santa Fe Trail. The former Colfax County courthouse in Springer is now the Santa Fe Trail Museum. The Springer Correctional Center is the town's main industry.

Springer, population 1,047, is 136 miles northeast of Santa Fe.

Spy's Guide to Santa Fe and Albuquerque, A

Overview of New Mexico's spy history. Author E.B. Held recounts how the assassination of Leon Trotsky was orchestrated from what is now the Plaza Bakery, how Los Alamos physicist Klaus Fuchs passed on America's atomic secrets in a meeting on a Santa Fe bridge, and how fired CIA agent Edward Lee Howard escaped from his FBI tail after eating dinner at a Canyon Road restaurant. Held also explores the possibility that Manhattan Project chief scientist J. Robert Oppenheimer was a Soviet agent (he was not) and details the full story of Wen Ho Lee's arrest and 10-month imprisonment. Held is a retired CIA clandestine operations officer. His book was published in 2011.

squash blossom necklace

Indian jewelry. The necklace typically features a pendant called a *naja* (Navajo for "crescent"), which is suspended from beaded strands. Experts say that the naja shape was copied from the decorative trappings on the horses of Spanish conquistadors, and that it was originally a Moorish design.

The necklace gets its name from the shape of its beads, which resemble squash blossoms. Originally, the Navajo fashioned the necklaces in silver. When the Zuni picked up the motif, they added turquoise and other stones to the traditional design.

Squash blossom necklace

A squash blossom necklace is featured on the United States Post Office's 2006 two-cent stamp.

St. Catherine Indian School

Abandoned Indian school. The Santa Fe institution was founded in 1887 by Philadelphia heiress Katharine Drexel, who became a nun in 1891. Drexel was devoted to the education of black and Indian children and established many schools, including Xavier University in New Orleans, in furtherance of that cause. In 2000, she became the second American to be canonized into sainthood. (The Indian school is sometimes called St. Kate's, but it was originally named for St. Catherine of Siena, not St. Katharine Drexel.)

Hispanic and Anglo kids who had trouble in the Santa Fe public schools were sometimes sent to St. Kate's to see if the nuns could straighten them out. Leroy Arthur Petry, a member of the school's last graduating class, was one of these. In 2011, the Army Ranger was awarded the Medal of Honor for his actions in Afghanistan. Petry is only the second living recipient of the Medal of Honor since the Vietnam War.

St. Kate's shut its doors in 1998, and the Sisters of the Blessed Sacrament, the religious order that Drexel founded, sold the buildings and 18 acres in 2005. The current owner has considered turning the school

St. Catherine
Indian
School

buildings into condominiums or selling the land to the Santa Fe National Cemetery, but these plans have not worked out.

St. Catherine Indian School is on Griffin Street, above Rosario Cemetery.

St. Francis Auditorium

Performance space in the New Mexico Museum of Art. The 450-seat auditorium is used for lectures and concerts, including those of the Santa Fe Chamber Music Festival and the Santa Fe Community Orchestra. Murals in the auditorium link the Spanish Pueblo-style museum building to St. Francis of Assisi and New Mexico's early Franciscan missions.

St. Francis Cathedral

Santa Fe's landmark Catholic church. (The Vatican designated the cathedral a basilica in 2005 in recognition of its historic importance. It is now officially named "The Cathedral Basilica of St. Francis of Assisi," but most people still refer to it as St. Francis Cathedral.)

St. Francis Cathedral, as originally planned

The cathedral was the pet project of Archbishop Jean Baptiste Lamy. The 25-year construction project began in 1869 when the cathedral walls were laid out around the parroquia, or parish church, that stood on the site. Church members attended services in the parroquia while the cathedral was being constructed around and above it. When the cathedral was complete, the parroquia was demolished and the debris was hauled out from inside the new building. Today, a small chapel dedicated to La Conquistadora is the only remaining remnant of the old parroquia. Archbishop Lamy was buried under the new cathedral's sanctuary floor after his death in 1888.

One of the curiosities of the building as it stands today is the difference in its towers – there are eight stone blocks visible on the north tower, while the south tower has none. The explanation lies in the archdiocese's perennial shortage of funds: when the north tower was completed in the 1880s, it was assumed that a spire would be added, and the eight stone blocks were installed to anchor it; by 1894, when the south tower was finally completed, it was accepted that the spires would not be forthcoming, and the eight stones were omitted. (An 1885 line drawing shows what the spires would have looked like. Many people feel that the cathedral looks better without them.)

The four Hebrew characters inscribed within a triangle over the cathedral's main entrance are another curiosity. The popular theory is that the inscription was Archbishop Lamy's expression of gratitude to the Jewish families who contributed to the cathedral's building fund. It is true that Lamy had many Jewish friends and that they contributed to

St. Francis Cathedral today

the fund. It is also true that the Jewish community contributed to the construction of Holy Faith Episcopal Church, and that a stained-glass Star of David was installed above Holy Faith's entrance in thanks for their help. This does not mean, however, that the popular theory about the cathedral is accurate.

Catholic priest and New Mexico historian Fray Angélico Chávez did not believe that the Hebrew letters within a triangle were a Jewish symbol. According to Chávez, the triangle around the *tetragrammaton*, as the four letters are called, makes it a Christian symbol, with the Hebrew letters representing Christianity's Judaic origins, and the triangle representing the Trinity. The symbol does appear in other Christian contexts, including in a chapel in the Palace of Versailles, so the story about it being tribute to Santa Fe's Jewish community may be apocryphal.

St. Francis Cathedral is one of downtown Santa Fe's three landmark churches. The others are Holy Faith Episcopal Church and First Presbyterian Church.

St. Francis Drive

Santa Fe's primary north-south artery. Before St. Francis Drive was completed in 1964, the route through the city to Española and points north was circuitous and time-consuming. The six-lane road was needed, but its construction required the demolition of many homes and the bisecting of Santa Fe's Westside. The area between Guadalupe Street and St. Francis Drive is now known as the "near Westside."

St. John's College

One of Santa Fe's two expensive, private colleges, the Santa Fe University of Art and Design being the other. St. John's opened in 1964 as the second campus of St. John's College of Annapolis, Maryland. Both campuses follow a Great Books curriculum in which students read, discuss, and write about the classics. Architect John Gaw Meem donated the 260-acre campus, and the school's library is named for him. Notable Johnnies, as St. John's students and alumni are called, include *Santa Fe Reporter* editor Andy Dudzik, environmentalist Sam Hitt, writer Duncan North, and entrepreneur Gerald Peters.

St. John's is on Camino de Cruz Blanca, near that road's intersection with Camino Cabra.

St. Michael's High School

Santa Fe's Catholic high school. St. Michael's is the city's oldest and largest private high school. (Runner-up Santa Fe Prep has less than half of St Michael's enrollment of about 800 students.)

St. Michael's dates back to 1859, when Archbishop Lamy invited four Christian Brothers from France to start a school for boys. The school moved to its present location on Siringo Road in 1967 and began admitting girls in 1968.

Students root for the Horsemen and the oxymoronic Lady Horsemen. Political blogger Heath Haussamen graduated from St. Michael's in 1997.

St. Vincent Hospital

See Christus St. Vincent Regional Medical Center and Old St. Vincent Hospital.

Staab, Julia (STOB)

(1844-1896) Notorious ghost. Berlin-born Julia Schuster Staab was the beautiful wife of Jewish merchant Abraham Staab. The couple's large house on Palace Avenue was a center of social activity for Santa Fe's business and political elites, and their seven children added to the lively atmosphere.

Julia's troubles began when she became inconsolable after her eighth child died soon after birth. She was so depressed that she took to her bed and stayed there until her death at age 52.

The ghost story suggests that Julia committed suicide or was murdered by her husband. Guests and staff at La Posada, the upscale hotel surrounding the Staab house, report seeing ghostly images around the hotel, particularly in the room where Julia died.

The Staabs' earthly remains are entombed in a mausoleum in Fairview Cemetery.

Stamm, Allen

(1912-2003) Prolific Santa Fe homebuilder. A native of Albuquerque and a graduate of the University of New Mexico, Stamm began building homes in Santa Fe in the mid-1930s. He served in the navy in World War II and reentered the construction business after the war. His postwar housing developments include Casa Linda (better known as the Kaune neighborhood), Casa Alegre, and Casa Solana, his largest project at over 750 homes. Most of his Spanish Pueblo-style houses feature wood floors, vigas, and kiva fireplaces.

In 1950, Allen Stamm and his family figured in one of Santa Fe's strangest and most sensational crimes. See CAMPBELL, NANCY.

state prison

See PENITENTIARY OF NEW MEXICO.

statehood

New Mexico's tenure as a state, which began in 1912. New Mexico was a territory for a long time, from 1846 to 1912, because various interests opposed statehood. An 1876 editorial in the *Milwaukee Sentinel* reflects the prejudice against New Mexico that was held by many Americans at that time. The editorial describes New Mexico as "the tag end of all that is objectionable in an imperfect civilization" and notes that "The scum and dregs of the American, Spanish, Mexican, and Indian people are there concentrated ...."

Some people within the Territory also opposed statehood. Mining and timbering interests were against it because they thought their taxes would go up. Catholic Church leaders were opposed because they thought the church would be weakened if too many Protestants rushed into the new state.

On the other hand, most Hispanics favored statehood because their majority population ensured that they would be represented in Congress. They were joined by large landowners, Thomas B. Catron among them, who assumed that statehood would increase the value of their real estate holdings.

Turquoise license plates commemorating New Mexico's 2012 statehood centennial were introduced in 2009.

Stewart, Betty

(1925-1994) Homebuilder and authentic local character. Stewart was raised on a ranch in Texas but made her name in Santa Fe. She is associated with Northern New Mexico-style buildings, which are distinguished from Santa Fe-style buildings primarily by their pitched roofs. One still sees real estate ads for "Betty Stewart-style" homes.

Stewart was openly gay, hard-drinking, and cantankerous. A story in Eli Levin's 2007 book *Santa Fe Bohemia, the Art Colony 1964-1980* tells of an encounter with Stewart. Levin was tending bar at Claude's on Canyon Road when an old lady wearing cowboy clothes came in and sat down. The manager told Levin who she was and instructed him to treat her well.

The band started playing, and Stewart beat time on the bar. After a while, she grabbed a "natty little middle-aged fellow, wearing a blazer and an ascot" and dragged him out onto the dance floor. The couple danced for a bit but were too drunk to do it well. All of sudden, for reasons unknown, Stewart threw the little man across the floor into the band's drum set. She then quietly exited the bar.

Stewart left a $1 million endowment to the Santa Fe Animal Shelter and Humane Society. Her portrait hangs on the wall in the shelter's Robin Sommers building.

Storyteller

Tableau of small clay figures in which a Pueblo woman, her mouth open as she speaks, sits surrounded by attentive children. The storyteller motif was developed by Helen Cordero of Cochiti Pueblo.

straw appliqué

The art and craft of decorating crosses and other items with gold-colored straw or corn husks. The "poor man's gilding" served as an inexpensive substitute for gold during New Mexico's Spanish Colonial Period. The straw appliqué technique was revived in the 1930s.

Straw appliqué

Studi, Wes (STEW-dee)

(1947-) Cherokee movie actor, musician, Vietnam veteran, political activist, and Santa Fe-area resident. Studi has appeared in numerous movies but is probably best known for his role as Magua, the vengeful Huron chief in *The Last of the Mohicans.* He plays bass, and his wife, Maura, sings lead vocals in a local band called Firecat of Discord.

Wes Studi

Sun Mountain

Broad hill south of Atalaya Mountain and just east of Old Santa Fe Trail. Camino del Monte Sol, "Sun Mountain Road," and the old Sunmount Sanatorium were both named for the 7,920-foot hill.

Sunmount Sanatorium

Santa Fe's health retreat for people with tuberculosis. Sunmount Tent City was established as a rustic resort in 1902. It was a struggling enterprise until 1906, when Dr. Frank Mera bought the property and turned it into a sanatorium for tubercular patients. (Frank's brother, Dr. Harry Mera, designed New Mexico's Zia flag.)

There were upwards of 60 sanatoriums in New Mexico in the early 20th century, but Mera succeeded in attracting a better class of "lunger" when he billed Sunmount as "The Sanatorium Different." The upscale facility offered lectures and readings by accomplished patients as well as by visiting luminaries like poet Carl Sandburg. Sunmount alumni include artist Carlos Vierra, poet Alice Corbin Henderson, and architect John Gaw Meem.

Sanatoriums lost business during the Depression and became obsolete when streptomycin was discovered as a cure for TB in the 1940s. Dr. Mera eventually sold the Sunmount property to the Archdiocese of Santa Fe. Today, the buildings and grounds at the intersection of Old Santa Fe Trail and Camino del Monte Sol are occupied by the Carmelite Monastery and the Immaculate Heart of Mary Retreat and Conference Center.

Sunmount Sanatorium Administration Building, circa 1910

Sunport

The Albuquerque airport. Santa Fe has a small municipal airport, but because service is limited, most visitors fly into the Albuquerque International Sunport and then drive or take a shuttle bus for the 60-mile trip to Santa Fe.

SWAIA (SWY-uh)

Acronym for the Southwestern Association for Indian Arts. The acronym is used more often than the full name.

swamp cooler

Low-cost, low-tech evaporative air cooler seen on the roofs of many New Mexico homes. Swamp coolers are essentially electric fans that draw air through water-moistened pads. They work well in the Southwest's low humidity.

- T -

T or C

Shorthand for the city of Truth or Consequences.

taco (TAH-co)

A tortilla, fried until crisp and filled with some combination of meat, cheese, beans, chopped lettuce, tomatoes, and onions. The New Mexico Air National Guard's 150th Fighter Wing, based at Kirtland Air Force Base, was nicknamed the "Tacos" during the Vietnam era.

Talavera tile (tah-lah-VAIR-uh)

Colorful Mexican tile. Talavera tiles feature Moorish designs and are patterned after tiles that were originally produced in Talavera de la Reina, Spain. The tiles are not strong enough for flooring but they are often used in backsplashes and other vertical surfaces.

tamale (*tuh-MA-lee)

A New Mexico Christmas tradition. Tamales are steamed in a corn husk that is discarded before eating. The tamale itself is corn dough, or *masa*, wrapped around various ingredients like chicken, pork, beef, cheese, and vegetables. Chiles are often included in New Mexican tamales.

*The singular of this word is actually *tamal*, pronounced tuh-MAL, but most people say *tamale*.

Tamalewood

Cutesy name for New Mexico and its burgeoning film industry. Luminous skies, uncluttered vistas, and cultural diversity have made the state a favorite among filmmakers since the Edison Company shot *Indian Day School* at Isleta Pueblo in 1898. The pace of film production in the state increased dramatically with the 2002 implementation of a 25 percent refund to film companies for direct, state-taxable production expenditures, including wages paid to state residents.

tamarisk (TAM-uh-risk)

Pernicious, non-native, riparian plant; the bane of the bosque. The genus *Tamarix*, also known as the salt cedar, was introduced into the western United States in the early 19th century as an ornamental shrub. It quickly spread out of control in marshes and along waterways, where it now displaces native plants and wildlife and consumes prodigious amounts of water. It is estimated that in any given year, tamarisk plants absorb roughly the same amount of water from the Colorado River Basin as is allocated to the state of Nevada.

Tanoan (tah-NO-un)

A group of languages spoken by Pueblo Indians. The Tanoan group includes the Tewa, Tiwa, and Towa languages. Tiwa is spoken at Isleta, Sandia, Picuris, and Taos pueblos, and Tewa is spoken at Nambé, Pojoaque, San Ildefonso, Ohkay Owingeh, Santa Clara, and Tesuque pueblos. Towa is spoken only at Jemez Pueblo. New Mexico's other pueblos speak Keres or Zunian.

Taos (*TA-os)

Northern New Mexico's rebellious second city. In the 17th, 18th, and 19th centuries, when Santa Fe was the center of authority for the Spanish, Mexican, and American governments, the town of Taos and nearby Taos Pueblo were at the center of every rebellion against that authority. The 1680 Pueblo Revolt, in which the Spanish were expelled from New Mexico, was organized in Taos Pueblo. The 1837 Chimayó Rebellion resulted in the beheading of the duly appointed Mexican governor and the installation of a rebel governor from Ranchos de Taos. The 1847 Taos Revolt against the new American government was a collaboration between Hispanic Taoseños and Indians from Taos Pueblo. And for most of the latter half of the 19th century, Taos's Padre Antonio José Martinez challenged the authority of Santa Fe's Archbishop Jean Baptiste Lamy.

Taos became less violent and more artsy in the 20th century. Anglo painters discovered the town in 1898 and established the Taos art colony. Mabel Dodge Luhan arrived in 1918 and set up a salon that attracted other creative types, including D.H. Lawrence, Georgia O'Keeffe, and Willa Cather. In the late 1960s and early 1970s, Dennis Hopper and the Taos hippies shocked the town with their alternative lifestyle.

The town, current population 5,716, is calmer now, but locals still take pride in its independence and eccentricity. Residents include former Governor Gary Johnson, author John Nichols, singer-songwriter Michael Martin Murphey, and mountain guide Dave Hahn. Part-timers include actress Julia Roberts and former defense secretary Donald Rumsfeld.

Taos is Northern New Mexico's second most popular tourist destination, after Santa Fe, and most visitors to Santa Fe make a day trip to Taos at some point in their stay. The town is on the Enchanted Circle, 70 miles north of Santa Fe via the "low road" that follows the Rio Grande. The High Road to Taos, which meanders through the villages of Chimayó, Truchas, Las Trampas, and Peñasco, runs about 76 miles.

*The syllables are slurred together so that the word sounds something like *towels*, only without the *l*.

Taos art colony

The first Anglo artists to become infatuated with Northern New Mexico. Painter Joseph Henry Sharp visited Santa Fe and Taos in the 1880s and 1890s and enthusiastically recommended New Mexico to his artist friends. In 1898, Bert Phillips and Ernest Blumenschein took Sharp's advice. They were on a sightseeing trip from Denver to Mexico when their wagon wheel broke, and Blumenschein lost the coin toss to see who would take the wheel into Taos for repair. Awed by the land around him as he slowly made his way into town, Blumenschein later wrote, "No artist had ever recorded the New Mexico I was now seeing. I was receiving ... the first great unforgettable inspiration of my life."

The art colony was born when Sharp, Blumenschein, and Phillips moved to Taos in the following years. They formed the Taos Society of Artists in 1915. Mabel Dodge Luhan, herself an amateur painter, vigorously promoted the town and its art colony after her arrival in Taos in 1918.

Taos Box

The stretch of white water that runs through the Rio Grande Gorge near Taos. (It is called a box because of the high canyon walls on either side of the river.) Commercial rafting operations based in Taos and Santa Fe offer guided excursions through the Taos Box.

Taos hippie

One of the many counterculture types who lived in or near Taos in the late 1960s and early 1970s. The New Buffalo commune, the first in the area, was established in 1967, and the Taos hippie population exploded after the 1969 release of the movie *Easy Rider*, which featured a commune scene based on New Buffalo. *Easy Rider* director Dennis Hopper bought the Mabel Dodge Luhan house in 1970, and, by 1971, there were nine communes around Taos.

The hippies had decidedly liberal ideas about sex and drugs so it was inevitable that there would be tension between the newcomers and the socially conservative Norteños. In May 1969, *The Taos News* reported a series of fights between Taoseños and hippies. One local said of the altercations, "Maybe things will settle down when the hippies catch on that somebody doesn't like them."

Scrapbook of a Taos Hippie (2000) by Iris Keltz records the recollections of some early hippies as well as contemporary articles from *The Taos News* and an alternative paper called the *Fountain of Light*. Lisa Law's *Flashing on the Sixties* includes photographs of the Taos hippie scene.

Taos hum

Mysterious, low-pitched hum. A few Taos residents first reported hearing the sound in the summer of 1992. In early 1993, Bill Richardson, who was at that time the congressman from Northern New Mexico, suggested that the noise might be related to some activity by the Department of Defense, but Senator Pete Domenici relayed assurances from the Pentagon that this was not the case. In August 1993, scientific investigators organized by UNM reported that there was a sonic vibration of 30 to 80 hertz, but they failed to isolate it. In a concurrent survey, two percent of Taos residents reported hearing the sound.

Interest in the phenomenon died out after a brief flurry of national publicity, including an article in the *Wall Street Journal.*

Taos News, The

Taos's weekly newspaper. The Thursday paper was founded in 1959 by *The New Mexican* publisher Robert McKinney and is today owned by his daughter, Robin McKinney Martin. Like *The New Mexican, The Taos News* endorsed Gore, Kerry, and Obama in the last three presidential races.

Taos Pueblo

The northernmost and best known of the Eight Northern Indian Pueblos. The 1680 Pueblo Revolt in which the united pueblos expelled the Spanish from New Mexico was organized in Taos Pueblo.

The pueblo's multistoried adobe homes, which appear much as they did before the Spanish arrived in 1598, have been the subject of innumerable paintings and photographs since the formation of the Taos art colony in the early 20th century. Well-known natives of Taos Pueblo include Tony Lujan, husband of Mabel Dodge Luhan, and musician

Taos Pueblo in 1880

Robert Mirabal. The Tiwa-speaking pueblo is 73 miles north of Santa Fe, three miles north of the town of Taos.

Taos Revolt

The bloody rebellion against the new American government during the Mexican-American War. Anxious to continue his march west after occupying Santa Fe in August 1846, General Stephen Watts Kearny appointed local civilians to head an American government. Though most New Mexicans seemed to accept American rule, unrest among Hispanics in the town of Taos and Indians in Taos Pueblo exploded in an orgy of violence in mid-January 1847.

Charles Bent, the newly appointed Territorial governor, was pierced with arrows and scalped in front of his family before finally being killed, and other officials were likewise tortured before being put to death. American troops garrisoned in Santa Fe marched to Taos and put down the rebellion in early February 1847. Scores of rebels were killed in the fighting and dozens more were executed after summary trials.

Kit Carson, whose wife, Josefa, witnessed the rebel atrocities, believed that Padre Antonio José Martinez had provoked or at least condoned the revolt. Martinez denied the accusation and eventually became a leader in the Territorial legislature.

Taos Ski Valley

The village built to serve the Taos Ski Valley Resort. At 9,200 feet, Taos Ski Valley is the highest incorporated municipality in New Mexico. There are fewer than 100 full-time residents, but visitors number in the hundreds of thousands during ski season. Mountain guide Dave Hahn works on the slopes as a ski patroller in the winter. Taos Ski Valley is 20 miles northeast of Taos.

Taos Society of Artists

See TAOS ART COLONY.

Taoseño/a (tah-o-SANE-yo/yah)

A person who lives in Taos.

tapas (TAH-puhs)

Appetizers. Spanish diners once used small plates to cover their drinks, and *tapa*, which means "lid" or "cover," refers to the small plates on which the appetizers are served. Diners usually order multiple tapas in lieu of a main course and share them among those at the table. El Farol, a popular bar and restaurant on Santa Fe's Canyon Road, is known for its tapas.

tecolote (teh-cuh-LO-tay)

"Owl." Owls are common in Northern New Mexico. The nocturnal predators are responsible for the disappearance of small pets in Santa Fe's outlying areas, including the Eldorado subdivision south of town.

Some Indians see owls as bad omens. Marta Handey, a volunteer at The Wildlife Center, once took a few birds to one of the pueblo schools for an educational presentation. The eighth graders enjoyed seeing the hawk and the falcon, but some of them covered their faces when she brought out an owl.

The Northern New Mexico village of Tecolote is 58 miles southeast of Santa Fe via I-25 north.

Tecolote Café

Longtime Santa Fe restaurant known for its breakfasts. The Tecolote Café was opened by Bill Jennison in 1980. (He named his diner for the village of Tecolote, not for the owl.) Jennison died in 2010, and the restaurant is now run by his daughter, Katie Adkins. It is open for breakfast and lunch. The Tecolote Café is on Cerrillos Road, just south of its intersection with Alta Vista Street.

Tejano/a (tay-HA-no/nuh)

Spanish term for a Texan. Visitors to New Mexico from the Lone Star State are better received now, but there was a time when they were openly disparaged. In the words of Tony Hillerman, *Tejano* was once "a pejorative term which covered Texans and all others with more money than manners." In the 2010 gubernatorial election, Diane Denish's campaign tried hard to diminish Susana Martinez's appeal to Hispanic New Mexicans. Martinez was born in El Paso, so the Denish camp called her

"Susana la Tejana." *Tejano* also refers to the style of music played along the Tex-Mex border. (See also TEXAS.)

Ten Thousand Waves

Luxurious, Japanese-style spa. Founded in 1981 by owner Duke Klauck, Ten Thousand Waves offers private and communal hot tubs, extensive spa services, and 13 rooms for overnight guests. The baths are particularly appealing to skiers coming down Hyde Park Road from Ski Santa Fe.

The communal tubs are bathing-suit optional for most of the day. Those who are uncomfortable with public nudity and creative body piercing should go after 8:15 p.m., when suits are required.

Ten Thousand Waves is on Hyde Park Road, three and a half miles north of the Santa Fe Plaza.

Tent Rocks National Monument

An eerie landscape of tent-shaped hoodoos (rock formations that have been created by wind and water erosion). The site is popular with tourists, who can easily walk through the striking formations on the 1.2-mile Cave Loop Trail. The 4,645-acre preserve is officially known as the Kasha-Katuwe Tent Rocks

Tent Rocks National Monument

National Monument. (*Kasha-Katuwe* means "white cliffs" in Keresan, the language spoken at nearby Cochiti Pueblo.) The monument is 40 miles southwest of Santa Fe via I-25, NM 16, and NM 22.

Territorial Period

From 1846 to 1912, when New Mexico was a United States Territory. The Americanization of New Mexico began with the opening of the

Santa Fe Trail in 1821 and continued through the rest of the Mexican Period, but it accelerated rapidly during the Territorial Period. Trade with the rest of the United States intensified, Anglo businessmen and land speculators rushed in to make their fortunes, and the Catholic hierarchy dispatched Bishop Jean Baptiste Lamy to reform the local church. New Mexico remained a territory longer than any of the 48 contiguous states because statehood was opposed by various factions, both within and without the territory.

Territorial Revival style

One of two distinct types of Santa Fe-style architecture. Territorial-style buildings have red brick cornices on their parapets and neoclassical window and door frames. These enhancements became possible during the Territorial Period, when kiln-dried bricks and milled wood were freighted in over the Santa Fe Trail. Architect John Gaw Meem revived the style in the late 1920s.

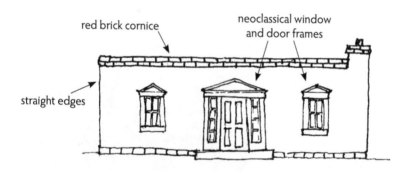

Territorial Revival Style

Territory, New Mexico

See NEW MEXICO TERRITORY.

Tesuque (*tuh-SUE-key)

Small village seven miles north of the Santa Fe Plaza. Santa Feans make the quick trip to Tesuque to visit the Shidoni foundry or to eat at the

Tesuque Village Market. Upscale homes, including those of actress Ali MacGraw, director Robert Redford, and novelist Cormac McCarthy, are nestled in the hills above Tesuque. The village is named for nearby Tesuque Pueblo. Santa Feans drive to the village via US 84/285 or the more scenic Bishop's Lodge Road.

Tesuque is a Spanish spelling of a Tewa word, so there are variations in its pronunciation, particularly the last syllable. The people who live in the pueblo for which the village is named as well as most Anglos say tuh-SUE-*key*. Spanish speakers say tuh-SUE-*kay*.

Tesuque Pueblo (*tuh-SUE-key)

The pueblo closest to Santa Fe. Tesuque Pueblo is one of the Eight Northern Pueblos. It operates Camel Rock Casino and the Pueblo of Tesuque Flea Market. According to pueblo members, *tesuque* means "place of cottonwood trees." The Tewa-speaking pueblo is 10 miles north of the Santa Fe Plaza, just west of US 84/285.

*The pueblo's name is pronounced tuh-SUE-*key*, not tuh-SUE-*kay*.

Tesuque Village Market (*tuh-SUE-key)

Neighborhood convenience store and casual dining restaurant in the village of Tesuque. TVM was owned by Jerry Honnell from 1989 to 2006, when he sold it to Michael Stein and Chris Foley. The diner, which is open for breakfast, lunch, and dinner, features wood-oven pizza. There are many first and second homes of the rich and famous nestled in the hills above the village, so it is not unusual to see a celebrity at TVM. Tesuque Village Market is seven miles north of the Santa Fe Plaza via US 84/285 or Bishop's Lodge Road.

*The market's name is pronounced tuh-SUE-*key*, not tuh-SUE-*kay*.

Teters, Charlene

(1952-) Indian political activist, artist, and editor. Teters is known for her protests against using Indians as mascots for sports teams. A member of the Spokane Tribe from Washington state, Teters first came to Santa Fe to attend the Institute of American Indian Arts (IAIA). In 1989, while pursuing an MFA at the University of Illinois, Teters objected to the school's Indian-chief mascot as demeaning to Native Americans. *In Whose Honor?*, a PBS documentary about her protest, made her the national spokesperson on the issue. Now back in Santa Fe, Teters teaches at IAIA.

Tewa (TAY-wuh)

Pueblo language spoken at Nambé, Ohkay Owingeh, Pojoaque, Santa Clara, San Ildefonso, and Tesuque pueblos.

Texas

The monster state to the east. In the 19th century, New Mexicans justifiably feared invasion by their larger neighbor. Texans did invade New Mexico in 1841 (see next entry) and again in 1862, albeit this time in the guise of Confederates (see GLORIETA PASS, BATTLE OF). In the 20th century, the worry was more about cultural domination, particularly as Texans led the tourist wave of the 1980s.

Norteños like to make fun of their neighbors' big hair and brash self-confidence, but the fact is that Texans have contributed much more than tourist dollars to Northern New Mexico. Texas oilman E. E. "Buddy" Fogelson and his wife, Greer Garson, generously supported the College of Santa Fe (now the Santa Fe University of Art and Design), and Texas-born homebuilder Betty Stewart developed Northern New Mexico-style architecture. Artists like sculptor Glenna Goodacre and musicians Bill Hearne and Michael Martin Murphey have also added to the region's cultural mix. But philanthropist Anne Marion has made the greatest contribution. Her funding of the Georgia O'Keeffe Museum and SITE Santa Fe in the late 1990s helped Santa Fe overcome its reputation as a market for regional kitsch. Thanks in large part to Ms. Marion, Santa Fe is now the second largest art market in the country.

New Mexicans usually think of Texans as Anglos, but two Hispanics born in the Lone Star State have had – or will have – great influence on New Mexico. Reies Lopez Tijerina led the Alianza movement in the 1960s, and Susana Martinez now presides over the state as the nation's first Hispanic female governor.

Texas-Santa Fe Expedition

Unsuccessful attempt by the fledgling Republic of Texas to establish control over New Mexico. In 1841, Texas President Mirabeau B. Lamar organized a contingent of merchants and soldiers and sent them on a march to Santa Fe. Lamar's exact intentions are unclear, but the Chimayó Rebellion of 1837 may have led him to believe that the 20-year-old Mexican government was unstable and that New Mexico was ripe for the taking.

The expedition did not make it to Santa Fe. The men got lost on the vast *Llano Estacado*, or "Staked Plains," of west Texas and eastern New Mexico and were easily rounded up by Mexican troops under the command of New Mexico Governor Manuel Armijo. Armijo forced the exhausted Texans on a long, painful march to Mexico City. They were released the following year, but the expedition remained a sore point between Texas and Mexico – and between the United States and Mexico after Texas was annexed by the U.S. in 1845. Historians cite the ill-fated Texas-Santa Fe Expedition and the rough treatment of the captured Texans as factors in the lead-up to the Mexican-American War.

Thank God for Mississippi

Exclamation of appreciation for the fact that Mississippi (or some other southern state) usually scores lower than New Mexico in social measures. When Governor Bill Richardson appeared on *Meet the Press* during his 2008 campaign for the Democratic presidential nomination, he was asked why he should be elected to lead the country when, after five years in office, his own state ranked 48th in people living below the poverty line, 47th in median family income, 49th in people without health insurance, and 46th in violent crime. (His answer was along the lines of "You should have seen it before.")

THE magazine

Free art tabloid. *THE* is Santa Fe's monthly magazine of "international art, photography, culture, and restaurant dining." The periodical was founded in 1993 by photographer Guy Cross, son of the late painter Doris Cross.

Third Congressional District

The newest of New Mexico's three congressional districts. Redistricting after the 1980 census resulted in the creation of the heavily Democratic district, which includes Northern New Mexico. It was first represented by Bill Richardson, who occupied the congressional seat from 1983 until 1997, when he was appointed ambassador to the United Nations.

Registered Democrats outnumber registered Republicans by almost two to one in the district. These numbers should ensure consistent Democratic

New Mexico Congressional Districts

representation, but this was not the case in 1997 when a special election was held for Richardson's replacement. The Democratic nominee, Eric Serna, was supported by most Hispanics but was seen as a political hack by Anglo progressives, who voted for the Green Party candidate, Carol Miller. The split in the Democratic party resulted in the election of Los Alamos Republican Bill Redmond. His tenure was short-lived, however, as Tom Udall reclaimed the seat for the Democrats in the 1998 regular election. He held it until 2008, when he was elected to the Senate. Udall was replaced by the Third District's current representative, Democrat Ben Ray Luján, Jr.

Thoreau (thuh-ROO, THROO)

New Mexico town notable only for its nonstandard pronunciation. *The Place Names of New Mexico* notes that Thoreau was named for naturalist Henry David Thoreau, but that locals insist that it was named for someone else – an army paymaster or a railroad contractor – whose name was pronounced as indicated above. The town is off I-40, 31 miles east of Gallup.

Thornburg, Garrett

(1946-) Founder of one of Santa Fe's most successful businesses. Originally from Minnesota, Thornburg graduated from Williams College and Harvard Business School before beginning a career in finance. He left New York, where he worked for Bear Stearns, and moved to Santa Fe in 1981. In 1982, he started Thornburg Investment Management. (Thornburg Mortgage was established in 1993 but that company was mortally wounded in the real estate recession and declared bankruptcy in 2009.) Thornburg Investment occupies a 100,000-square-foot "campus" on Ridgetop Road, near the intersection of US 84/285 and NM 599.

Thornburg is known for his philanthropy. He has contributed to the St. Vincent Hospital Foundation, the St. Elizabeth Shelter, the Santa Fe Community Foundation, the Partners in Education program, and other Santa Fe nonprofits. He is married to Catherine Oppenheimer, founder of the National Dance Institute of New Mexico.

Tia Sophia's

One of the Maryol family's restaurants. The downtown Santa Fe restaurant was established in 1975 by Jim and Ann Maryol. *Tia* means "aunt," but the restaurant was named for Jim's mother, Sophia. Today, it is owned and operated by his son, Nick Maryol.

Tia Sophia's is on West San Francisco Street, across the street from the Lensic.

Tierra Amarilla (tee-AIR-uh ah-ma-REE-uh)

The county seat of Rio Arriba County. Tierra Amarilla made headlines in June 1967 when members of the Alianza Federal de Mercedes led by land reform activist Reies Lopez Tijerina staged a raid on the Rio Arriba County Courthouse. The activists wounded two officers in a gun battle and briefly held two people hostage before surrendering.

Tierra Amarilla means "yellow earth." TA, as the village is sometimes called, is on US 84, 91 miles north of Santa Fe.

Tierra o Muerte!

(tee-AIR-uh o MWAIR-tay)

"Land or Death!", the rallying cry of the Alianza Federal de Mercedes. A billboard proclaiming this sentiment stands on US 84 near the turnoff for Tierra Amarilla.

tierra sagrada (tee-AIR-uh suh-GRAH-duh)

"Sacred land." The term can be seen on a bridge over US 84/285 north of Santa Fe.

Sign near Tierra Amarilla

Tijerina, Reies Lopez (tee-heh-REE-nuh, rays LO-pez)

(1926-) The 1960s political activist known as *El Tigre del Norte*, "The Tiger of the North." The fiery, Texas-born preacher founded and led the Alianza Federal de Mercedes, an organization dedicated to the return of millions of acres of land that it claimed had been illegally taken from Hispanic New Mexicans in violation of the Treaty of Guadalupe Hidalgo. Tijerina was jailed for his actions during the Alianza's raid on the Tierra Amarilla courthouse.

Tijerina's later speeches and writings reflect some bizarre theories about race, religion, and politics. In a speech at St. John's College, he concluded that Thomas B. Catron, a leader of the Santa Fe Ring and the most successful land-grabber in New Mexico history, must have been Jewish because "It takes a well-developed race to do what they did to the Spanish people." Tijerina now lives in El Paso.

tinwork

The art and craft of using a nail or punch to stamp designs on tin. Tinwork is considered a Spanish Colonial art form, although it really flourished in the Mexican Period (1821-1846) when tin cans brought in over the Santa Fe Trail were used to create sconces, boxes, and frames for pictures and mirrors. Just as straw appliqué is considered the "poor man's gilding," tinwork is considered the "poor man's silver."

Tinwork

Tiny's

Old-time Santa Fe restaurant. Tiny's was started in downtown Santa Fe in 1950 by Walter "Tiny" Moore, his wife, Lucille, and their daughter and son-in-law, Betty and Jimmie Palermo. The restaurant moved a few times before settling in its present location in 1971. The restaurant is now operated by Jimmie's son, J.R. Palermo, and his wife, Pamela. Their children constitute the fourth generation to work in the family business.

Tiny's is in the Crossroads Center, at the intersection of Cerrillos Road and St. Francis Drive.

tio/a (TEE-o/ah)

"Uncle" and "aunt."

Tiwa (TEE-wuh)

Language spoken at Isleta, Picuris, Sandia, and Taos pueblos.

Tomasita's (tom-uh-SEE-tuh's)

One of Santa Fe's busiest restaurants. Tomasita's, which is named for its first cook, was founded in 1974 by Georgia Maryol. The restaurant began life in a building on Hickox Street (the same building later housed Dave's Not Here and is now home to the Tune-Up Café) before moving to its current Guadalupe Street location in 1976.

Tomasita's New Mexican food is appreciated by Bill and Hillary Clinton, who make a point of eating there when they are in Santa Fe. The restaurant has reciprocated by naming one of its dining rooms the "Hillary Clinton Room."

Tomasita's is in the Railyard, in what was once the Santa Fe depot for the Chili Line.

Torreon

torreon (tore-ray-OWN)

A defensive tower common during the Spanish Colonial Period. The Poeh Center in Pojoaque features a prominent torreon.

tortilla (tor-TEE-uh)

"Little cake," a flat bread made from corn or wheat flour. Tortillas are the basic ingredient in many Latin American dishes, including tacos, burritos, and enchiladas. Northern New Mexico is known for blue corn tortillas.

tostada (toe-STAH-duh)

An open-faced tortilla, toasted and topped with beans, salsa, cheese, and chopped lettuce and tomato. Chiles are a common ingredient in New Mexican tostadas.

Towa (TOE-wuh)

Language spoken only at Jemez Pueblo. The people of Pecos Pueblo were also Towa speakers, but they abandoned their town and joined Jemez in 1838. *Towa* means "the people" in the Tewa language. The Towa Golf Course at the Buffalo Thunder Resort is owned and operated by Pojoaque Pueblo, whose people speak Tewa rather than Towa.

¡Traditions! shopping center

Hard-luck shopping center at the Budaghers exit off I-25, midway between Albuquerque and Santa Fe. The mall, which is currently unoccupied, is buffeted by incessant winds and is too far from the two cities to draw business from either. ¡Traditions! opened in 1993 as the New Mexico Outlet Center.

Trampas

See LAS TRAMPAS.

Tramway

See SANDIA PEAK TRAMWAY.

trastero (tra-STAIR-o)

A tall, carved Spanish Colonial cabinet or cupboard.

Travis, Randy

(1959-) Country singer and Santa Fe-area resident. When not on the road, Travis lives on a 220-acre ranch that the *Santa Fe Reporter* deems the third most valuable property in the area. Travis moved to Santa Fe in 1999.

Treaty of Guadalupe Hidalgo (gwah-duh-LOO-pay he-DOLL-go)

1848 treaty ending the Mexican-American War. The treaty ceded Mexico's northern territory, including New Mexico, to the United States and established the Rio Grande as Texas's southern border.

The treaty also guaranteed the existing property rights of Hispanic New Mexicans, though this proved easier to promise than to accomplish. Spanish and Mexican communal land grants were difficult to reconcile with the Anglo concept of private property. The resultant claims and counterclaims, fraud, and deceit enabled speculators like Thomas B. Catron to acquire vast tracts of land. Hispanic descendants of the original landowners have since argued, sometimes violently (see ALIANZA), that they are entitled to compensation for land taken from their ancestors in violation of the treaty.

Trementina Base (treh-men-TEE-nuh)

The Church of Scientology's unpublicized repository for the archived writings and recordings of its founder, L. Ron Hubbard.

A large symbol resembling two interlocking crop circles has been etched into the surface of the property. The symbol, which is visible from space, is meant to guide future Scientologists to the archives from other places in the universe. The site's landing strip and underground vaults are near the small San Miguel County village of Trementina, 119 miles east of Santa Fe.

Tres Piedras (TRACE pee-AY-druss)

"Three rocks," a small Northern New Mexico community. The "rocks" are granite formations that are popular with rock climbers. Tres Piedras is 82 miles north of Santa Fe and 28 miles south of the Colorado border, at the intersection of US 285 and US 64.

tribal sovereignty

An Indian community's limited right to self-government. The United States government recognizes tribes and pueblos as "domestic dependent nations" that are more sovereign than states but less sovereign than other countries. Tribal sovereignty applies only within Indian country, which is a legal term used to describe the geographical bounds of a self-governing

Indian community. The practical effect of tribal sovereignty is that Indian people in Indian country are largely exempt from state laws and taxes but are subject to tribal and federal laws and taxes.

tricultural model

The conceit that New Mexico is comprised of distinct Anglo, Hispanic, and Indian cultures. The tricultural model is flawed because it ignores the history of extensive intermarriage between its three ethnic components and because it lumps African-Americans, Asians, and East Indians in with Anglos. Historians believe that the model became useful when New Mexico was lobbying for statehood at the turn of the 20th century and mainstream America was opposed to mongrelization of the races.

The tricultural model is appreciated by some. In an interview in *Santa Fean* magazine, Indian activist Russell Means said, "Santa Fe is the only city that celebrates three cultures in harmony and individuality. It should be touted to the world."

Trinidad, Colorado

The small town long known as the "Sex Change Capital of the World." Dr. Stanley Biber (1923-2006) came to practice at the United Mine Workers clinic in Trinidad in 1954. In 1969, a patient asked him to perform a sex-change surgery, and Biber developed the procedures to do so. After performing thousands of sex-change operations and training dozens of surgeons, Biber retired in 2003 and turned his practice over to Dr. Marci Bowers, a gynecologist and a transsexual woman. Bowers still maintains an office in Trinidad but has moved her surgical practice to San Mateo, California.

Trinidad is 197 miles north of Santa Fe, on I-25 eight miles north of the New Mexico state line.

Trinity Site

Site of the world's first atomic explosion. On July 16, 1945, scientists from Los Alamos National Laboratory test-exploded the first atomic bomb on land that is now part of the White Sands Missile Range. Trinity Site is in south-central New Mexico, 182 miles from Santa Fe. It is open to the public only twice a year, on the first Saturdays in April and October.

Truchas (TROO-chuss)

Northern New Mexico village on the High Road to Taos. Truchas is named for the nearby *Rio de Truchas*, "River of Trout." The isolated village was the setting for director Robert Redford's 1988 film version of *The Milagro Beanfield War*. Truchas is on NM 76, 36 miles north of Santa Fe.

View from Truchas Peak

Truchas Peak

New Mexico's second-highest mountain, at 13,102 feet. Although Wheeler Peak is 59 feet higher, Truchas is considered harder to climb because of its location in the center of the Pecos Wilderness. Motor vehicles are banned from the Wilderness, so an attempt to summit Truchas requires a long hike to the base of the mountain. Most people take two or more days to make the climb.

Trujillo (troo-HEE-o)

Old New Mexico name. The Trujillo family of Chimayó is known for its weaving.

trustafarian (trust-uh-FAIR-ee-un)

A derogatory term for a young person, often sporting dreadlocks, who adopts a counterculture persona while living on inherited money. Santa Fe counts many idle rich among its full- and part-time residents – some are early retirees and some are living off trust funds established by more industrious forebears. Trustafarian is a whimsical combination of *trust-funder* and *Rastafarian*.

Truth or Consequences

Southern New Mexico city named for a TV show. In 1950, host Ralph Edwards challenged any city in the country to rename itself after his game show. Hot Springs, New Mexico, obliged and is now called Truth or Consequences. The city, population 6,475, still has its hot springs, but most visitors come to go boating and fishing on Elephant Butte Lake.

T or C, as it is also known, is 208 miles south of Santa Fe off I-25, at the southern end of the lake.

tuberculosis

The disease that helped populate New Mexico. In the late 19th and early 20th centuries, TB sufferers were advised to move to a drier climate, and people as diverse as Billy the Kid's mother, architect John Gaw Meem, and Senator Bronson Cutting came to New Mexico in search of a cure. The number of patients is inexact because TB was stigmatized, but UNM professor Chris Wilson estimates in *The Myth of Santa Fe* that up to one-third of the Anglo artists and intellectuals who moved to Santa Fe in the 1920s came because of "health problems," which usually meant tuberculosis.

(Casual observation reveals a similar phenomenon occurring today among people affected by SAD, or seasonal affective disorder. Incapacitated by depression in gloomier climes, many SAD sufferers become re-energized and productive in New Mexico's abundant sunshine.)

Tucumcari (TOO-come-care-ee)

The county seat of Quay County. The origin of Tucumcari's name is a matter of much speculation. Local lore ascribes it to Indian lovers named Tocom and Kari, but *The Place Names of New Mexico* discounts that theory. The name more likely comes from a nearby mountain that the Comanches called *tukamukaru*, or "lookout."

Tucumcari, population 5,363, is 181 miles southeast of Santa Fe via US 285 south and I-40 east.

Turn Left at the Sleeping Dog

John Pen La Farge's recollected history of Santa Fe. The author is the son of Pulitzer Prize winner Oliver La Farge, and he grew up surrounded by some of Santa Fe's most interesting people. *Turn Left at the Sleeping Dog*, published in 2001, reflects the city's evolution between 1920 and 1955 as recalled by writers, artists, and assorted characters-about-town. The title refers to directions given to a visiting motorist by Richard Bradford, author of *Red Sky at Morning*.

Turner, Ted

(1938-) The largest private landowner in New Mexico, and in the United States. Turner owns 1.1 million acres in New Mexico and almost two million acres nationwide. His New Mexico holdings include the Armendaris Ranch on Elephant Butte Lake, the Vermejo Park Ranch near Raton, and the Ladder Ranch near Truth or Consequences. Turner is a dedicated conservationist who has removed miles of barbed wire and encouraged the growth of elk and bison herds on his property.

Turner's ex-wife, Jane Fonda, owns the 2,200-acre Forked Lightning Ranch in Pecos.

turquoise

New Mexico's state gem. The Cerrillos turquoise mine 10 miles south of Santa Fe is the oldest mine of any kind in North America, and stones from the site were widely traded in pre-Columbian times. Turquoise is not, however, an exclusively New World gemstone. A turquoise bracelet found on a 7,000-year-old Egyptian mummy represents one of the earliest examples of jewelry. The blue-green stone was called *turquoise*, "Turkish stone," by the French, who acquired it from Turks, who brought it to Europe from Persia.

Turquoise stones found in Southwestern jewelry come in five grades:

Natural – A stone that is naturally hard and colorful. Less than three percent of the turquoise on the worldwide market is natural.

Stabilized – A stone that has been injected with clear epoxy to increase its hardness. Most turquoise stones have been stabilized.

Treated – A stone that has been injected with a colored epoxy to enhance its color. The color may look artificial, so a treated turquoise should be significantly less expensive than a natural or stabilized stone.

Reconstituted – A faux "stone" created from turquoise powder. Turquoise chalk that is too soft to be made into jewelry is ground up and then shaped into stones.

Imitation – A fake turquoise stone, which may be either another stone dyed to look like turquoise, or a plastic epoxy resin colored to look like turquoise.

Turquoise Trail

The National Scenic Byway that runs south for 62 miles from Santa Fe to just past the town of Tijeras, a little south of I-40. The Trail follows NM 14 for most of its length. It passes through the old mining towns of Cerrillos, Madrid, and Golden.

Tusas Mountains (TOO-suss)

Northern New Mexico mountain range. The Tusas are the southern extension of the San Juan Mountains. They are mostly in northeastern Rio Arriba County, west of the Rio Grande and north of the Rio Chama. *Tusa* means "prairie dog" in New Mexico Spanish.

- U -

Udall, Stewart

(1920-2010) Congressman from Arizona, Secretary of the Interior in the Kennedy and Johnson administrations, and father of Senator Tom Udall. Stewart Udall lived in Santa Fe for the last years of his life, and he took an active interest in local conservation. In the early 1990s, he successfully opposed residential development on Atalaya Mountain. In 1997, he was interviewed by *The New York Times* about yet another millionaire's attempt to build a trophy house on a prominent hill. Udall said, "Vail, Aspen, Telluride, Jackson – those are communities with different histories ... to do this right in the middle of the city violates everything that Santa Fe is about."

Udall's memorial service was held at Santa Fe's Paolo Soleri amphitheater.

Udall, Tom

(1948-) One of New Mexico's United States senators. Udall, a Democrat, served as New Mexico's attorney general for eight years before being elected to Congress from Northern New Mexico's Third Congressional District in 1998. In 2008, he won the Senate seat vacated by retiring Republican Pete Domenici. Udall will become New Mexico's senior senator when Jeff Bingaman retires and his replacement takes office in 2013.

Tom Udall comes from a distinguished political family. He is the son of Stewart Udall and the nephew of Morris "Mo"

Tom Udall

Udall, who served in Congress for 30 years. Tom's first cousin, Mark, is a United States senator from Colorado.

United World College

Prep school in Montezuma, New Mexico, just north of Las Vegas. The United World Colleges were founded in 1962 as institutions where students from around the world could gather to live and learn together. The New Mexico branch, officially known as the Armand Hammer United World College of the American West, is one of 10 such schools. (The others are in Canada, Hong Kong, India, Italy, Norway, Singapore, Swaziland, Venezuela, and Wales.) The Montezuma campus has about 200 students, including 150 from outside the United States, who range in age from 16 to 19. Montezuma Castle is owned by the school.

University of New Mexico (UNM)

New Mexico's largest post-secondary educational institution. The Albuquerque university has the only medical and law schools in the state. The UNM Lobos maintain a fierce sports rivalry with the Aggies of New Mexico State University. Notable alumni include authors Edward Abbey (*The Monkey Wrench Gang*) and N. Scott Momaday (*The House Made of Dawn*), as well as Chicago Bears linebacker Brian Urlacher.

Unser family

New Mexico racing dynasty. In the 1940s, patriarch Jerry Unser, Sr., operated a garage and junkyard on Route 66 west of Albuquerque. His sons learned to race in cars patched together from junkyard wrecks.

Jerry Unser, Jr., was killed practicing for the 1959 Indianapolis 500. Bobby Unser won the Indy 500 three times, and Al Unser, Sr., won four times. In 1992, Al Unser, Jr., became the first son of an Indy winner to win the race. Albuquerque's Unser Boulevard and the Unser Racing Museum on Montaño Road are named for the family.

US 84/285

The extension of St. Francis Drive that becomes the highway between Santa Fe and Española. The six-lane divided highway is the main route out of town for trips to Bandelier National Monument, Los Alamos, and both the high and low roads to Taos. It is also the commuter corridor for Norteños who work in Santa Fe.

A study conducted in the 1990s concluded that, at that time, US 84/285 was one of the 10 most dangerous roads in the United States. It has become much safer since its reconstruction in the 2000s, although tailgating and weaving in and out of traffic are still rampant, particularly during commuter rush hours.

- V -

VLA

See VERY LARGE ARRAY.

Vadito (vah-DEE-toe)

Northern New Mexico community whose name means "little ford" or "little crossing." Vadito is on NM 75, 55 miles north of Santa Fe.

Valle Grande (VIE-yay GRAHN-day)

"Big Valley," the largest of the grassy valleys in Valles Caldera National Preserve. NM 4, which runs along the south rim of the Valles Caldera, offers the best view of the Valle Grande. People who bring binoculars may spot a herd of elk moving through the valley.

Vallecitos (vie-yay-SEE-toes)

Northern New Mexico community in Rio Arriba County. The name means "little valleys." Vallecitos is on NM 111, 16 miles north of Ojo Caliente and 67 miles north of Santa Fe.

Valles Caldera National Preserve (VIE-yays call-DAIR-uh)

The "Caldera Valleys" National Preserve. The 89,000-acre expanse is centered on the enormous Valles Caldera, an ancient volcano that measures 12 to 14 miles across. The caldera contains Redondo Peak (elevation 11,254 feet) and over 27 miles of streams. It is home to over 4,000 elk, as well as 17 threatened or endangered species.

Formerly known as the Baca Ranch, the Jemez Mountain property was purchased by the federal government in 2000 for $101 million. The preserve has since been governed by a nine-member board that operates outside the jurisdiction of any other government land management agency, although there is talk of turning it over to the National Park Service.

Vargas, Don Diego de

The Spanish governor who reclaimed New Mexico after the Pueblo Revolt. For some reason, this governor is usually referred to as *De* Vargas, while Don Juan de Oñate and Don Pedro de Peralta are known as Oñate and Peralta. See also DE VARGAS, DON DIEGO.

vato (VAH-toe)

Slang word for "guy" or "dude." New Mexico music stations used to play a Freddie Fender song with a line that goes, "Hey, baby, *que paso?* Thought I was your only vato."

vecino/a (vay-SEE-no/nah)

"Neighbor." Some historians use the word to mean a citizen of New Mexico in the Spanish Colonial Period.

vega (VAY-guh)

"Meadow." Las Vegas, New Mexico, and Las Vegas, Nevada, are both named for meadows.

Velarde (vuh-LAR-day)

Northern New Mexico village known for its apple orchards. The small farming community, which is named for its founding family, is on NM 68 (the low road to Taos), 39 miles north of Santa Fe.

Pablita Velarde (1918-2006) was a renowned Pueblo Indian painter.

Visitors at the Very Large Array

Very Large Array (VLA)

The world's largest radio telescope. The installation consists of 27, two-and-a-half-ton, movable dish antennae arrayed to receive radio signals from space. The VLA is 182 miles southwest of Santa Fe on US 60, 19 miles west of Magdalena.

viejo/a (vee-AY-ho/ha)

"Old" or, as a noun, "old man" or "old woman."

viga (VEE-guh)

Round log that extends from one adobe wall to another to provide support for the ceiling and roof of a Santa Fe-style building. Smaller latillas or rajas are placed on top of the vigas to make up the next layer in the roof system.

Vigil (vee-HILL)

Prominent New Mexico surname. The Northern New Mexico village of Cundiyo was once known as the "Village of the Vigils" because everyone who lived there was named Vigil.

Villa Linda Mall (VEE-uh)

The former name of Santa Fe Place. The mall was known as Villa Linda from its opening in 1985 until the name change in 2005. Some Santa Feans still use the old name.

virga (*VER-guh)

Wispy precipitation that evaporates before it reaches the ground.

*Care should be taken with pronunciation. The Spanish word *verga* (pronounced VAIR-gah) is a vulgar word for penis.

Visualize Turn Signal Use

Old bumper sticker encouraging notoriously negligent Santa Feans to use turn signals. The phrase evolved to this practical form through the sublime "Visualize World Peace" and the ridiculous "Visualize Whirled Peas."

- W -

Wagon Mound

Northern New Mexico village named for a nearby butte that looks like a covered wagon. The butte became a landmark for travelers on the Santa Fe Trail, and a community

Wagon Mound

gradually grew up near it. Fray Angélico Chávez was born in Wagon Mound in 1910. The community currently has a population of 314.

Wagon Mound is 110 miles northeast of Santa Fe via I-25.

Wallace, Lew

(1827-1905) Territorial governor and author of *Ben Hur*. Wallace was appointed governor in 1878 to break up the Santa Fe Ring and to end the Lincoln County War but was unable to do either. He is quoted as lamenting, "Every calculation based on experience elsewhere fails in New Mexico." Wallace did manage to finish writing the novel *Ben Hur* while living in the Palace of the Governors. He happily left New Mexico in 1881 upon his appointment as United States Minister to the Ottoman Empire. The Lew Wallace Building on Old Santa Trail commemorates the frustrated governor.

water right

A permit from the state allowing the use of a certain amount of water from a certain source for a certain purpose. Water rights are usually measured in acre-feet, the amount of water needed to cover one acre of land to a depth of one foot (325,851 U.S. gallons).

In the eastern United States, where water is plentiful, those who own land along rivers and streams have riparian water rights that allow them unrestricted consumption of the water flowing past their land. In most western states, including New Mexico, water rights are issued by the state, which ranks them under a prior appropriation system in which senior rights take precedence over junior rights. The states' seniority systems are complicated by the existence of federal water rights, including those for Indian lands, that trump state water rights. Junior water rights holders may not receive any water in dry years, when "paper water rights" exceed the available "wet water." Lawsuits like New Mexico's lengthy Aamodt case are attempts to reconcile potentially conflicting water rights.

New Mexico water law should not be attempted by amateurs. Those purchasing water rights or land with rights attached are advised to consult a knowledgeable attorney.

West Side Locos

Santa Fe's most visible teenage gang. Members are generally native Santa Feans, most of them Hispanic, with a few *gueros locos*, "crazy white boys," thrown in. As the name implies, the gang originated on the city's Westside, though as more and more old Santa Fe families move to the Southside, a Westside residence is no longer a requirement for membership.

Gang mischief is usually confined to flashing signs and spraying "WSL" on other people's property, but there have been ugly incidents of violence. The worst occurred on the Plaza at the beginning of Fiesta weekend in 1997. On Friday night, after the burning of Zozobra, an 18-year-old shouting "West Side!" fired shots into the crowd. Three people were hit, and a 20-year-old died from his wounds. The burning of Zozobra was moved to Thursday night after the shooting. Nowadays, the Locos frequently fight with immigrant kids from Mexico or Central America who live on the Southside.

Santa Fe's property crime statistics, which had always been bad, became much worse in the 2000s when gang members began committing burglaries on a large scale.

Westphall, Victor

(1913-2003) Founder of the country's first monument honoring Vietnam veterans. Westphall's son, Marine First Lieutenant David Westphall, was killed in combat in 1968. In 1971, Westphall erected a 50-foot-tall memorial to David on his property near Angel Fire. The monument became the Vietnam Veterans Memorial State Park in 2005.

Victor Westphall was also a respected historian. He earned a Ph.D. in history at the University of New Mexico in 1956 and published a number of books on New Mexico history, including *Thomas Benton Catron and his Era* (1973).

Westphall and his wife, Jeanne, are buried on the grounds of the Vietnam Veterans Memorial State Park.

Westside

The historically less affluent side of Santa Fe, now in the slow process of gentrification. Boundaries are inexact, but the Westside has been described as the area west of Guadalupe Street, south of West Alameda Street, and north of Cerrillos Road. Agua Fria Street and Hickox Street run down the middle of the Westside. The area between Guadalupe Street and St. Francis Drive is sometimes called the "near Westside."

The Westside is a mix of older houses and small commercial buildings. Zoning has been haphazard, and appreciation has been much slower than on the Eastside. This is changing, however, as significant numbers of homebuyers opt for an older house close to downtown over a newer one on Santa Fe's burgeoning Southside.

Wheeler Peak

New Mexico's highest mountain. The 13,161-foot peak is northeast of Taos in the Sangre de Cristo Mountains. It is named for U.S. Army Major George Wheeler, who surveyed the West in the 1870s. Wheeler Peak in Nevada, that state's second-highest mountain, is also named for Major Wheeler.

Most people begin the seven-and-one-half-mile hike to the summit of Wheeler Peak at the Taos Ski Valley parking lot.

Wheelwright, Mary Cabot

(1878-1958) Wealthy Boston Brahmin who founded a Santa Fe museum. According to the *Dictionary of American Biography*, Wheelwright did not attract suitors as a young woman because she was "dyspeptic, gawky, and opinionated." She lived at home with her mother until age 40 but traveled widely after her mother's death. She became fascinated with the Southwest, particularly with Navajo culture, which she sought to protect by founding what is now the Wheelwright Museum of the American Indian.

Wheelwright bought the 148-acre Los Luceros ranch, near Española, in 1923 and lived there part time until her death in 1958.

Wheelwright Museum of the American Indian

Private museum on Santa Fe's Museum Hill. The facility originated as a collaboration between Mary Cabot Wheelwright and a Navajo medicine man named Hosteen Klah. Worried that Navajo culture might not survive the government's policy of Indian assimilation, Wheelwright and Klah created a museum to preserve Navajo cultural and religious traditions. Wheelwright funded the building and Klah contributed songs, stories, sand paintings, and religious artifacts. The Museum of Navajo Ceremonial Art, as they named it, opened in 1937. In 1977, Navajo elders decided that they had become capable of protecting their own culture and asked that the religious items be returned to the tribe. The museum readily complied, then changed its name to the Wheelwright Museum of the American Indian.

The Wheelwright Museum is on Camino Lejo, near its intersection with Camino Corrales. The building itself is in the shape of an elongated hogan. Hosteen Klah is buried on the museum grounds.

Where the emeriti come to die

Comment on Santa Fe retirees. Professors emeriti from all over the country retire to the City Different, and many immediately begin sharing their opinions on local matters in letters to the editor. This happens so often that editorial-page staffers at *The New Mexican* have taken to calling Santa Fe the place "where the emeriti come to die."

White, Amelia

(1878-1972) Santa Fe socialite and philanthropist. Amelia Elizabeth and her younger sister, Martha, were the daughters of wealthy New York newspaper publisher Horace White. They moved to Santa Fe after serving as nurse's assistants in Europe during World War I. In the 1920s and 1930s, the sisters hosted lavish parties at their Garcia Street home, which they called *El Delirio*, "The Madness."

Amelia White

Martha died in 1937, but "Miss Elizabeth," as Amelia was known, remained a force in the city for another 35 years. She was active in Indian health issues and was instrumental in founding the Laboratory of Anthropology, the Old Santa Fe Association, the Santa Fe Animal Shelter, and the Santa Fe Indian Market. She served on the board of what is now the School of Advanced Research (SAR) for 25 years and willed El Delirio to the school, which is now headquartered there. Santa Fe's Amelia White Park is at the intersection of Old Santa Fe Trail and Camino Corrales.

White Rock

Bedroom community for Los Alamos. White Rock was originally a housing area for workers building the Lab and the Los Alamos townsite. It was virtually abandoned in the late 1950s but was later revived and currently has a population of 5,725. Alleged spy Wen Ho Lee lived in White Rock.

White Sands National Monument

White Sands

Vast expanse of glistening white sand dunes in

southern New Mexico. The dunes are composed of pure gypsum crystals.

Most of the dunes are in the White Sands Missile Range. At 3,200 square miles (more than three times the land area of the state of Rhode Island), the Missile Range is the largest military installation in the country. The Trinity Site, where Los Alamos scientists exploded the first atom bomb, is at the northern end of the Range.

The White Sands National Monument encompasses 115 square miles of the gypsum dunes. The monument is open to the public, although it does close one or two days a week when the Missile Range is conducting tests. White Sands National Monument is 326 miles south of Santa Fe via I-25 south and US 70 east.

Wildlife Center, The

New Mexico's only animal hospital for large mammals and endangered species. The Wildlife Center was founded in 1986 to rehabilitate birds but now treats all native animals. Of the approximately 1,400 injured birds, reptiles, and mammals brought to the facility each year, about 60 percent survive. Most of the survivors are returned to the wild. Those too crippled or too accustomed to humans to be released are transferred to animal sanctuaries or kept at the center as educational animals.

The Wildlife Center is 22 miles north of Santa Fe, off US 84/285 just south of Española.

Valerie Plame Wilson

Wilson, Valerie Plame

(1963-) Former CIA operations officer and current Santa Fe resident. In 2003, Plame Wilson's husband, former ambassador Joe Wilson, criticized the Bush administration's rationale for the invasion of Iraq. Journalists who had been tipped off by members of the administration identified her as a CIA officer, and the disclosure ended her covert career with the agency. Plame Wilson and her family left Washington, D.C., and moved to Santa Fe in 2007. That same year, she published her story in a book titled *Fair Game*. A movie version of the book starring Naomi Watts and Sean Penn was released in 2010.

Valerie Plame Wilson appeared on the cover of the May 2010 issue of *Santa Fean* magazine. In the accompanying interview, she said, "I have lived many, many places in the world, and I have never felt as at home as I do in Santa Fe." The former spy currently serves as part-time director of community relations for the Santa Fe Institute and as a member of the board of the United Way of Santa Fe County.

windy season

Spring, particularly from mid-March to early May, when strong winds stir up allergens and increase the danger of forest fires. The Cerro Grande fire that devastated Los Alamos in May 2000 was accelerated by 50-mile-per-hour gusts. A newcomer to the Eldorado neighborhood south of Santa Fe who wrote a memoir of her first year in New Mexico titled it *Blown Away* in honor of the wind.

WIPP

Acronym for the Waste Isolation Pilot Plant. The WIPP site is a 2,150-foot-deep, man-made salt cavern 26 miles east of Carlsbad. It received its first shipment of nuclear waste in March 1999 after years of protests by opponents. The federal Department of Energy plans to deposit nuclear waste from Los Alamos and other sources in the cave for 30 years before permanently sealing it. NM 599, also known as the Santa Fe Relief Route, was built primarily to provide a detour around the city for trucks carrying waste from Los Alamos to the WIPP site.

wolf, Mexican gray

Endangered wolf species. In 1998, despite fierce opposition from cattlemen, gray wolves were reintroduced into a remote area along the New Mexico-Arizona border by the United States Fish and Wildlife Service. The wolf packs were released in the Gila Wilderness in an effort to keep them isolated from cows and people, but they have not thrived as hoped. Federal wildlife officials who counted the population in 2011 could find only 50 wolves.

- X, Y, Z -

xeriscape (ZEER-es-cape)

To landscape for an arid climate, dry landscaping. A xeriscaped yard contains drought-tolerant native plants that do not require much water. Most grasses do not qualify.

"Zeroscaping" is what some people facetiously call the practice of removing all plants and replacing them with rocks.

yah-ta-hey (yah-tah-HAY)

The written approximation of a traditional Navajo greeting.

Yazzie (YAH-zee)

One of the most common Navajo names. Like Begay, Yazzie originated with a misunderstanding by Anglo registrars at Indian schools. The registrar would ask the parent, "Who is this?" and, upon hearing *yazzie*, which means "little," as in "little one," the registrar would record it as the child's last name.

Yogi Bhajan (bah-ZHAHN)

(1930-2004) The late founder and spiritual leader of New Mexico's Sikh community. In 1969, Harbhajan Singh Puri moved from Punjab, in northern India, to Los Angeles to teach yoga. As the Sikhs' web site explains, "Yogi Bhajan's penetrating insight, infinite compassion, tireless service, and delightful sense of humor immediately endeared him to the eager young people who flocked to his Kundalini Yoga classes." In response to his students' questions about his religion, Yogi Bhajan opened an ashram, and, in 1972, moved it from Los Angeles to Española. Governor Bill Richardson ordered flags throughout the state to be flown at half-mast when Yogi Bhajan died in 2004.

yucca (YUCK-uh)

New Mexico's official state flower. For centuries, the roots of the yucca plant have been used to make soap.

zaguán (zah-GWAHN)

An open vestibule, or a breeze-way between buildings. The building called El Zaguán on Canyon Road offers the best local example. (See also El Zaguán.)

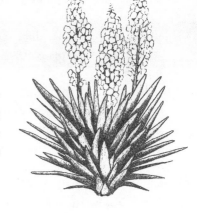

Yucca

zapata (za-PAH-tuh)

Literally "shoe;" in architectural terms, the double-sided support that sits atop a post to carry the weight of a beam. (The single-sided support that extends from a wall is called a corbel.)

Zeckendorf, Bill

(1929-) New York and Santa Fe real estate developer. William Zeckendorf, Jr., himself the son of a famed developer, played a major role in New York's commercial building boom of the 1980s before suffering serious losses in the 1990s. His Santa Fe projects have been more successful. Zeckendorf and his wife, Nancy, a former ballerina with the Santa Fe Opera, built the Eldorado Hotel in 1985 and, in 1991, they collaborated with Picuris Pueblo in the development of the Hotel Santa Fe. They are also partners in the exclusive Sierra del Norte residential development.

The Zeckendorfs are active in community affairs and were the driving force behind the 2000-2001 renovation of the Lensic Theater. They were both named Living Treasures in 2011.

Bill Zeckendorf's interest in Santa Fe comes honestly. His great-grandfather, William Zeckendorf, and his great-great uncles, Aaron and Louis, established a business in the city in 1854.

Zia (ZEE-uh)

New Mexico's ubiquitous sun symbol. The circular sun with linear rays extending in the four cardinal directions adorns the state flag, license plate, driver's license, and quarter.

Zia

The motif is an adaptation of a symbol found on a Zia Pueblo water jar. In 1925, Dr. Harry Mera, a physician and archaeologist, used it in a redesign of the New Mexico state flag. In 2001, the North American Vexillological Association, a scholarly organization of flag experts, recognized New Mexico's red-and-yellow Zia flag as the best among those of the American states and Canadian provinces. In 2011, New Mexico's centennial license plate, which also features a Zia, was deemed the country's best by the Automobile License Plate Collectors Association.

Zia Diner

Casual, all-purpose Santa Fe restaurant. The Zia is open for breakfast, lunch and dinner, seven days a week. It is probably best known for its comfort foods – meat loaf, hot turkey, and liver and onions.

Beth Koch opened the restaurant in 1986 in a building that once served as the coal warehouse for the Santa Fe Railway. It continues to benefit from its proximity to the railroad, as people who have taken the train from Albuquerque or Rio Rancho walk to the restaurant from the nearby Rail Runner depot.

The Zia Diner is on Guadalupe Street, diagonally across the street from Cowgirl BBQ.

Zia Pueblo

Pueblo best known as the source of the Zia sun symbol. The Keresan-speaking pueblo once sought reimbursement for use of the symbol but now simply requests that people ask permission before copying it. Zia Pueblo is off US 550, 63 miles southwest of Santa Fe.

Zozobra (zo-ZO-bruh)

The 50-foot-tall effigy of Old Man Gloom that is burned at the Fort Marcy complex on the Thursday night before Fiesta weekend. The burning of Zozobra, Spanish for "worry," was added to the festivities in 1924 by artist Will Shuster. (Some sources say it was 1925 or 1926; Shuster himself was unsure of the exact year.) Shuster fashioned the body of the first effigy and Gustave Baumann created the head. Because it has movable arms, Zozobra is technically a puppet, and *Guinness World Records* has certified it as the world's tallest marionette.

Zozobra

The annual burning of Zozobra draws 25,000 paying spectators.

Zuni Pueblo (ZOO-nee)

Largest, most populous, and westernmost of New Mexico's 19 pueblos. The Zuni are believed to have descended from the Mogollon rather than the Anasazi, and the Zuni language is different from the Tewa, Tiwa, Towa, and Keresan languages spoken at the other 18 pueblos.

Zuni Pueblo was the subject of intense study by Anglo anthropologists in the late 19th and early 20th centuries. There were so many social scientists around at that time that the Zunis joked that a typical Zuni family consisted of a father, a mother, two children, and an anthropologist.

Zuni Pueblo, population 6,302, is on NM 53, 210 miles southwest of Santa Fe.

~ Illustration Credits ~

Page

Page

Page

Mark H. Cross is a native of Virginia with a master's degree in American history from George Mason University. He moved to Santa Fe in 1996.

Mark has written book reviews for *The New Mexican* and worked as a proofreader and editor for the New Mexico Legislature. He lives on Santa Fe's Westside with Beth Nommensen and their two dogs.

CPSIA information can be obtained
at www.ICGtesting.com
Printed in the USA
FSHW021230240620
71316FS

9 780983 419426